DE SMITH'S Judicial Review

First Supplement to the
6th Edition

SWEET & MAXWELL   THOMSON REUTERS

First edition	1959
Second impression	1960
Third impression	1961
Second edition	1968
Third edition	1973
Fourth edition	1980
Second impression	1986
Third impresion	1987
Fifth edition	1995
Supplement to the fifth edition	1998
Sixth edition	2007
Supplement to the sixth edition	2009

Published in 2009 by Sweet & Maxwell Limited of
100 Avenue Road,
London NW3 3PF
http://www.sweetandmaxwell.co.uk
Typeset by LBJ Typesetting Ltd of Kingsclere
Printed and bound in Great Britain
by MPG Books Ltd, Bodmin, Cornwall

No natural forests were destroyed to make this product; only farmed
timber was used and re-planted

A CIP catalogue record for this book is available from the British Library

ISBN: 9780421691001

DE SMITH'S JUDICIAL REVIEW

FIRST SUPPLEMENT TO THE SIXTH EDITION

Andrew Le Sueur
Professor of Public Law, Queen Mary University of London
Director of Studies, Institute of Law, Jersey
Barrister

Catherine M. Donnelly
Lecturer in Law, Trinity College, Dublin
Barrister, Blackstone Chambers and
Law Library Dublin

Ivan Hare
Barrister, Blackstone Chambers

CONSULTANT EDITORS

The Rt Hon The Lord Woolf
Former Lord Chief Justice of England and Wales
Judge of the Court of Final Appeal, Hong Kong

Jeffrey Jowell Q.C.
Professor of Law
Faculty of Laws, UCL
Barrister, Blackstone Chambers

London
Sweet & Maxwell
2009

PREFACE

The 6th edition of *de Smith's Judicial Review* was published at the end of 2007. It sought to state the law as it stood on June 1, 2007, though some later developments (as to the end of October 2007) were incorporated at proof stage. This supplement updates the main work to state the law as at September 1, 2009, with some additional material incorporated at proof stage in late October.

As in the main work, we have been selective in the cases that have been included. They either develop a principle or provide a particularly useful illustration of a principle or practice. We have not confined ourselves to reported cases; where we thought it appropriate to do so, reference is made to unreported judgments. Practitioners will, of course, need to bear in mind the strictures on citation of authorities set out in Appendix A to the 6th edition.

We are grateful to our "foreign correspondents" who have brought to our attention developments in their jurisdictions during this period.

- Australia: Professor Cheryl Saunders, University of Melbourne.
- Canada: Professor David Mullan, Professor Emeritus, Queen's University, Canada.
- India: Soli J. Sorabjee, Attorney-General of India 1998–2004.
- New Zealand: Jason N. E. Varuhas, Sidney Sussex College, University of Cambridge.
- South Africa: Professor Cora Hoexter, University of Witwatersrand, Johannesburg.

We note with sadness that our former New Zealand correspondent, Professor Michael Taggart, died in August this year. Mike's full and interesting contributions to the previous two editions were greatly valued by the authors and readers and his rich work, cited throughout the present edition, shows that public law has lost one of its greatest exponents.

We thank Ruchi Parekh and Niamh Cleary who provided research assistance; and Varda Bondy who cast a critical eye over Ch.1. All errors and omissions are, of course, our responsibility.

Andrew Le Sueur
Catherine Donnelly
Ivan Hare
October 2009

v

TABLE OF CONTENTS

Preface

Table of Cases

Table of Statutes

Table of Statutory Instruments

Table of Civil Procedure Rules

Table of European Legislation

Part I
THE CONTEXT OF JUDICIAL REVIEW

CHAPTER 1

THE NATURE OF JUDICIAL REVIEW

THE CONSTITUTIONAL CONTEXT OF JUDICIAL REVIEW

The purpose of judicial review

[Add to end of n.17]   1–006

For an analysis of the various meanings attributed to the term constitutionalism, see further J. Murkens, "The Quest for Constitutionalism in Public Law Discourse" (2009) 29 O.J.L.S. 1.

[Add to end of n.25]   1–010

See also M. Bevir, "The Westminster Model, Governance and Judicial Reform" (2008) 61 Parl. Aff. 559; R. Masterman, "Juridification, Sovereignty and Separation of Powers" (2009) Parl. Aff. 499; M. Bevir, "Juridification and Democracy" (2009) Parl. Aff. 493.

CONSTITUTIONAL JUSTIFICATIONS OF JUDICIAL REVIEW

Justification by constitutional principles

Reconciliation between parliamentary sovereignty and the rule of law

[Add to end of n.42]   1–019

See also D. Jenkins, "Common law declarations of unconstitutionality" (2009) 7 Int. J. Constitutional Law 183 (arguing that British courts have an inherent power to issue non-binding, common law "declarations of unconstitutionality" when Parliament legislates against constitutional norms); S. Lakin, "Debunking the Idea of Parliamentary Sovereignty: The Controlling Factor of Legality in the British Constitution" (2008) 28 O.J.L.S. 709 (contending that the idea of Parliamentary sovereignty is misconceived and arguing that the British constitution instead rests on the ideal of government under law or the principle of legality); Sir John Laws, "Constitutional

Guarantees" (2008) 29 Stat. L.R. 1; and M, Gordon, "The Conceptual Foundations of Parliamentary Sovereignty: Reconsidering Jennings and Wade" [2009] P.L. 519.

1–020 *[Add to end of n.46]*

See also A.L. Young, "Hunting Sovereignty: *Jackson v Her Majesty's Attorney-General*" [2006] P.L. 187; A. McHarg, "What is Delegated Legislation" [2006] P.L. 539.

Certainty and flexibility

1–024 *[Add to para.1–024 after ". . . Namibia and South Africa.[59]"]*

. . . and there is a similar provision in the new Cayman Island Constitution 2009: see Cayman Islands Constitution Order 2009 (SI 2009/1379), Sch.2 art.19:

> "19.—(1) All decisions and acts of public officials must be lawful, rational, proportionate and procedurally fair. (2) Every person whose interests have been adversely affected by such a decision or act has the right to request and be given written reasons for that decision or act".

The Human Rights Commission for Northern Ireland has recommended a new Bill of Rights for Northern Ireland including a right to "civil and administrative justice", which includes the right to "administrative action that is lawful, procedurally fair, rational, proportionate and taken within a reasonable time". It also includes the right of access to public information and imposes a duty on public authorities to give reasons for their decisions and, where feasible, provide appropriate mechanisms for internal review or appeal of their decisions. See Northern Ireland Human Rights Commission, *A Bill of Rights for Northern Ireland* (December 2008), p.44.

[Add new para.1–024A after para.1–024]

1–024A In March 2009, the UK Ministry of Justice published a Green Paper entitled *Rights and Responsibilities: developing our constitutional framework* (Cm 7577), as part of the Labour Government's "Governance of Britain" constitutional reform proposals. Noting that "the law of judicial review has evolved to require administrative decisions and actions which are lawful, rational and procedurally fair" (para.3.39), the Green Paper stated that

> "The Government considers that to include these core principles in a Bill of Rights and Responsibilities would place the rules governing fair decision-making at the heart of the UK's constitutional arrangements, making them more accessible to the citizen, and helping to enhance confidence in our system of government" (para.3.40).

The Green Paper continued:

"However, there are a number of ways in which the principles of good administration might be framed in a Bill of Rights and Responsibilities, ranging from a general statement of a right of individuals to decision-making which is lawful, rational and procedurally fair, to a more detailed statement of the principles drawn from the existing law and the values which underpin fair decision-making and good administration. One way might be to express the principles to be applied by the courts in judicial review cases in statutory form so that Parliament and the people it represents had the opportunity to endorse the scope for judicial scrutiny of the actions of the executive" (para.3.46).

CONSTITUTIONAL AND INSTITUTIONAL LIMITS OF JUDICIAL REVIEW (JUSTICIABILITY)

[Add to end of n.63]   1–025

And see J. Jowell, "What Decisions Should Judges Not Take?" in M. Andenas and D. Fairgrieve (eds), *Tom Bingham and the Transformation of the Law* (Oxford: OUP, 2009), Ch.9; A. Kavanagh, "Judging Judges under the Human Rights Act: Deference, Disillusionment and the 'War on Terror'" [2009] P.L. 287.

Limitations inherent in the courts' constitutional role

[Add new para.1–029A after para.1–029]   1–029

The constitutional role of the courts was brought into sharp focus in *R. (on* 1–029A
the application of Gentle) v Prime Minister [2008] UKHL 20; [2008] 2 W.L.R. 879. A nine-member panel of the House of Lords, on an appeal by mothers of British soldiers killed in Iraq, was called upon to consider whether it was unlawful for the Government to refuse to hold an independent inquiry into the circumstances that led to the British invasion of Iraq in 2003. The mothers contended, unsuccessfully in the end, that they had a right to such an inquiry under art.2 ECHR ("Everyone's right to life shall be protected by law", on which see further Ch.13). Lord Bingham noted that art.2 ECHR had never previously been held to apply to the "process of deciding on the lawfulness of a resort to arms" and stated ([8]):

"It must (further) have been obvious [to those drafting the ECHR] that an enquiry such as the appellants claim would be drawn into considera-tion of issues which judicial tribunals have traditionally been very reluctant to entertain because they recognise their limitations as suitable bodies to resolve them. This is not to say that if the appellants have a legal right the courts cannot decide it. The respondents accept that if the appellants have a legal right it is justiciable in the courts, and they do not seek to demarcate areas into which the courts may not intrude. They do, however, say, in my view rightly, that in deciding whether a right exists it is relevant to consider what exercise of the right would entail. Thus the restraint traditionally shown by the courts in ruling on what has been called high policy—peace and war, the making of treaties, the conduct of foreign relations— does tend to militate against the existence of the right: *R. v Jones (Margaret)* [2006] UKHL 16, [2007] 1 A.C. 136 at [30], [65]–[67]."

Baroness Hale of Richmond said:

"it is now common ground that if a Convention right requires the court to examine and adjudicate upon matters which were previously regarded as non-justiciable, then adjudicate it must. The subject matter cannot preclude this (although, as is already clear, I do agree with the Court of Appeal that it is a factor tending against interpreting a right in such a way as to require the courts to do this)" (at [60]).

Lord Carswell said counsel for the mothers

"did not ask the House to pronounce directly on the legality of the invasion and it would not be proper for your Lordships to attempt to do so. The question is one which has been the subject of much debate and more speculation, but it is clear that the proper place for it is in the court of public opinion and the forum of Parliament, not before this House sitting in its judicial capacity. It is equally clear, however, that the appellants' quest for a public inquiry into the process by which the decision to join in the invasion was reached is an attempt to get as near as possible inquiring into that very issue" (at [62]).

In *Secretary of State for Environment, Food and Rural Affairs v Downs* [2009] EWCA Civ 664; (2009) 153(27) S.J.L.B. 29; the Court of Appeal refused to hold unlawful a decision of the Secretary of State not further to regulate the environmental effects of crop-spraying. It was held that the regulatory framework for pesticides falls within a "difficult social and technical sphere in which a balance must be struck between the competing interests of the individual and the community as a whole".

Limitations inherent in the courts' institutional capacity

Matters which are in essence matters of preference

1–031   *[Add to end of para.1–031]*

In *R. (on the application of Wheeler) v Office of the Prime Minister* [2008] EWHC 936 (Admin); [2008] 2 C.M.L.R. 57 the claimant sought judicial review of the Government's decision not to hold a referendum on whether the United Kingdom should ratify the Treaty of Lisbon. Dismissing the claim, the Divisional Court doubted whether the correctness of the Government's assessment that the Lisbon Treaty was materially different from the Constitution Treaty (in respect of which a referendum had been promised) was justiciable as that "depends on political perspective and political judgment", adding: "At best, it is a matter to be approached on a Wednesbury basis; and on that basis we are far from persuaded that the assessment is an unreasonable on a *Wednesbury* basis" (at [37]). In *R. (on the application of Bancoult) v Secretary of State for Foreign and Common-wealth Affairs (No.2)* [2008] UKHL 61; [2008] 3 W.L.R. 955 at [130] Lord Rodger of Earslferry took the view that it is not for the courts to substitute their view for that of the Foreign Secretary advising Her Majesty in Council that executive legislation was for the "peace, order and good government" of the British Indian Ocean Territories:

> "it is not for the courts to declare the law invalid on that ground. Once they enter upon such territory they could very easily get into the area of challenging what is essentially a political judgment, which is not for the courts of law. However distasteful they may consider a provision such as those under consideration in the present case, I think that the rule of abstinence should remain unqualified and the courts should not pronounce on the validity of such a provision on the ground that it is not for the peace, order and good government of the colony in question".

Matters that are polycentric

[Add to end of n.89]   1–033

See also J. King, "Institutional Approaches to Judicial Restraint" (2008) 28 O.J.L.S. 409 and "The Pervasiveness of Polycentricity" [2008] P.L. 101.

[Add to end of para.1–035]   1–035

In *R. (on the application of Corner House Research) v Director of the Serious Fraud Office* [2008] UKHL 60; [2008] 3 W.L.R. 568, the House of Lords held that the courts should be slow to interfere in prosecutorial decisions outside of exceptional cases. One of the reasons given by Lord Bingham in support of that proposition was, quoting a judgment of the Supreme Court of Fiji: "The polycentric character of official decision-making in such matters including policy and public interest considerations are not susceptible of judicial review because it is within neither the constitutional function nor the practical competence of the courts to assess their merits" (*Matalulu v DPP* [2003] 4 L.R.C. 712 at 735–76). With respect, the concept of polycentricity does not justify judicial abstinence on the ground that the decision involves taking into account a number of different considerations. The essence of the polycentric problem is the fact that it has interacting points of influence described above, and is therefore not easily amenable to an either/or, or yes/no decision. Nevertheless, the deference to the Director's decision in *Corner House* was ultimately based less on polycentricity than the fact that it involved government policy in the area of national security (albeit ignoring the implications of such an approach for the rule of law, as argued below, at para 3–055). See R. Hopkins and C. Yeginsu, "Storm in a Teacup: Domestic and International Conservatism from the Corner House Case" (2008) 13 J.R. 267; J. Jowell, "Caving In: Threats and the Rule of Law" (2008) 13 J.R. 273.

Comparative approaches to justiciability

Australia

1–037 *[Add new para.1–037A after para.1–037]*

1–037A Surprisingly, the High Court of Australia has still yet to confirm that the prerogative powers are not inherently unreviewable, although commentators expect it to do so when an appropriate opportunity occurs. However, recent cases have taken tentative steps in developing jurisprudence in this area. In *Thomas v Mowbray*, in the context of anti-terrorism legislation, Gleeson C.J. stated that there was nothing in "the threat of terrorism, or the matters of inference or prediction involved in considering terrorist threats and control orders, that renders this subject non-justiciable or in some other way unsuited to be a subject of judicial review" (*Thomas v Mowbray* (2007) 233 C.L.R. 307 at [28] (Gleeson C.J.)). In *Hicks v Ruddock*, Tamberlin J. held in an interlocutory proceeding that it was "arguable" that the Australian Government had a justiciable duty to consider whether to provide diplomatic protection to an Australian citizen imprisoned in Guantanamo Bay (*Hicks v Ruddock* (2007) 156 F.C.R. 574). In *Habib v Commonwealth (No. 2)*, Perram J. observed that if there is a justiciable duty to consider whether to provide diplomatic protection, a failure to consider doing so does not sound in damages. Such a remedy would require the courts to determine the effect of diplomatic overtures by the Australian Government, which goes beyond the competence of the courts (*Habib v Commonwealth (No.2)* (2009) 254 A.L.R. 250).

The position in Australia is complicated by the existence of a written constitution that expressly vests the executive power of the Commonwealth in the Queen and exercisable by the Governor-General (s.61), and which confers constitutional review jurisdiction on the courts (ss.75–76). It has been suggested that the exercise of prerogative powers should be susceptible to review because they now find their source in s.61, and so questions regarding their exercise are at heart constitutional questions to be answered by the judiciary (*Re Ditfort; Ex p. Deputy Commissioner of Taxation* (1988) 19 F.C.R. 347). This approach is consistent with the apparent prevailing view that the Commonwealth executive power in s.61 includes, but is not limited to, the historical prerogative powers (*Ruddock v Vadarlis* (2001) 110 F.C.R. 491; *Pape v Commissioner of Taxation* [2009] HCA 23 (unreported, French C.J., Gummow, Hayne, Heydon, Crennan, Kiefel and Bell JJ., July 7, 2009)). It is bolstered by the constitutional jurisdiction of the High Court in s.75(v) to deal with matters in which certain remedies are sought against an "officer of the Commonwealth" and in s.75(iii) to deal with matters in which the Commonwealth is a party. Both are capable of covering an exercise of executive power in the nature of the prerogative (although whether the Governor-General is an officer of the Commonwealth remains unclear). Alternatively, it has been suggested that questions of justiciability should collapse into the determination of whether a constitutional "matter" exists so as to enliven jurisdiction (see B. Tamberlin and L. Bastin, "David Hicks in the Australian Courts: Past and Future Legal Issues" (2008) 82 Aust.L.J. 774). Ultimately, the impact of the Constitution on questions of justiciability remains unsettled.

Canada

[Insert new para.1–038A after para.1–038] **1–038**

In *Smith v Canada (Attorney General)* 2009 FC 228, the Federal Court **1–038A** held that the government's decision to no longer assist the applicant's attempts to avoid the death penalty in the US was justiciable in at least a limited sense. In so holding, the Court accepted that it had no authority to review the substance of the government's decision, in the exercise of prerogative power, to change its policy as to the circumstances under which it would intervene on behalf of someone seeking clemency from a foreign power. However, to the extent that issues arose as to whether the policy should be applied in a particular case, the court held that it was entitled to review the government's decision on procedural fairness and legitimate expectation grounds. That judgment is currently under appeal to the Federal Court of Appeal.

India

[Add to end of n.116] **1–039**

And see *Bhikhubhai Vithalbhai Patel v State of Gujarat*, 2008 (4) S.C.C. 144; *N.D. Jayal v Union of India*, 2004 (9) S.C.C. 362.

New Zealand

[Add new para.1–040A after para.1–040] **1–040**

In *Boscawen v Attorney-General* [2009] 2 N.Z.L.R. 229, the Court of **1–040A** Appeal considered a challenge to the Attorney-General's decision not to make a report to Parliament under s.7 of the Bill of Rights Act 1990

("NZBORA"), which imposes an obligation on the Attorney-General to report to Parliament, generally upon the introduction of a Bill, where any provision in a Bill appears to be inconsistent with the rights enumerated in the NZBORA. The appellants argued that the Attorney General was "wrong in law" to hold the view that no provision of the Bill was inconsistent with the NZBORA. The central issue for the court was whether it could review the s.7 duty. The High Court, consistent with previous jurisprudence, had found that the duty was non-justiciable because judicial review would be contrary to both art.9 of the Bill of Rights 1688 (which applies in New Zealand) and the principle of comity between the courts and Parliament. Significantly the Court of Appeal did not find that the duty was non-justiciable nor did it express a concluded view on the effect of art.9 of the Bill of Rights 1688. It grounded its decision on the principle of comity and preferred to limit its conclusion to the facts of the case: "We conclude that it would be contrary to the comity principle for the Court to intervene in the Attorney-General's role under s.7 in the circumstances of this case" (at [42], emphasis added). Addressing the hypothetical scenario of the Attorney General refusing to report in the case of a glaring inconsistency and in plain dereliction of his or her duty, the court said that nothing in its judgment should be taken to limit the way a court should approach such a scenario (at [41]). The court also pointed out that such a scenario raises questions of process, whereas the case before it raised a difference of view about the legal assessment made by the Attorney General. The court gave several reasons why it thought it would be inappropriate to intervene in the exercise of the Attorney-General's discretion in this case (although most of these reasons would be applicable to any future challenge):

(a) There may be genuine disagreement about human rights issues and it is pertinent that Parliament entrusted the s.7 obligation to the Attorney General, not the courts (at [18]–[20]).

(b) The reporting duty is part of the legislative process (even if the Attorney General is part of the Executive) and is therefore covered by the established principle of comity (at [32]).

(c) Review by the court could create a major impediment to the legislative process (at [34]–[35]).

(d) Intervention by a court would place it "at the heart of a political debate actually being carried out in the House" and force a confrontation between the Attorney General and the courts (at [36]).

(e) A question would arise over how a court decision on the compatibility of legislation with the NZBORA, in the review of the s.7 duty, would affect future litigation challenging the Act's compatibility with the NZBORA (at [37]).

(f) The courts are poorly situated to undertake a review of a whole piece of legislation (at [38]).

(g) The court would not countenance criticism of the legislative process as a basis for intervention (at [39]).

In *New Zealand Maori Council v Attorney General* [2008] 1 N.Z.L.R. 318, the Court of Appeal reaffirmed the general principle that "the courts will not grant relief which interferes or impacts on actions of the Executive preparatory to the introduction of a Bill to Parliament, because to do so would be to intrude into the domain of Parliament" (at [60]). The case concerned a settlement deed between certain Maori groups and the Crown related to certain historical breaches of the Treaty of Waitangi. The only commitment under the deed was to introduce a settlement Bill and the court held this to be unenforceable in the courts, saying that the deed was a political compact.

South Africa

[Add to n.129]   1–043

And see also *Ekhurhuleni Metropolitan Municipality v Dada NO*, 2009 (4) S.A. 463, SCA.

THE INCIDENCE AND IMPACT OF JUDICIAL REVIEW

[Add to end of n.134]   1–044

On settlement of threatened and actual claims for judicial review, see V. Bondy and M. Sunkin, *The Dynamics of Judicial Review Litigation: the resolution of public law challenges before final hearing* (London: Public Law Project, 2009); "Accessing Judicial Review" [2008] P.L. 647; and "Settlement in Judicial Review Proceedings" [2009] P.L. 237. The findings of these studies include that "increasing numbers of judicial review claims are now being resolved in favour of claimants by settlement without the need for trial in the Administrative Court"; and there is "widespread conscientious concern amongst both claimant and defendant solicitors to resolve disputes in a timely fashion". They conclude that the reforms to the judicial review claim procedure introduced following recommendations of the Bowman Committee (on which, see para.15–096)—including the pre-action protocol and "acknowledgment of service" procedures (whereby defendants must respond in summary form to a claim if they wish to be heard on the permission application)—may well have led to "a significant change in the dynamics of judicial review litigation".

[Update Table 1 as follows]

Table 1: The judicial review caseload

Year	Leave/ permission appli- cations received	Success rate at fil- ter stage	Full hear- ings disposed of during the year	Allowed	Dismissed	With- drawn
2006	6,458	11.6%	310	42.3%	53.2%	4.5%
2007	6,690	12.6%	336	48.2%	48.8%	3%

Note: the "success rate" in this table is calculated on the basis of applications received, not applications considered, i.e. it does not reflect the number of claims that were resolved by consent after issue but before permission consideration.

[Add to end of n.135]

Judicial and court statistics are now published by the Ministry of Justice: *http://www.justice.gov.uk/publications/6012.htm*. The data in Table 1 do not include claims other than for judicial review under CPR Pt 54. The Administrative Court determines a very substantial number of other types of claim, e.g. applications for reconsideration under s.103a of the Nationality, Immigration and Asylum Act 2002 (of which there were 3,306 in 2006 and 3,730 in 2007).

The case load

1–045 *[Add new n.137A after ". . .there has been a significant decrease in the number permitted to proceed to a full hearing"]*

See further V. Bondy and M. Sunkin, "Accessing Judicial Review" [2008] P.L. 647. The authors chart a long-term decline in the grant of permission, with a particularly steep decline since 2000. They suggest that "despite the diminishing grant rate, the overall picture may be one in which access to substantive justice in terms of satisfactory outcomes has improved" (p.666). This is because of the high incidence of settlements in favour of claimants that occur prior to permission being considered.

1–047 *[Add to end of n.144]*

See also T. Poole and S. Shah, "The Impact of the Human Rights Act on the House of Lords" [2009] P.L. 347.

[Add to end of para.1–047]

On October 1, 2009 the jurisdiction of the House of Lords, along with the devolution issue jurisdiction of the Judicial Committee of the Privy Council, was transferred to the Supreme Court of the United Kingdom, established under Pt 3 of the Constitutional Reform Act 2005.

Central government responses to judicial review

[Add to end of n.158]   1–050

If there is a change of governing party at the 2010 general election, there are indications that ministerial attitudes to the judiciary will be as dismal as they were, at times, during the previous Labour administrations. David Cameron MP, Leader of Her Majesty's Official Opposition, said in a speech delivered at Imperial College, London on June 25, 2009, entitled "Giving power back to the people": "It [i.e. 'real accountability'] means reining in and reversing the regulation of our lives by unaccountable judges who are changing Britain's legal landscape with their judgments in the courtroom". (See *http://www.conservatives.com/News/Speeches/2009/06/David_ Cameron_Giving_power_back_to_the_people.aspx*).

ADMINISTRATIVE JUSTICE AND PROPORTIONATE DISPUTE RESOLUTION

[Add to end of n.179]   1–057

During 2007 it became plain that the Administrative Court was beset with such serious difficulties in listing cases that the principle of the rule of law was at risk. In *R. (on the application of Casey) v Restormel BC* [2007] EWHC 2554 Admin); [2008] A.C.D. 1, Munby J. spoke of the indefensible delay that had occurred in that case as amounting to a denial of justice in the sense in which that phrase was used in Ch.40 of Magna Carta (which declares that "to no one will we sell, to no one we will deny or delay, right or justice"). In late 2007, the Public Law Project (a national legal charity which aims to improve access to public law remedies for those whose access is restricted by poverty, discrimination or other similar barriers) sent a letter before claim to the Ministry of Justice arguing that the unacceptable level of delays was unlawful. In April 2008, Collins J., the Lead Judge of the Administrative Court, issued a statement that the number of courts sitting from April to the end of the Trinity term would be substantially increased (see *http://www.hmcourts-service.gov.uk/cms/admin.htm*; and further C. Haley, "Action on Administrative Court Delays" (2008) 13 J.R. 69 and R. Clayton, "New Arrangements for the Administrative Court" (2008) 13 J.R. 164).

INTERNAL COMPLAINT SYSTEMS

1–061 *[Add to n.189]*

And see J. Gulland, "Independence in complaints procedures: lessons from community care" (2009) 31 Journal of Social Welfare & Family Law 59 ("Most people do not make formal complaints at all and very few people seek an independent review of their complaint. When they do seek such a review, they expect it to be transparently independent of the body complained about. The article concludes that the current system of local authority complaints review panels or committees does not provide the independent element that complainants seek").

[In text of para.1–061]

Delete "The National Health Service (Complaints) Regulations 2004" and substitute: The Local Authority Social Services and National Health Service Complaints (England) Regulations 2009.

[In n.191]

Delete "SI 2004/768" and substitute: SI 2009/309; and see also the Local Authority Social Services and National Health Service Complaints (England) (Amendment) Regulations 2009 (SI 2009/1768).

1–064 *[Add citation in n.200]*

Tsfayo v United Kingdom is now reported at [2007] H.L.R. 19; [2007] B.L.G.R. 1; (2009) 48 E.H.R.R. 18.

MEDIATION

1–065 *[In para.1–065 insert new n.201a after ". . . the Public Law Project commenced a study on value and limits of mediation in this context".]*

See V. Bondy and L. Mulcahy, *Mediation and Judicial Review: an empirical research study* (London: Public Law Project, 2009). The study concluded that "there is no single explanation for why there are so few mediations of public law disputes, nor it is possible to create a checklist of factors that would identify public law cases that are suitable for mediation" (p.89). An important context is that the vast majority of situations in which a claimant threatens judicial review, as well as of issued claims, are resolved before reaching the point of a full hearing in the Administrative Court: it is estimated that of 1,000 letters before claim written, only 46 cases will reach a full adjudication (p.19). The study found that there was no evidence to support the view that lawyers' lack of use of mediation in public law cases might be motivated by financial considerations. In cases where mediation was used or contemplated, lawyers took the view that they should be present and involved in the process to protect their clients' rights and interests especially where the clients were individuals challenging powerful public bodies. They also believe that mediators needed to understand the legal framework to the dispute in the context of public law challenges (p.59). There was a view that mediation "took too long to be of any help in urgent cases" (p.63). The study found no clear evidence to support a view that mediation is cheaper than judicial review litigation and urged caution in drawing comparisons in the costs of mediation in commercial disputes (p.69).

OMBUDSMEN AND SIMILAR GRIEVANCE-HANDLING SCHEMES

[Add to end of n.204]   1–066

See also R. Moules, *Actions against Public Officials: Legitimate Expectations, Statements and Misconduct* (London: Sweet & Maxwell, 2009), Ch.10; J. Halford, "It's Public Law, But Not As We Know It: Understanding and Making Effective Use of Ombudsman Schemes" (2009) 14 J.R. 81.

[Add to table on p.43 headed "Examples of non-statutory ombudsmen . . . 1–068
dealing with the public sector" in the box next to "Prison and Probation Ombudsman for England and Wales"]

In January 2008, the Government proposed in the Criminal Justice and Immigration Bill to put the Prison and Probation Ombudsman on a statutory footing; but the Government withdrew the plans following criticisms, including from ombudsmen.

The Parliamentary Ombudsman

[Add to end of n.215]   1–069

For views of the current PCA, see: A. Abraham, "The Ombudsman as Part of the UK Constitution: A Contested Role?" (2008) 61 Parl. Aff. 206; "The Ombudsman and Individual Rights" (2008) 61 Parl. Aff. 370; "The Ombudsman and the Executive: The Road to Accountability" (2008) Parl. Aff. 535; "The Future in International Perspective: The Ombudsman as Agent of Rights, Justice and Democracy" (2008) 61 Parl. Aff. 681; "The ombudsman and 'paths to justice': a just alternative or just an alternative?" [2008] P.L. 1.

1–075 *[Add to end of n.221]*

And on appeal, see *R. (on the application of Bradley) v Secretary of State for Work and Pensions* [2008] EWCA Civ 36; [2008] 3 W.L.R. 1059 (considered below); and see further R. Kirkham, B. Thompson and T. Buck, "When Putting Things Right Goes Wrong: Enforcing the Recommendations of the Ombudsman" [2008] P.L. 510.

Health Service Ombudsman for England

1–076 *[Delete text of para.1–076 and substitute]*

The PCA does not have jurisdiction to deal with complaints arising from the National Health Service. Instead, such complaints are dealt with by the HSC—a post that is in practice combined with that of the PCA (Health Service Commissioners Act 1993 (as amended)). In Wales, health service complaints are dealt with the by Public Services Ombudsman for Wales (see Public Services Ombudsman (Wales) Act 2005). A simpler two-stage complaints process was introduced by the Health and Social Care Act 2008 on April 1, 2009, removing the requirement to complain to the Health Service Commission (now abolished) before approaching the Health Service Ombudsman. Under the new scheme, complaints are made first to the local NHS body or practice; thereafter, if a person is dissatisfied with the way in which the local NHS body or practice has dealt with the complaint, a complaint may be made to the Health Service Ombudsman.

The reforms also introduced an integrated approach to both health and social care complaints. Complaints about social care (which is a local authority rather than NHS function) not resolved locally may be brought to the attention of the Local Government Ombudsman, which can work together on complaints that cross the boundaries of both systems.

Local Government Ombudsman

1–077 *[Delete second sentence in para.1–077 and substitute the following]*

There are three Commissioners, each with a distinct jurisdiction. Until reforms contained in the Local Government and Public Involvement in Health Act 2007 are implemented, cases continue to be allocated on the basis of geographical area; in future, each Commissioner will be able to specialise in categories according to subject matter. Part 9 of the 2007 Act also introduced changes to the operation of the LGO: the LGO may now look at service failure in addition to maladministration; the LGO now has a limited power to investigate where an apparent case of maladministration comes to light even though they have received no complaint about the matter; complaints about the procurement of goods and services are now within jurisdiction; the LGO may issue a "statement of reasons" instead of a report if they are satisfied with the council's proposals to remedy its failures; there are new powers to publish LGO's decisions other than reports; and complaints no longer need to be in writing.

[Add new n.227a in para.1–078 after ". . . before calling on the LGO to investigate."]   1–078

In April 2009, the LCO introduced a formal policy called "Council First", under which complaints are required to exhaust all stages of a local authority internal complaints process (which typically have three tiers) before having recourse to the LGO. The policy includes exceptions to this, including where matters are urgent (such as school admissions and homelessness) and where complaints are regarded as falling into a category of vulnerability (such as care services for children and adults): see *Local Government Ombudsman Annual Report 2008–09*.

Reform of the ombudsmen

[Add to end of para.1–080]   1–080

As noted above, Pt 9 of the Local Government and Public Involvement in Health Act 2007 introduced a package of reforms to the LGO; and the Health and Social Care Act 2008 brought about changes to the remit of the Health Service Commissioner.

Judicial review and the ombudsmen

[Delete para.1–082 and substitute the following]   1–082

Generally, there is a high level of compliance by public authorities with ombudsmen reports. Occasionally, however, a public authority subject to a formal investigation by an ombudsman may be inclined to disagree with findings contained in a report and may be disinclined to implement recommendations made (see further R. Kirkham, B. Thompson and T. Buck, "When Putting Things Right Goes Wrong: Enforcing the Recommendations of the Ombudsman" [2008] P.L. 510). Other than publicity, the LGO has no powers to compel action from a public authority following an adverse report. The PCA has express power to lay a report before Parliament where "it appears . . . that the injustice" investigated "has not or will not be remedied" (Parliamentary Commissioner for Administration Act 1967 s.10(3)) but there are no legal powers of enforcement. The extent to which a public authority may reject findings and recommendations of the ombudsmen is governed by the different statutory and constitutional frameworks in which these ombudsmen operate (the Parliamentary Commissioner for Administration Act 1967 in the case of the PCA and the Local Government Act 1974 in relation to the LGO).

The leading authority on judicial review of the PCA is now the Court of Appeal in R. *(on the application of Bradley) v Secretary of State for Work and Pensions* [2008] EWCA Civ 36; [2008] 3 W.L.R. 1059 (on which see J. Varuhas, "Governmental Rejections of Ombudsman Findings: What Role for the Courts?" (2009) 72 M.L.R. 102). It was common ground that *recommendations*, as opposed to findings at of "maladministration" and "injustice" were not binding on the Secretary of State. The Department disagreed with the PCA's factual findings and conclusions in relation to guidance issued about occupational pensions. Sir John Chadwick drew a distinction between the PCA and the LGO: "there is no separation of powers in local government which corresponds to the separation, in national government, between the powers of the executive and the powers of parliament" (at [58]) and (per Wall L.J. at [137]) "a Minister who rejects the Ombudsman's findings of maladministration will have to defend him or herself in Parliament, and will be subject to Parliamentary control". The constitutional question was whether this should lead "to the conclusion that, when enacting the [Parliamentary Commissioner for Administration] 1967 Act, Parliament intended to preclude a Minister who was called to account before either House from explaining, as part of his justification for the decision to provide no remedy in respect of the complaint which has been the subject of investigation, his reasons for rejecting the Parliamentary Commissioner's finding of maladministration".

Sir John Chadwick held (at [70]) that the following principles can be derived from the judgments in R. *v Warwickshire CC Ex p. Powergen Plc* (1998) 75 P. & C.R. 89 and R. *v Secretary of State for the Home Department Ex p. Danaei* [1997] EWCA Civ 2704; [1998] Imm. A.R. 84:

"(i) the decision maker whose decision is under challenge (in the former case, the local highway authority; in the latter, the Secretary of State) is entitled to exercise his own discretion as to whether he should regard himself as bound by a finding of fact made by an adjudicative tribunal (in the former case, the planning inspector; in the latter, the special adjudicator) in a related context; (ii) a decision to reject a finding of fact made by an adjudicative tribunal in a related context can be challenged on *Wednesbury* grounds; (iii) in particular, the challenge can be advanced on the basis that the decision to reject the finding of fact was irrational; (iv) in determining whether the decision to reject the finding of fact was irrational the court will have regard to the circumstances in which, and the statutory scheme within which, the finding of fact was made by the adjudicative tribunal; (v) in particular, the court will have regard to the nature of the fact found (e.g. that the immigrant was an adulterer), the basis on which the finding was made (e.g. on oral testimony tested by cross-examination, or purely on the documents), the form of the proceedings before the tribunal (e.g. adversarial and in public, or investigative with no opportunity for cross-examination), and the role of the tribunal within the statutory scheme."

This compelled the conclusion that "properly understood, . . . the two cases provide no support for the proposition that, as a matter of law, it is not open to a body which has been the subject of a finding of maladministration by the Parliamentary Ombudsman to reject that finding; rather, the cases are authority for the proposition that it is open to such a body, acting rationally, to reject a finding of maladministration" (see at [71]). The "fundamental point" is the "rejection of the proposition that the decision of this court in *R. v Local Commissioner for Administration Ex p. Eastleigh BC* [1988] 1 Q.B. 855 is authority for the proposition that the Secretary of State is bound by the Parliamentary Ombudsman's findings of maladministration and must treat them as correct unless and until they are quashed in judicial review proceedings" (per Wall J. at [135]). The question is not whether the Secretary of State himself "considers that there was any maladministration, but whether in the circumstances his rejection of the Ombudsman's finding to this effect is based on a cogent reason" (per Sir John Chadwick at [72]). The court concluded in relation to one finding that the minister had advanced sound arguments but no such reasons existed in relation to another finding; accordingly, the department was required to reconsider its response.

In *R. (on the application of Equitable Members Action Group) v Her Majesty's Treasury* [2009] EWHC 2495 (Admin), the Divisional Court said of the "cogent reasons" requirement: "That is not a precise test, but it would be wrong in our view for us at this level to attempt a further definition of the 'cogent' reasons test or to suppose that there is some exhaustive list of such reasons. What is required instead is a careful examination of the facts of the individual case—with the focus resting upon the decision to reject the findings of the Ombudsman, rather than the Ombudsman's findings themselves" ([66]).

The legal and constitutional position of the LGO is rather different from that of the PCA, so the scope for a local authority wanting to disagree with the findings and recommendations of the LGO may be more limited. The LGO, unlike the PCA, has no power to pursue a failure to implement a recommendation in Parliament. In *Bradley*, Wall L.J. said that "the system . . . depends on the convention that local authorities will be bound by the findings of the LGO. It must follow inexorably that if a local authority wishes to avoid findings of maladministration made by a LGO, it must apply for judicial review to quash the decision" (at [139]).

TRIBUNALS

Tribunals after the Tribunals, Courts and Enforcement Act 2007

[Add to end of n.267]   1–088

The New Zealand Law Commission and the Ministry of Justice have been working on proposals for a "unified tribunal framework" over the last few years. That work culminated in the production of a study paper in December 2008 for feedback and comment, which set out the Commission's preferred model for tribunal reform. See *http://www.lawcom. govt.nz/ProjectGeneral.aspx?ProjectID=131.*

Review and appeal in the new tribunal system

1–090   *[Add to end of n.270]*

See generally, R. Carnwath, "Tribunal Justice—a New Start" [2009] P.L. 48; and P. Cane, "Judicial Review in the Age of Tribunals" [2009] P.L. 479.

1–093   *[Add new para.1–093A to end of para.1–093]*

What approach should be adopted by a court reviewing a decision made by an expert tribunal?

1–093A   In *Secretary of State for the Home Department v AH (Sudan)* [2007] UKHL 49; [2008] 1 A.C. 678—in relation to the Asylum and Immigration Tribunal—Baroness Hale of Richmond stated

> "the ordinary courts should approach appeals from them with an appropriate degree of caution; it is probable that in understanding and applying the law in their specialised field the tribunal will have got it right: see *Cooke v Secretary of State for Social Security* [2001] EWCA Civ 734, [2002] 3 All ER 279, [16]. They and they alone are the judges of the facts. It is not enough that their decision on those facts may seem harsh to people who have not heard and read the evidence and arguments which they have heard and read. Their decisions should be respected unless it is quite clear that they have misdirected themselves in law. Appellate courts should not rush to find such misdirections simply because they might have reached a different conclusion on the facts or expressed themselves differently" (at [30]).

Lord Hope of Craighead agreed: "A decision that is clearly based on a mistake of law must, of course, be corrected. Its reasoning must be explained, but it ought not to be subjected to an unduly critical analysis" (at [19]). The position is different where the judicial body being appealed from is a court: "appellate courts would not be performing their task properly if they were to exercise the same self-denying ordinance to decisions by judges sitting in the ordinary courts. Subject to the familiar rules that recognise the advantage that a judge enjoys who has seen and heard the witnesses, his decision is open to the widest scrutiny that is possible within the limits that the law places on the jurisdiction of the appeal court" (*RB (Algeria) v Secretary of State for the Home Department* [2009] UKHL 10; [2009] 2 W.L.R. 512, Lord Hope of Craighead at [219]–[221] in relation to the Special Immigration Appeal Commission, which was presided over by a senior judge). And while the expertise of a specialist tribunal (such as the Asylum and Immigration Tribunal) "as assessors of in-country evidence and as judges experienced in fact finding exercises about events in foreign countries" is to be respected, "on basic issues of fairness", such a tribunal is "no more specialist than any other judicial tribunal" (see *VH (Malawi) v Secretary of State for the Home Department* [2009] EWCA Civ 645 at [73] (Pill L.J.).

Immigration and asylum

[Add to end of para.1–094]   1–094

In May 2009, the Government announced that immigration and asylum tribunal adjudication will be transferred to the unified tribunal system in early 2010. The Asylum and Immigration Tribunal will cease to exist and will be replaced by Immigration and Asylum Chambers of the First-Tier Tribunal and of the Upper Tribunal. See further para.17–009.

PUBLIC INQUIRIES AND INQUESTS

Coroners and Inquests

[Add to end of n.303]   1–101

The Coroners and Justice Bill (introduced to Parliament in 2008–09) will, if enacted, create a new statutory framework for the work of Coroners.

CATEGORIES OF JUDICIAL REVIEW

[Add to end of para.1–103 a new n.303A]   1–103

For a fascinating alternative analysis, see R. Rawlings, "Modelling Judicial Review" (2008) 61 C.L.P. 95. Rawlings argues that judicial review in England and Wales is a "multi-streamed" jurisdiction.

CHAPTER 2

CLAIMANTS, INTERESTED PARTIES AND INTERVENERS

THE "SUFFICIENT INTEREST" REQUIREMENT

Charity proceedings

[In para.2–010] 2–010

Delete "Charity Commissioners" and substitute "Charity Commission for England and Wales".

Delete "Standing rules are imposed by the Charities Act 1993 s.31(1). . ."; and substitute "Standing rules are imposed by the Charities Act 1993 s.33(1) . . .".

[Add new para.2–010A] 2–010A

The Charity Commission for England and Wales, a non-ministerial government department, is a public authority. The Charities Act 2006 created the Charity Tribunal to which appeals against specified decisions of the Charity Commission may be made. The tribunal "shall apply the principles which would be applied by the High Court on an application for judicial review": Charities Act 1993 Sch.1C.

CAPACITY AND STANDING

Unincorporated associations and companies

[Add to end of n.37] 2–012

Permission for judicial review was refused in relation to a decision said to have been made by the "Buckingham Pubwatch Scheme" (an unincorporated association of publicans) to ban the claimant from licensed premises for several years was held, at a permission hearing, not to be amenable to judicial review: it had no constitution, no finances, no fixed membership, no rules and its decisions were binding on its members only to the extent that they treat them as binding, on which again there are no rules: *R. (on the application of Proud) v Buckingham Pubwatch Scheme* [2008] EWHC 2224 (Admin).

Child claimants and abuse of process

2–015 *[Add to end of para.2–015]*

There may be circumstances in which a child should be made a party to judicial review proceedings and even separately represented: see *E (A Child) v Chief Constable of Ulster* [2008] UKHL 66; [2008] 3 W.L.R. 1208 [6], [42] (judicial review challenge to police handling of sectarian demonstrations outside a school in which the mother but not her young daughter was a party to the application).

How and When is Standing Relevant?

2–016 *[Add to end of para.2–016]*

A "rolled-up" hearing, combining all these stages, may be ordered where a judge considers that there is or may be an arguable claim but a defence, such as lack of standing or delay, "should be kept open or some additional evidence is needed to show that the claim is indeed an arguable one and it is desirable that it should be dealt with substantively rather than rejected as unarguable": *R. (on the application of Hasan) v Secretary of State for Trade and Industry (now Business, Enterprise and Regulatory Reform)* [2007] EWHC 2630 (Admin) at [7] (Collins J.).

Assessing the Claimant's Interest

The legislative framework

2–026 *[Add new para.2–026A after para.2–026]*

2–026A Legislation may make express provision in relation to the scope of "sufficient interest" in order to clarify, restrict or expand the category of those who have "sufficient interest". For example, the Local Government Act 1988 s.19(7) provides that "in proceedings for judicial review . . . the persons who have a sufficient interest in the matter shall include any potential contractor" (in relation to challenges to decisions about the contracting-out of local authority service provision): see *First Real Estates (UK) Ltd v Birmingham City Council* [2009] EWHC 817 (Admin); *R. v Enfield LBC Ex p. TF Unwin (Roydon)* 46 B.L.R. 1; *R. v Bristol City*

Council Ex p. D L Barrett & Sons, CO/4181/1999. In a different context, the Human Rights Act 1998 s.7 restricts the scope of "sufficient interest" by introducing a requirement that a person who seeks to rely on a breach of a Convention right has standing only if he or she is a "victim": see para.2–024 below.

Impact and proximity interests

[Insert after first sentence of para.2–029]   2–029

But as the Court of Appeal has made plain, the relevance of a claimant's personal rights "is not that without them there would be no claim for judicial review. Any person or body with a sufficient interest can seek judicial review. The claimants' interest is that they say they were among those who suffered violations of their right not to be inhumanly or degradingly treated; but there is no requirement of law that their claim for judicial review must be confined to their private law or personal interests": *R. (on the application of AM) v Secretary of State for the Home Department* [2009] EWCA Civ 219 at [34]. The Court of Appeal held, finding that the Home Secretary had acted unlawfully in failing to meet obligations to fully investigate events during a disturbance at an immigration removal centre, that "arguments about the degree of involvement or suffering of the particular claimants, unless these were to found a submission that they are mere meddlers who lack standing, are largely irrelevant. What matters is whether the entirety of what they have now brought to the court's attention requires, or at some point required, the Home Secretary to set up an inquiry" (at [35]).

[Add to end of para.2–030]   2–030

A regular user of a bridle-way adjacent to a ruined cottage was held to have no standing to challenge a decision of a local authority to take enforcement action to require repair and restoration work to the cottage to be dismantled: *R. (on the application of Friend) v East Devon DC* [2009] EWHC 1013 (Admin) (H.H. Judge Kirham: "His interest is essentially that of a passer-by and a lover of the local landscape. He has no interest in the land itself. Mr Friend has not demonstrated a sufficient direct personal interest in the outcome. Further, I am not persuaded that there is a serious issue of general or public importance to be considered here").

Public interest

[Add to end of para.2–031]   2–031

A Palestinian farmer who lived in a village near Bethlehem, whose land was appropriated to the Israeli Land Department, was held to have standing to challenge ministerial decisions to grant Standard Individual Export Licences (SIELs) for Military List items exported to Israel: *R. (on the application of Hasan) v Secretary of State for Trade and Industry* [2007] EWHC 2630 (Admin) (Collins J. at [8]: "A Palestinian living in a part of the occupied territories affected by Israel's attempts to contain attacks upon its citizens and so indirectly affected by any trade in military equipment to Israel is not a busybody and has in my view sufficient interest to pursue this claim"); on appeal, where standing was not considered, see [2008] EWCA Civ 1311.

Presence or absence of other challengers

2–033   *[Add to end of n.96]*

But in *R. (on the application of Al-Haq) v Secretary of State for Foreign and Commonwealth Affairs* [2009] EWHC 1910 (Admin) at [62] Cranston J. expressed doubt whether a non-governmental organisation based in the Occupied Palestinian Territory/the West Bank would have standing in a claim seeking a declaration that the UK Government was in breach of its obligations in international law in respect of the Israeli Government's actions in Gaza:

> "as a matter of principle it seems to me that if declaring an act or decision to be unlawful will affect a particular individual or group, and if none of them decides to challenge it, the courts must generally refuse to permit someone more remote from the act or decision to do so. In this case no one in the United Kingdom has sought judicial review of United Kingdom foreign policy regarding Israel's actions in Gaza. Then, as a practical matter, there is the Secretary of State's argument that if the claimant is correct, it would follow that any NGO, anywhere in the world, would have standing to bring a claim for judicial review in similar circumstances".

The application for permission was refused on grounds of non-justiciability.

HUMAN RIGHTS ACT 1998 AND THE VICTIM REQUIREMENT

2–041   *[Add new para.2–041A after para.2–041]*

Public Contracts Regulations

2–041A   The Public Contracts Regulations 2006 (SI 2006/5) make provision in domestic law for European Union rules on public procurement; breach of rules by a "contracting authority" may be challenged by way of a judicial review claim. The courts have taken the approach that in order to have standing in this context, a claimant must be an "economic operator". Thus, the fact that a would-be claimant was a mother of school-age children living in the London Borough of Camden did not provide her with sufficient interest to make a judicial review claim on the ground that the public procurement rules had not been followed in a decision under s.482 of the Education Act 1996 relating to the establishment of an Academy sponsored by UCL: "The nature of the legal protections conferred by the procurement regime created by the 2006 Regulations is such that they can be invoked only in private law proceedings by affected economic operators and no such has come forward" (*R. (on the application of Chandler) v Secretary of State for Children, Schools and Families* [2009] EWHC 219 (Admin); [2009] ACD 50 at [140], Forbes J.).

Strasbourg case law on meaning of "victim"

[Add at end of n.133]   2–052

See H. Davis, "Public authorities as 'victims' under the Human Rights Act" (2005) 64 C.L.J. 315.

Application of "victim" requirement in the HRA

[Add to text of para.2–053 after n.136]   2–053

In *Re Northern Ireland Commissioner for Children and Young People's Application for Judicial Review* [2007] NIQB 115, Gillen J. was "reluctantly" drawn to the conclusion that the Commissioner, a statutory body, was not a "victim" in a challenge to a ministerial decision to lay before Parliament delegated legislation which provided for a defence of reasonable chastisement of a child to a charge of assault—the court could not "permit a complaint against this law *in abstracto* simply because the Commissioner feels, however sincerely, it contravenes the Convention unless she is a victim" (at [15]). The court held that it could not be plausibly argued that the applicant in this case has been "affected" simply because the legislation offends against her concept of what is appropriate for children's rights notwithstanding the aims and terms of her empowering legislation. The court noted that it was still open to the Commissioner to provide assistance to individuals to take cases relating to HRA 1998 who are victims, to intervene by way of third-party intervention, and as amicus curiae. The court nonetheless went on to consider whether there had been a violation of rights and freedoms under art.3, art.6, art.8 and art.14 ECHR and held that there was not.

[Add to end of para.2–053]

In *Somerville v Scottish Ministers* [2007] UKHL 44; [2007] 1 W.L.R. 2734, the House of Lords considered s.100(1) of the Scotland Act 1998, which in similar terms to s.7 of the HRA 1998 restricts reliance on Convention rights in legal proceedings to those who are "victims". Lord Scott of Foscote commented that:

> "Bearing in mind that Convention incompatibility is a ground on which any enactment of the Scottish Parliament, any subordinate legislation made by the Scottish Ministers or the Scottish Executives or any act of any member of the Scottish Executive may be held to be outside devolved competence and therefore ultra vires, the need to place a strict limit on those entitled to raise such a point in litigation seems to me easy to understand" (at [75]).

In *Eastaway v Secretary of State for Trade and Industry* [2007] EWCA Civ 425; [2007] B.C.C. 550 at [51] the Court of Appeal reiterated that "A person can be a victim under Strasbourg jurisprudence even though the violation has been brought to an end". The appellant had given an undertaking to the Secretary of State in May 2001 not to act as a company director for four and a half years. In 2004, the European Court of Human Rights had held that the art.6 ECHR rights of the appellant had been breached by the length of proceedings; he was awarded compensation for his legal costs and non-pecuniary damage. In the present case the appellant sought to have the undertaken given in 2001 set aside, even though it had expired. Arden L.J., for the court, held that:

> "The definition of 'victim' in s.7(7) turns on whether proceedings could be brought in the Strasbourg court in respect of the act complained of. The act complained of would be the continuance of the disqualification proceedings when no fair trial was possible. Thus the statutory hypothesis in s.7(7) of the HRA must, in my judgment, be applied not to the proceedings which have already been brought in the Strasbourg court, but to some new proceedings brought on the same basis as his new complaint and at the same time" (at [54]).

The appellant did not, however, have an arguable case.

STANDING OF "PERSONS AGGRIEVED"

2–055 *[Add to end of n.144]*

The Competition Appeal Tribunal, in a review under s.120 of the Enterprise Act 2002 of a decision of the Secretary of State for Business, Enterprise and Regulatory Reform not to refer to the Competition Commission under s.45 of the 2002 Act a proposed merger of banks, held that although "the relevant tests for standing in claims for judicial review in England and Wales and under s.120 of the Act are phrased differently, and thus the ease with which an applicant can establish standing may well differ, we see no reason why the factors that inform the question of standing should be wholly different" (*Merger Action Group v Secretary of State for Business, Enterprise and Regulatory Reform* [2008] CAT 36; 2009 S.L.T. 10 at [41]). Moreover, "it would be undesirable to interpret 'person aggrieved' in this context in such a way as to limit the possibility of challenge to a merger decision by shutting out those with a less immediate connection to the subject-matter of the dispute than, for example, competitors in the market place but who may well also be adversely affected, albeit in a different way" (at [47]).

INTERESTED PARTIES AND INTERVENERS

Interested parties

[Add to end of n.175]

2–063

The term "interested party" has different meanings in other contexts, e.g. Licensing Act 2003 s.13(3) and Gambling Act 2005 s.158.

[Add to end of para.2–063]

Doubt has been expressed as to whether an interested party is entitled to advance a particular argument without the grant of permission: (*R. (on the application of Fraser) v National Institute for Health* [2009] EWHC Admin 452 at [114]. Moreover, the court held that "In order to succeed with a claim for judicial review the interested party has to show a sufficient interest in the matter in issue" ([115]) and went on to find that the interested party in that case (a challenge to publication of a guideline by the National Institute for Health and Clinical Excellence on the treatment of Chronic Fatigue Syndrome/Myalgic Encephalomyelitis) "fails for insufficiency of interest" because the ground of challenge was without legal merit.

Interveners

[Add new n.183a at end of para.2–064]

2–064

See *E (A Child) v Chief Constable of Ulster* [2008] UKHL 66; [2008] 3 W.L.R. 1208 at [3] (Lord Hoffmann: "An intervention is however of no assistance if it merely repeats points which the appellant or respondent has already made. An intervener will have had sight of their printed cases and, if it has nothing to add, should not add anything. It is not the role of an intervener to be an additional counsel for one of the parties. This is particularly important in the case of an oral intervention. . . . In future, I hope that interveners will avoid unnecessarily taking up the time of the House in this way").

COMPARATIVE PERSPECTIVES

Canada

2–075   *[Add to end of para.2–075]*

Irving Shipbuilding Inc v Canada (Attorney General), 2009 FCA 116 demonstrates the unwillingness of the Canadian courts to be drawn unnecessarily into challenges based on a lack of standing. The Federal Court of Appeal there rejected an argument that a sub-contractor of an unsuccessful bidder lacked standing to challenge the award of a government contract on the grounds of procedural unfairness. Rather, the application for judicial review fell to be determined on the basis of whether the sub-contractor was entitled to procedural fairness. The court held that it was not.

India

2–077   *[Add to end of para.2–077]*

A person acting bona fide and having sufficient interest in proceedings will alone have standing. If a writ petitioner is not acting bona fide and yet there is scope for dealing with public interest litigation that can be done by appointing an amicus in his place only in exceptional circumstances: see *Holicow Pictures (P) Ltd v Prem Chand Mishra*, 2007 (14) S.C.C. 281.

Chapter 3

DEFENDANTS AND DECISIONS SUBJECT TO JUDICIAL REVIEW

Scope

[Insert after last sentence of n.8]   3–001

For recent statutory use of the terminology "public authority", see e.g: Health and Social Care Act 2008 Sch.4 para.3 (similar definition to that used in the Human Rights Act 1998); Human Fertilisation and Embryology Act 2008 ss.8–9 (the Human Fertilisation and Embryology Authority may give assistance to "a government department, a public authority or the holder of a public office"—but are these not all "public authorities"?); Education and Skills Act 2008 s.128 (". . .the Secretary of State, or such other public authority as may be prescribed").

Range of Public Authorities Subject to Judicial Review

Central government

[Delete first sentence in n.13 and substitute the following]   3–003

For an overview of central government, see A. Le Sueur, "The Nature, Powers and Accountability of Central Government", Ch.3 in D. Feldman (ed.), *English Public Law*, 2nd edn (Oxford: OUP 2009).

Local and devolved government

[Delete text of n.21 and substitute]   3–004

For an overview of local government, S.H. Bailey, "The Structure, Powers and Accountability of Local Government", Ch.4 in D. Feldman (ed.), *English Public Law*, 2nd edn (Oxford: OUP 2009).

Criminal justice system

3–005 *[In para.3–005 add new n.24a after ". . . Director of the Serious Fraud Office"]*

In *R. (on the application of Corner House Research) v Director of the Serious Fraud Office* [2008] UKHL 60; [2008] 3 W.L.R. 568, the House of Lords considered a challenge to the legality of a decision of the Director to halt a criminal investigation into allegations of bribery against a defence contractor after a threat was made by an official of Saudi Arabia that, if the investigation continued, Saudi Arabia would cease to cooperate with the UK on counter-terrorism and would not enter into the contract. Lord Bingham of Cornhill stated (at [30]–[31]) that it was:

> "accepted that the decisions of the Director are not immune from review by the courts, but authority makes plain that only in highly exceptional cases will the court disturb the decisions of an independent prosecutor and investigator: *R. v Director of Public Prosecutions, Ex p. C* [1995] 1 Cr.App.R. 136, 141; *R. v Director of Public Prosecutions, Ex p. Manning* [2001] Q.B. 330, [23]; *R. (on the application of Bermingham and others) v Director of the Serious Fraud Office* [2006] EWHC 200 (Admin), [2007] Q.B. 727, [63]–[64]; *Mohit v Director of Public Prosecutions of Mauritius* [2006] UKPC 20, [2006] 1 W.L.R. 3343, [17] and [21] citing and endorsing a passage in the judgment of the Supreme Court of Fiji in *Matalulu v Director of Public Prosecutions* [2003] 4 L.R.C. 712, 735–736; *Sharma v Brown-Antoine and others* [2006] UKPC 57, [2007] 1 W.L.R. 780, [14(1)–(6)]. The House was not referred to any case in which a challenge had been made to a decision not to prosecute or investigate on public interest grounds.
>
> The reasons why the courts are very slow to interfere are well understood. They are, first, that the powers in question are entrusted to the officers identified, and to no one else. No other authority may exercise these powers or make the judgments on which such exercise must depend. Secondly, the courts have recognised (as it was described in the cited passage of *Matalulu*) 'the polycentric character of official decision-making in such matters including policy and public interest considerations which are not susceptible of judicial review because it is within neither the constitutional function nor the practical competence of the courts to assess their merits'. Thirdly, the powers are conferred in very broad and unprescriptive terms".

See further J. Jowell, "Caving In: Threats and the Rule of Law" (2008) 13 J.R. 273 (arguing that it was "surprising that the House of Lords in *Corner House* positively encourages the view that the rule of law is on a par with any other 'relevant consideration' taken into account by the prosecutor" and expressing hope "that this does not signal an abrupt lapse into the unnecessarily deferential administrative law of yesteryear"). For a different view, see R. Hopkins and C. Yeginsu, "Storm in a Teacup: Domestic and International Conservatism from the Corner House Case" (2008) 13 J.R. 267.

[Add to end of n.26] 3–006

Proposals for reform of the Attorney General's role in relation to prosecutions were included in the Constitutional Renewal Bill, introduced to Parliament in the 2008–09 session (and likely to be carried over to the 2009–10 session).

Administrative justice system

[Add to end of para.3–007] 3–007

A social security commissioner's refusal to grant permission to appeal against the disallowance of an appeal by the Social Security Appeal Tribunal is in principle amenable to judicial review, though the courts should be very slow to interfere with such decisions: *Head v Social Security Commissioner* [2009] EWHC 950 (Admin); [2009] Pens. L.R. 207.

Courts

Criminal cases

[Add to end of n.40] 3–009

I. Steele, "Judicial Review of the Crown Court and Section 29(3) of the Supreme Court Act 1981" (2008) 13 J.R. 180; J. Horder, "Rationalising Judicial Review in Criminal Proceedings" (2008) 13 J.R. 207. So, e.g. a decision of the Crown Court to issue the warrants to enter and search properties under the Police and Criminal Evidence Act 1984 is amenable to judicial review: see *R. (on the application of Faisaltex Ltd) v Crown Court Sitting at Preston* [2008] EWHC 2832 (Admin); [2009] 1 Cr. App. R. 37.

[Add to end of para.3–009]

It has been held that where the "magistrate is acting not as an Examining Magistrate, but deciding a preliminary issue as to jurisdiction, his ruling upon that is final and can properly be challenged by way of case stated or judicial review": *R. (on the application of Donnachie) v Cardiff Magistrates' Court* [2007] EWHC 1846 (Admin) at [6], citing *R. v Clerkenwell Metropolitan Stipendiary Magistrate Ex p. DPP* [1984] 2 All E.R. 193.

Legislation

3–011 *[Add to end of n.46]*

In *Tabernacle v Secretary of State for Defence* [2009] EWCA Civ 23; (2009) 106(7) L.S.G. 18 the Court of Appeal held that byelaws made by the Ministry of Defence, which sought to prevent a long-established peace camp near the Atomic Weapons Establishment at Aldermaston, violated arts 10 and 11 ECHR, contrary to s.6 of the Human Rights Act 1998. Challenges were made to delegated legislation providing for freezing orders in respect of assets thought to be related to terrorism. In *A v HM Treasury* [2008] EWCA Civ 1187; [2009] 3 W.L.R. 25, the Court of Appeal held the Terrorism (United Nations Measures) Order 2006 (SI 2006/2657) was ultra vires the United Nations Act 1946 but did not quash the whole Order, instead severing the offending words; the Al-Qaida and Taliban (United Nations Measures) Order 2006 (SI 2006/2952) was held to be lawful. In *R. (on the application of Hay) v HM Treasury* [2009] EWHC 1677 (Admin), Owen J. quashed the Al Qaida and Taliban (United Nations Measures) Order 2006 (SI 2006/2952) insofar as it related to the claimant (see further para.5–037).

[Add to end of n.48]

Javed was approved by the Privy Council in *Toussaint v Attorney General of St Vincent and the Grenadines* [2007] UKPC 48; [2007] 1 W.L.R. 2825 at [18]: the Court of Appeal "said, correctly in the Board's view, that both art.9 of the Bill of Rights and the wider common law principle accommodate the right and duty of the court to review the legality of subordinate legislation. The court can review the material facts and form its own judgment on the legality of subordinate legislation tabled in both Houses of Parliament and approved there, even though the result might be discordant with statements made in parliamentary debate".

[Add to end of n.51]

In *R. (on the application of C) v Secretary of State for Justice* [2008] EWCA Civ 882; [2009] 2 W.L.R. 1039, the Court of Appeal considered the court's approach to the exercise of its discretion to withhold a relief notwithstanding that the court accepts that delegated legislation is legally flawed. The court noted observations of Webster J. in *R. v Secretary of State for Social Services Ex p. Association of Metropolitan Authorities* [1986] 1 W.L.R. 1 at 15 that ". . . it is not necessarily to be regarded as the normal practice, where delegated legislation is held to be ultra vires, to revoke the instrument, but . . . the inclination would be the other way, in the absence of special circumstances making it desirable to revoke that instrument . . . in principle, I treat the matter as one of pure discretion".

The Court of Appeal did not endorse this approach. Buxton J. at [41] stated: "As with any administrative decision, the court has discretion to withhold relief if there are pressing reasons for not disturbing the status quo. It is, however, wrong to think that delegated legislation has some specially protected position in that respect. If anything, the imperative that public life should be conducted lawfully suggests that it is more important to correct unlawful legislation, that until quashed is universally binding and used by the public as a guide to conduct, than it is to correct a single decision, that affects only a limited range of people". See also Keene L.J. at [85].

The Court of Appeal in *A v HM Treasury* [2008] EWCA Civ 1187; [2009] 3 W.L.R. 25 considered the validity of the Al-Qaida and Taliban (United Nations Measures) Order 2006 (SI 2006/2952) and the Terrorism (United Nations Measures) Order 2006 (SI 2006/2657), the purpose of which was to provide what were described as "draconic" powers to freeze the assets of persons suspected of aiding terrorism. The majority held that the former was valid and the latter was valid if three words were excised.

[Add to para.3–012 after n.53]   3–012

The principle of parliamentary sovereignty does not prevent the courts reviewing primary legislation made under prerogative powers: *R. (on the application of Bancoult) v Secretary of State for Foreign and Commonwealth Affairs* [2008] UKHL 61; [2008] 3 W.L.R. 955; see further n.148 below.

Jurisdiction, Justiciability and Discretion

Jurisdiction of the Administrative Court

[Add after second sentence in n.67]   3–016

In *Fun World Co Ltd v Municipal Council of Quatre Bornes* [2009] UKPC 8, Lord Scott (dissenting as to the outcome of the appeal) noted at [55] the "distinction between jurisdiction in the strict sense and procedural propriety", citing *Guaranty Trust Company of New York v Hannay & Co* [1915] 2 K.B. 536, in which Pickford L.J. commented at 563: "The word 'jurisdiction' and the expression 'the court has no jurisdiction' are used in two different senses which I think often leads to confusion. The first and, in my opinion, the only really correct sense of the expression that the court has no jurisdiction is that it has no power to deal with and decide the dispute as to the subject matter before it, no matter in what form and by whom it is raised. But there is another sense in which it is often used, i.e. that although the court has power to decide the question it will not according to its settled practice do so except in a certain way and under certain circumstances". See also *R. (on the application of St Helens BC) v Manchester Primary Care Trust* [2008] EWCA Civ 931; (2008) 11 C.C.L. Rep. 774: "Judicial review is a flexible, but not entirely unfenced jurisdiction. This stems from certain intrinsic features. The court's relevant function is to review decisions of statutory and other public authorities to see that they are lawful, rational and reached by a fair and due process" (May L.J. at [13]).

Public functions outside the court's jurisdiction

3–019 *[Add to end of n.75]*

The Parliamentary Standards Act 2009 created a body corporate known as the Independent Parliamentary Standards Authority and an officer known as the Commissioner for Parliamentary Investigations. The bill led to a great deal of debate about the extent to which the new regulatory framework for MPs' salaries and allowances might be subject to judicial review: see e.g. House of Lords Constitution Committee, *Parliamentary Standards Bill: implications for Parliament and the courts*, 11th Report of 2008–09 (HL 134). The Committee stated: "It should not be assumed that those decisions or actions of the IPSA and new Commissioner which are not 'proceedings in Parliament' will automatically fall within the court's jurisdiction. The Court of Appeal's judgment in *Fayed* was based on broad constitutional understandings about the appropriate division of responsibility between the courts and Parliament, a borderline that is based on sound constitutional principles. The fact that investigations and other regulatory decisions are now to be placed on a statutory footing (rather than based on a Resolution of the House of Commons) does not, in and of itself, have the consequence that they will in future be judicially reviewable. The courts will determine the extent of their jurisdiction having regard to the constitutional principles governing a parliamentary democracy" (para.26). And see also *R. (on the application of Bradley) v Secretary of State for Work and Pensions* [2007] EWHC 242 (Admin); [2007] Pens. L.R. 87 at [26]–[35] (obiter: to allow the evidence of a witness to a select committee to be relied on in court would inhibit the freedom of speech in Parliament and thus contravene art.9 of the Bill of Rights but reference to a select committee report would not infringe art.9; not commented upon in the subsequent CA judgment at [2008] EWCA Civ 36; [2009] Q.B. 114); in *R. (on the application of Equitable Members Action Group) v Her Majesty's Treasury* [2009] EWHC 2495 (Admin), [70], the Divisional Court recorded that the claimant had quoted and relied upon evidence given to the Public Administration Select Committee by the Economic Secretary to the Treasury—the court put it out of their minds and no further reference was made to it; *R. (on the application of Wheeler) v Office of the Prime Minister* [2008] EWHC 936 (Admin); [2008] 2 C.M.L.R. 57

at [45]–[54] (introduction of a bill into Parliament clearly forms part of the proceedings within Parliament; for a court to order a minister to introduce a bill, or an amendment to a bill, "would plainly be to trespass impermissibly on the province of Parliament"); and *Corporate Officer of the House of Commons v Information Commissioner* [2008] EWHC 1084 (Admin); [2008] A.C.D. 71 at [2] (claim about right under Freedom of Information Act 2000 to access to information about MPs' allowances did not engage with "proceedings in Parliament" and therefore art.9 of the Bill of Rights was not engaged).

[Add to end of n.82]

The Privy Council considered the characteristics of a "superior court" in *Suratt v Attorney General of Trinidad and Tobago* [2007] UKPC 55; [2008] 1 A.C. 655, Baroness Hale of Richmond citing with approval at [49] John Burke (ed.), *Jowitt's Dictionary of English Law*, 2nd edn, (1977), p.493: "Courts are of two principal classes—of record and not of record. A court of record is one whereof the acts and judicial proceedings are enrolled for a perpetual memory and testimony, and which has the power to fine and imprison for contempt of its authority. . . Courts are also divided into superior and inferior, superior courts being those which are not subject to the control of any other courts, except by way of appeal".

[Add to end of n.92]   3–021

In *R. (on the application of Al-Haq) v Secretary of State for Foreign and Commonwealth Affairs* [2009] EWHC 1910 (Admin), the Divisional Court on a permission application considered whether the court had jurisdiction to determine a claim by a non-governmental organisation for a declaration that the UK Government was in breach of the UK's obligations under customary international law in respect of the Government of Israel's actions in Gaza. The court did not have jurisdiction: the matters raised were of high policy; the breach of international law was not plain and acknowledged; it would "entail determinations of knotty issues of law and fact"; it would breach the principle of comity; the claimant was not "asserting a readily identifiable right, such as a right in certain circumstances to claim asylum or the right to a fair trial". (The court ordered that the judgments in this permission application may be cited). See also P. Sales and J. Clement, "International Law in Domestic Courts: The Developing Framework" (2008) 124 L.Q.R. 388.

No Decision or Decisions without Legal Effect

Informal action

[Add to end of n.107]   3–026

Note that aspects of the statutory scheme (Pt 7 of the Care Standards Act 2000) that came into force after C was decided were held by the House of Lords to be incompatible with art.6 ECHR: see *R. (on the application of Wright) v Secretary of State for Health* [2009] UKHL 3; [2009] 2 W.L.R. 267. See also *R. (on the application of Shrewsbury and Atcham BC) v Secretary of State for Communities and Local Government* [2008] EWCA Civ 148; [2008] 3 All E.R. 548. The circumstances in which a public body may take action not positively authorised by legislation (or, in the case of ministers, a prerogative power) are considered at 5–022.

Decisions without direct legal effect

3–027 *[Add to end of n.111]*

And for further examples see: *R. (on the application of BAPIO Action Ltd) v Secretary of State for the Home Department* [2008] UKHL 27; [2008] 1 A.C. 1003 (ministerial guidance issued to employing bodies in the NHS on recruitment of international medical graduates was unlawful); *R. (on the application of A) v Secretary of State for Health* [2009] EWCA Civ 225; (2009) 12 C.C.L. Rep. 213 (NHS guidance on how NHS trusts should exercise discretion to grant or withhold treatment to failed asylum seekers was unlawful for lack of clarity).

[Add to end of para.3–027]

In *R. (on the application of Shrewsbury and Atcham BC) v Secretary of State for Communities and Local Government* [2008] EWCA Civ 148; [2008] 3 All E.R. 548, the Court of Appeal considered a judicial review challenge by councils relating to the Secretary of State's decision to replace two-tier local government in some parts of England with unitary authorities. The Secretary of State decided not to use powers under the Local Government Act 1992 but instead to introduce a bill with new powers (which was enacted as the Local Government and Public Involvement in Health Act 2007). The court described as "misconceived" the view of the claimant councils that they could confine their challenge to alleged flaws in the decision-making processes that had taken place before the 2007 Act was in force and before orders giving effect to the Secretary of State's decision were laid before Parliament. Carnwath L.J. stated:

> "[32] Judicial review, generally, is concerned with actions or other events which have, or will have, substantive legal consequences: for example, by conferring new legal rights or powers, or by restricting existing legal rights or interests. Typically there is a process of initiation, consultation, and review, culminating in the formal action or event ('the substantive event') which creates the new legal right or restriction. For example, the substantive event may be the grant of a planning permission, following a formal process of application, consultation and resolu-

tion by the determining authority. Although each step in the process may be subject to specific legal requirements, it is only at the stage of the formal grant of planning permission that a new legal right is created.

[33] Judicial review proceedings may come after the substantive event, with a view to having it set aside or 'quashed'; or in advance, when it is threatened or in preparation, with a view to having it stayed or 'prohibited'. In the latter case, the immediate challenge may be directed at decisions or actions which are no more than steps on the way to the substantive event. In the planning example, judicial review may be directed at a local authority resolution to grant permission while it is still conditional on, say, the completion of a highways agreement, even though the resolution can have no legal effect until the issue of the formal permission.

[34] In the present case, the substantive event, if it occurs, will be the taking effect of the necessary orders under the 2007 Act, bringing about the creation of the new authorities and the abolition of the old. Decisions or actions taken in advance of that event, whether before or after the Act, were no more than preparatory steps to that end. There is the difference, however, that steps taken after the Act were on their face formal steps in a statutorily defined procedure, whereas those taken before the Act were not. It was of course open to the Boroughs to commence proceedings at the earlier stage, and to use the March and July decisions as the focus of that challenge. But that challenge had no purpose in itself, except as a means of pre-empting the possibility of formal steps leading to a substantive order under the Act in due course.

[35] Once the Act has been passed and formal decisions have been taken, the focus of the challenge inevitably shifts. To put it another way, there would be no purpose in the court 'setting aside' the pre-Act decisions, while leaving the post-Act decisions in place, since it is only the latter which provide the direct legal foundation for the making of the Parliamentary orders. At best, such an order by the court would create great uncertainty as to its practical consequences. In my view, therefore, it would have been wrong in principle to allow the challenge to proceed in the form proposed by [counsel for the councils]. Had he refused to amend, I would have been inclined to treat that in itself as sufficient reason to deny a remedy."

AMENABILITY TESTS BASED ON THE SOURCE OF POWER

Prerogative powers

Nature of prerogative powers

[Add to end of n.121]   3–032

and on appeal to the House of Lords: *R. (on the application of Bancoult) v Secretary of State for Foreign and Commonwealth Affairs* [2008] UKHL 61; [2008] 3 W.L.R. 955 (on which, see further n.148).

Shift from jurisdiction to justiciability to set limits on court's powers to supervise legality prerogative powers

3–035 *[Add to end of n.145]*

R. (on the application of Shields) v Secretary of State for Justice [2008] EWHC 3102 (Admin) (despite the establishment of the Criminal Cases Review Commission, through which questions as to whether there had been miscarriages of justice in the UK were now normally referred, the prerogative to grant a free pardon remained intact and was available in respect of a prisoner repatriated under the Convention on the Transfer of Sentenced Persons 1983).

[Add to end of n.148]

On appeal to the House of Lords in *R. (on the application of Bancoult) v Secretary of State for Foreign and Commonwealth Affairs* [2008] UKHL 61; [2008] 3 W.L.R. 955, it was affirmed that prerogative legislation (even though classified as primary legislation) was subject to review on ordinary principles of legality, rationality and procedural impropriety in the same way as any other executive action. See further M. Richard, "Judicial Review of Prerogative Orders in Council" (2009) 68(1) C.L.J. 14; M. Cohn, "Judicial Review of Non-Statutory Executive Powers after Bancoult: a Unified Anxious Model" [2009] P.L.260; M. Elliott and A. Perreau-Saussine, "Pyrrhic public law: Bancoult and the sources, status and content of common law limitations on prerogative power" [2009] P.L. 697.

[Add to end of para.3–035]

The Extra Division, Inner House, Court of Session has doubted whether the "achievement" of arms on payment of a fee can truly be viewed as the conferment of any "honour" in the sense meant by Lord Roskill in *GCHQ*: *Kerr of Ardgowan v Lord Lyon King Of Arms* [2009] CSIH 61.

[After para.3–035 insert "not" into the following sub-heading]

Prerogative powers in respect of which the court may not have supervisory jurisdiction

JUDICIAL REVIEW OF PUBLIC FUNCTIONS

[In para.3–042 add after n.176]   3–042

; the Law Society of Northern Ireland (in the exercise of its power of attorney over the property of a deceased solicitor, to create a mortgage of the interest of the deceased in the former matrimonial home to the Law Society of Northern Ireland as trustees of the solicitors' compensation fund): *Brangam, Re Judicial Review* [2008] NIQB 11.

[In para.3–043 add]

[. . . London Metal Exchange Ltd;[174]] the Office of the Independent Adjudicator for Higher Education[174a];

[174a] *R. (on the application of Siborurema) v Office of the Independent Adjudicator* [2007] EWCA Civ 1365; [2008] E.L.R. 209. The OIA was formed as a company limited by guarantee in 2003, to fulfil the function of providing a procedure by which students could make a complaint about decisions of Higher Education Institutions ("HEIs") affecting them, other than matters of academic judgment. The scheme of handling complaints was set up by statute and the OIA had been designated as the operator. The aspiration of the OIA to be an informal substitute for court proceedings was not inconsistent with the presence of supervision by way of judicial review.

[In para.3–043 add after n.181]   3–043

A decision said to have been made by the "Buckingham Pubwatch Scheme" (an unincorporated association of publicans) to ban the claimant from licensed premises for several years was held, at a permission hearing, not to involve any public functions—"licensees are entitled to make decisions from time to time as to who they admit and whom they serve intoxicating liquor to, provided of course that there is no unlawful discrimination": *R. (on the application of Proud) v Buckingham Pubwatch Scheme* [2008] EWHC 2224 (Admin). This brief judgment given at a permission hearing does not deal with law on "common callings" (on which, see further A. Reichman, *Human Rights in Private Law* (Oxford: Hart Publishing, 2001), p.248).

Various characteristics of a public function

"But for"

[Add to end of n.186]   3–046

See further C. Campbell, "The Nature of Power as Public in English Judicial Review" (2009) 68 C.L.J. 90 at 92.

Statutory underpinning

3–047   *[Add to end of n.188]*

See further C. Campbell, "The Nature of Power as Public in English Judicial Review" (2009) 68 C.L.J. 90 at 96.

AMENABILITY OF FUNCTIONS RELATING TO PRE-CONTRACTUAL AND CONTRACTUAL POWERS

Identifying the "additional public element"

Situations where there was a sufficient "additional public element"

3–064   *[In para.3–064 add after n.241]*

; the Northern Ireland Department for Social Development's decision to terminate the claimant's appointment as a preferred developer for the Queen's Quay project, which is a "key strategic site in a development in which the citizens of Belfast have a major interest given the huge investment of public money and land": *Sheridan Millennium Ltd, Re Judicial Review* [2008] NIQB 8.

Employment situations

3–068   *[Add to n.255]*

And see *Re The Prison Officers Association's Application for Judicial Review* [2008] NIQB 35.

AMENABILITY AND THE HUMAN RIGHTS ACT

"Functions of a public nature" under the HRA

3–075   *[Add to end of n.282]*

In *R. (on the application of Weaver) v London & Quadrant Housing Trust* [2009] EWCA Civ 587 , Elias L.J. noted that "The concept of 'functions' is not altogether straightforward, nor is the distinction between functions and acts", continuing "In *Hazell v Hammersmith and Fulham London BC* [1992] 2 A.C. 1 29F Lord Templeman said that the word 'functions', at least as to be construed in s.111 of the Local Government Act 1972, embraced 'all the duties and powers of a local authority; the sum total of the activities Parliament has entrusted to it'. This would suggest that a function is a sub-species of those duties and powers; although whether and when a specific power or duty can be equated with a function is more problematic" (at [29]).

The YL decision in the House of Lords

[Add to end of n.294]   3–081

And see Lord Pannick, "Functions of a Public Nature" (2009) 14 J.R. 109.

[Add new para.3–081A after para.3–081]

The debate over the amenability of social care provision to the Human 3–081A Rights Act 1998 has moved forward with enactment of the Health and Social Care Act 2008 s.145. This seeks to ensure that people who are receiving publicly arranged care in a private sector care home fall within the ambit of the Human Rights Act in relation to that provision. The provision was brought into force on December 1, 2008 (except in relation to a person who is an adult placement carer within the meaning of the Care Homes (Wales) Regulations 2002 (SI 2008/2994) reg.46). The text of s.145 is as follows:

"**Human Rights Act 1998: provision of certain social care to be public function**

(1) A person ('P') who provides accommodation, together with nursing or personal care, in a care home for an individual under arrangements made with P under the relevant statutory provisions is to be taken for the purposes of subsection (3)(b) of section 6 of the Human Rights Act 1998 (c. 42) (acts of public authorities) to be exercising a function of a public nature in doing so.

(2) The 'relevant statutory provisions' are—
  (a) in relation to England and Wales, sections 21(1)(a) and 26 of the National Assistance Act 1948 (c. 29),
  (b) in relation to Scotland, section 12 or 13A of the Social Work (Scotland) Act 1968 (c. 49), and
  (c) in relation to Northern Ireland, Articles 15 and 36 of the Health and Personal Social Services (Northern Ireland) Order 1972 (S.I. 1972/1265 (N.I. 14)).

(3) In subsection (1) 'care home'—
  (a) in relation to England and Wales, has the same meaning as in the Care Standards Act 2000 (c. 14), and
  (b) in relation to Northern Ireland, means a residential care home as defined by Article 10 of the Health and Personal Social Services (Quality, Improvement and Regulation) (Northern Ireland) Order 2003 (S.I. 2003/431 (N.I. 9)) or a nursing home as defined by Article 11 of that Order.

(4) In relation to Scotland, the reference in subsection (1) to the provision of accommodation, together with nursing or personal care, in a care home is to be read as a reference to the provision of accommodation, together with nursing, personal care or personal support, as a care home service as defined by section 2(3) of the Regulation of Care (Scotland) Act 2001 (asp 8).

(5) Subsection (1) does not apply to acts (within the meaning of section 6 of the Human Rights Act 1998 (c. 42)) taking place before the coming into force of this section."

Although s.145 on the face of it applies only to care homes, the fact of Parliament's evident disapproval of the majority approach in *YL* must leave open the question whether that approach should be re-examined. (On this point, see Lord Pannick, "Functions of a Public Nature" (2009) 14 J.R. 109, para.16).

Overview of the case law up to and including YL

3–082 *[Add new para.3–082A after para.3–082]*

3–082A The following table summarises the principal decisions on "functions of a public nature" after the House of Lords decision in *YL*.

Case	Date	Court	"function"	"act"	Outcome
R. (on the application of Weaver) v London & Quadrant Housing Trust [2009] EWCA Civ 587	7/09	CA (Elias L.J. and Lord Collins of Mapresbury; Rix L.J. dissenting)	management and allocation of housing stock by a registered social landlord	termination of a tenancy	act of terminating a tenancy in social housing did not constitute an act of a private nature, and was in principle subject to human rights considerations
Yarl's Wood Immigration Ltd v Bedfordshire Police Authority [2008] EWHC 2207 (Comm); [2009] 1 All E.R. 886 at [51]	9/08	QBD Commercial Court (Beatson J.)	management of contracted-out immigration detention centre (Immigration and Asylum Act 1999)	Was a function of a public nature	

As the Court of Appeal noted in *London & Quadrant Housing Trust*, holding that decisions of a registered social landlord to terminate tenancies falls within the ambit of s.6 of the Human Rights Act 1998 and will afford only limited practical protection in the light of *Doherty v Birmingham City Council* [2008] UKHL 57; [2008] 3 W.L.R. 636 (in which it was held that in relation to art.8 ECHR, a social landlord's decision to evict a tenant from social housing would in most cases be justified by a pressing social need and proportionate).

The *Yarl's Wood Immigration* case involved a claim for damages under the Riot (Damages) Act 1886 against a police authority, following a riot and a serious fire. The claimants were a company under contract with the Home Office to run a detention centre under the terms of the Immigration and Asylum Act 1999 s.149 and the Detention Centre Rules 2001 (SI 2001/238), and a company to which the day-to-day operation of the centre had been sub-contracted. The court held that the claimants were "public authorities for the purposes of the judicial review jurisdiction and as functional or hybrid public authorities within s.6(3)(b) of the Human Rights Act" (at [51]) and that accordingly they fell outside the scope of the 1886 Act.

Relevance of the judicial review case law on public functions

[Add to end of n.319]

3–084

In *R. (on the application of Weaver) v London & Quadrant Housing Trust* [2008] EWHC 1377 (Admin); [2009] 1 All E.R. 17 at [64]–[66], the Divisional Court considered whether the decision of a registered social landlord to terminate a tenancy was amenable to the Human Rights Act 1998 (in respect of which it was said by the claimant that art.8 had been breached) and to judicial review (it was said that a legitimate expectation had been violated). Richards L.J. held that "I think it better to leave the question of amenability to judicial review out of account when considering the issue of public authority [under the HRA], not least to avoid a danger of circularity of reasoning" at [60]. Richards L.J, later opined at [64] that "It would be strange if a function had a public character sufficient to engage the application of the 1998 Act yet insufficient to engage the court's normal public law jurisdiction"; the Court of Appeal concurred: [2009] EWCA Civ 587 at [83].

Relevance of the ECtHR case law

[Add to end of n.324]

3–085

In *R. (on the application of Weaver) v London & Quadrant Housing Trust* [2009] EWCA Civ 587; [2009] 1 All E.R. 17 at [118], Rix L.J. (dissenting) attached importance to the fact that "there is no case, at any rate none has been cited, in Strasbourg jurisprudence in which the non-governmental provider of social housing has been the cause or object of a complaint of victimhood within the meaning of the Convention".

Possible factors indicating a "function of a public nature"

3–086   *[Add to end of n.332]*

See further C. Campbell, "The Nature of Power as Public in English Judicial Review" (2009) 68 C.L.J. 90 at 102, where it is suggested that the courts' approach of relying on indicia is problematic as it may have the effect of creating a presumption that a function is private unless it is shown to be public.

[In para.3–086 insert the following material into the table]

Factor	Comment
Public funding—often necessary but never sufficient.	"[T]here is a substantial public subsidy which enables the [registered social landlord] to achieve its objectives. This does not involve, as in YL, the payment of money by reference to specific services provided but significant capital payments designed to enable the [RSL] to meet its publicly desirable objectives" (*London & Quadrant Housing Trust* at [68])
Statutory powers.	Registered Social Landlords "have certain statutory powers, identical to those enjoyed by local authorities but not private landlords, empowering them to take action in respect of the conduct of their tenants. For example, they may apply for anti-social behaviour orders under Pt 1 of the Crime and Disorder Act 1998, or for a parenting order under the Anti-Social Behaviour Act 2003 in respect of the parents of children causing a nuisance" (*London & Quadrant Housing Trust* at [16]).
Coercive and regulatory powers.	
Delegation—standing in the shoes of a public authority.	"[A]lthough not directly taking the place of local government, the [registered social landlord] in its allocation of social housing operates in very close harmony with it, assisting it to achieve the authority's statutory duties and objectives" (*London & Quadrant Housing Trust* at [69]).
Public service.	Provision of subsidised housing was "a public service" (*London & Quadrant Housing Trust* at [70]); it followed that not all tenants of a registered social landlord would fall within the ambit of s.6—those who were paying market

	rents for properties were not protected (see at [81]).
Public rights of access.	
Core State responsibilities.	"[T]he provision of subsidised housing, as opposed to the provision of housing itself, is, . . . a function which can properly be described as governmental. Almost by definition it is the antithesis of a private commercial activity. The provision of subsidy to meet the needs of the poorer section of the community is typically, although not necessarily, a function which government provides" (*London & Quadrant Housing Trust* at [70]). But cf. *R. (on the application of Ahmad) v The Mayor and Burgesses of Newham LBC* [2009] UKHL 12 at [12] where Baroness Hale of Richmond emphasises that the provision of housing (as opposed to its allocation) is not a government function.
Beyond core state responsibilities: the assumption of responsibility by the state.	
The public interest.	A registered social landlord was "acting in the public interest and has charitable objectives" (*London & Quadrant Housing Trust* at [70]).
Democratic accountability.	
Government control.	
Regulation.	"[T]he regulation to which [a registered social landlord] is subjected is not designed simply to render its activities more transparent, or to ensure proper standards of performance in the public interest. Rather the regulations over such matters as rent and eviction are designed, at least in part, to ensure that the objectives of government policy with respect to this vulnerable group in society are achieved and that low cost housing is effectively provided to those in need of it. Moreover, it is intrusive regulation on various aspects of allocation and management, and even restricts the power to dispose of land and property" (*London & Quadrant Housing Trust* at [71]).
Risk of breaching rights.	

Step 2—assessing the nature of the particular act complained of

3–087 *[Add to end of para.3–087]*

The following have been held to be acts of a public nature: the termination of a tenancy by a registered social landlord, see *R. (on the application of Weaver) v London & Quadrant Housing Trust* [2009] EWCA Civ 587. The Court of Appeal in that case rightly stressed that in deciding whether a particular "act" is public or private, the court must look at the context in which the act occurs. Both the source and nature of the "act" must be considered, but it would be wrong to think that a private (e.g. contractual) source inevitably has the consequence of characterising the "act" as private. As Elias L.J. stated:

> "if an act were necessarily a private act because it involved the exercise of rights conferred by private law, that would significantly undermine the protection which Parliament intended to afford to potential victims of hybrid authorities. Public bodies necessarily fulfil their functions by entering into contractual arrangements. It would severely limit the signifi-cance of identifying certain bodies as hybrid authorities if the fact that the act under consideration was a contractual act meant that it was a private act falling within s.6(5)"

at [77]; and see Lord Collins of Mapesbury at [102].

TERRITORIAL REACH OF JUDICIAL REVIEW AND THE HRA

Public functions exercised outside the United Kingdom

3–094 *[In para.3–094 add new n.349a after ". . .the Bailiwicks of Jersey and Guernsey"]*

[349a] In *R. (on the application of Barclay) v Lord Chancellor and Secretary of State for Justice* [2008] EWCA Civ 1319, the Court of Appeal held that it had jurisdiction to determine a judicial review challenge brought by the Barclay brothers against decisions of the Secretary of State for Justice/Lord Chancellor (to approve and refer legislation providing for a new constitution for Sark to the Privy Council) and the decision of the Committee for the Affairs of Jersey and Guernsey to recommend that Royal Assent be given by the Privy Council. At the time of writing, a judgment of an appeal heard by the House of Lords is pending.

[In para.3–094 add new n.349b after ". . .the British Overseas Territories"]

[349b] See e.g. *R. (on the application of Bancoult) v Secretary of State for Foreign and Commonwealth Affairs* [2008] UKHL 61; [2008] 3 W.L.R. 955; and *R. (on the application of Misick) v Secretary of State for Foreign & Commonwealth Affairs* [2009] EWHC 1039 (Admin); [2009] A.C.D. 62, a former Premier of the Turks and Caicos Islands unsuccessfully sought permission to challenge the legality of the Turks and Caicos Islands Constitution (Interim Amendment) Order 2009 (SI 2009/701).

Territorial jurisdiction and the HRA

[Add to end of n.353]   3–095

The House of Lords held that, in giving the instruction under the 1985 Order, the Secretary of State was acting on behalf of Her Majesty exercising Her powers as sovereign of SGSSI, not the United Kingdom. See further A. Twomey, "Responsible Government and the Divisibility of the Crown" [2008] P.L. 742, who argues that in *Quark Fishing* the House of Lords failed to recognise that "the criterion for recognising the divisibility of the Crown in this sense is not the existence of a separate government, but rather the source of responsibility for advice to the monarch with respect to matters concerning the relevant territory" (p.743). Twomey argues that the court neglected the crucial questions in the case— "On whose advice was the Queen acting giving these instructions? To whom was that person responsible for the advice?" (p.761). The better analysis, she contends, is that the Secretary of State was acting in relation to the United Kingdom rather than "as the mouthpiece of the Queen of South Georgia". The European Court of Human Rights dismissed a complaint as inadmissible: *Quark Fishing Ltd v United Kingdom (Admissibility)* (15305/06) 22 B.H.R.C. 568. See also J. Finnis, "Law Constraints: Whose Common Good Counts?" Oxford Legal Studies Research Paper No.10/2008 (available at SSRN: *http://ssrn.com/ abstract = 1100628* [last accessed June 12, 2009]).

[Add to end of n.355]   3–096

In *R. (on the application of Al-Saadoon) v Secretary of State for Defence* [2009] EWCA Civ 7; [2009] U.K.H.R.R. 638 the Court of Appeal considered the position of the claimant Iraqi nationals whom the Secretary of State ordered to be transferred from the custody of British forces into the custody of the Iraqi Higher Tribunal (IHT) to be tried for the murder of two British servicemen (war crimes). The claimants argued that the transfer would be unlawful because, if convicted by the IHT, they risked the death penalty, contrary to art.1 of Protocol No.13 to the ECHR. The jurisdictional question therefore arose as to whether the claimants could rely on s.6 of the

Human Rights Act 1998. The Court of Appeal held that they could not. Laws L.J., noting of the extra-territorial reach of art.1 ECHR that "its scope has no sharp edge; it has to be ascertained from a combination of key ideas which are strategic rather than lexical" (at [37]), held:

". . . there are four core propositions, though each needs some explanation. (1) It is an exceptional jurisdiction. (2) It is to be ascertained in harmony with other applicable norms of international law. (3) It reflects the regional nature of the Convention rights. (4) It reflects the indivisible nature of the Convention rights. The first and second of these propositions imply (as perhaps does the term jurisdiction itself) an exercise of sovereign legal authority, not merely de facto power, by one State on the territory of another. That is of itself an exceptional state of affairs, though well recognized in some instances such as that of an embassy. The power must be given by law, since if it were given only by chance or strength its exercise would by no means be harmonious with material norms of international law, but offensive to them; and there would be no principled basis on which the power could be said to be limited, and thus exceptional."

Laws L.J. rejected the submission that in *Al-Skeini* the House of Lords' acceptance of art.1 jurisdiction in that case was essentially based on de facto control over the territory in question: "It is impossible to reconcile a test of mere factual control with the limiting effect of the first two propositions I have set out, and, indeed, that of the last two". His Lordship continued (at [38]–[39]):

"If a State Party is to exercise art.1 jurisdiction outside its own territory, the regional and indivisible nature of the Convention rights requires the existence of a regime in which that State enjoys legal powers wide enough to allow its vindication, consistently with its obligations under international law, of the panoply of Convention rights—rights which may however, in the territory in question, represent an alien political philosophy.

The ECHR's natural setting is the *espace juridique* of the States Parties; if, exceptionally, its writ is to run elsewhere, this *espace juridique* must in considerable measure be replicated. In short the State Party must have the legal power to fulfil substantial governmental functions as a sovereign State. It may do so within a narrow scope, as in an embassy, consulate, military base or prison; it may, in order to do so, depend on the host State's consent or the mandate of the United Nations; but however precisely exemplified, this is the kind of legal power the State must possess: it must enjoy the discretion to decide questions of a kind which ordinarily fall to a State's executive government. If the art.1 jurisdiction is held to run in other circumstances, the limiting conditions imposed by the four propositions I have set out will be undermined."

The Court of Appeal concluded that before December 31, 2008 the United Kingdom was not exercising any power or jurisdiction in relation to the claimants "other than as agent for the Iraqi court"—it was "not exercising, or purporting to exercise, any autonomous power of its own as a sovereign State". After December 31, 2008 the British forces enjoyed no legal power to detain any Iraqi (Laws L.J. at [40]).

In *R. (on the application of Smith) v Secretary of State for Defence* [2009] EWCA Civ 441, the Court of Appeal addressed the question whether a British soldier on military service in Iraq was subject to the jurisdiction of the United Kingdom within the meaning of art.1 ECHR so as to benefit from the rights guaranteed by the Human Rights Act 1998 while operating in Iraq or whether he is only subject to the jurisdiction for those purposes when he is on a British military base or in a British hospital. The Secretary of State for Defence conceded, on the basis of the House of Lords judgment in *R. (on the application of Al-Skeini) v Secretary of State for Defence* [2007] UKHL 26; [2008] 1 A.C. 153, that the HRA extended to military bases and hospitals in Iraq. The claimants contended that the meaning of "jurisdiction" in art.1 ECHR was not confined to geographical jurisdiction but "jurisdiction may be personal and that a soldier in Iraq is within the personal jurisdiction of the UK" (at [15]). The Court of Appeal held at [30] that the soldiers were indeed within the jurisdiction of the HRA:

"We stress that we are not saying that such a soldier is within the jurisdiction merely because the army may owe soldiers a duty of care. We recognise that that is a different question. However, it is accepted that a British soldier is protected by the HRA and the Convention when he is at a military base. In our judgment, it makes no sense to hold that he is not so protected when in an ambulance or in a truck or in the street or in the desert. There is no sensible reason for not holding that there is a sufficient link between the soldier as victim and the UK whether he is at a base or not. So too, if he is court-martialled for an act committed in Iraq, he should be entitled to the protection of art.6 of the Convention wherever the court martial takes place: see in this regard *per* Lord Brown in *Al-Skeini* at [140]. In these circumstances we accept the submission . . . that there would have to be compelling reasons of principle for drawing a distinction for the purposes of jurisdiction under art.1 of the Convention between the soldier while at his base and the soldier when he steps outside it, at any rate so long as he is acting as a soldier and not, in the old phrase, on a frolic of his own. In our judgment, no such compelling reasons have been advanced on behalf of the Secretary of State."

[Add to end of n.357]

On *R. (on the application of Al-Skeini) v Secretary of State for Defence* [2007] UKHL 26; [2008] 1 A.C. 153, in which the House of Lords held that ECHR obligations were owed to people detained by the British military in Iraq, see further D. Feldman, "The Territorial Scope of the HRA 1998" (2008) 67 C.L.J. 8 (arguing that the majority view "is, on the facts, a well balanced approach to an increasingly common problem in national and international law").

[Add to end of para.3–096]

Powers conferred on the British military by a resolution of the United Nations Security Council may, however, operate to qualify the ECHR rights that would otherwise protect a person. In *R. (on the application of Al-Jedda) v Secretary of State for Defence* [2007] UKHL 58; [2008] 1 A.C. 332, the claimant, who had both British and Iraqi nationality, was detained for several years without charge or trial by British troops at detention facilities in Iraq on grounds that he was suspected of involvement in terrorism; he contended (unsuccessfully) that his detention was contrary to art.5 ECHR. The House of Lords held that:

> "the UK may lawfully, where it is necessary for imperative reasons of security, exercise the power to detain authorised by [United Nations Security Council resolutions], but must ensure that the detainee's rights under art.5 are not infringed to any greater extent than is inherent in such detention"

(Lord Bingham of Cornhill at [39]).

> Whatever remains of the art.5 ECHR right, qualified in this way, "thereafter must be observed. This may have both substantive and procedural consequences" (Baroness Hale of Richmond at [126]).

PROCEDURAL EXCLUSIVITY

Procedural exclusivity in the era of the Civil Procedure Rules

3–103 *[Add to end of n.375]*

In *Ford-Camber Ltd v Deanminster Ltd* [2007] EWCA Civ 458; (2007) 151 S.J.L.B. 713, the claimant objected to proposals for the stopping-up of a private access road (over which it had a right of way) on an industrial site undergoing redevelopment and the provision of alternative access from a new road. Whether the stopping-up of the road could lawfully be done turned in part on whether the site had at a relevant time in the past been owned by a public authority responsible for redevelopment. The claimant contended that a sale and buy back arrangement that had taken place was in effect a sham, which did not satisfy the requirements of the Local Government, Planning and Land Act 1980; it was said that the decision to acquire the land had not been properly authorised by the public authority's board and has been vitiated by the taking of a fee. The Court of Appeal noted (at [38]) that in both *Clark v University of Lincolnshire and Humberside* [2000] 1 W.L.R. 1988 and *Rhondda Cynon Taff County Borough Council v Watkins* [2003] EWCA Civ 129: "the authority whose acts were impugned was a party to the action. It is a very different matter to raise, in a property dispute between A and B, a claim or defence based on public law matters alleged to have vitiated some act of A's predecessor in title, C, where C was a public body whose act had not been challenged by direct judicial review".

The Court of Appeal went on to deal with the public law matters.

In *Jones v Powys Local Health Board* [2008] EWHC 2562 (Admin); (2009) 12 C.C.L. Rep. 68, Plender J. struck out, as an abuse of process, a civil claim in the High Court which sought reimbursement of fees paid for the care and accommodation of the claimant's deceased father at a nursing home. The board had previously decided that the father did not meet the eligibility criteria for free accommodation and health care except for a two-month period immediately preceding his death.

In *Bloomsbury International Ltd v Sea Fish Industry Authority and DEFRA* [2009] EWHC 1721, Hamben J. refused to strike out a restitutionary claim brought by ordinary civil claim by importers of sea fish and sea fish products who had paid a levy to the SFIA, which they now said was demanded under delegated legislation that was contrary to European Union law. DEFRA contended that the examination of the public law issue of the vires of the regulations was the "primary focus" or "dominant issue". The court noted that the claim was brought in an ordinary action because the only claim being made was a private law claim for a monetary remedy and under CPR Pt 54.3(2) a claim for judicial review cannot be made where only a monetary remedy is being sought.

COMPARATIVE PERSPECTIVES

Scotland

[Add to end of n.380]   3–106

See further S. Thomson, "Golf clubbing judicial review to death" (2008) 33 S.L.T. 221 (in which it is argued that "a tripartite relationship analysis is a false analysis which serves no useful purpose other than to explain prior case law which has provided redress in contexts other than public law cases"; the author argues that an "honest return to a private/public law distinction is the sensible and sustainable option").

Australia

[Add to end of para.3–108]   3–108

Australian cases have yet to adopt a general test to determine whether a decision is subject to judicial review proceedings, and the ad hoc approaches adopted in individual cases are unsatisfactory (see generally C. Campbell,

"The Public/Private Distinction in Australian Administrative Law" in M. Groves and H. Lee (eds), *Australian Administrative Law* (2007) 34; M. Aronson, "Private Bodies, Public Power and Soft Law in the High Court" (2007) 35 Fed. L.R. 1). The question of the public/private divide is likely to be developed in Australia in the context of the Human Rights Act 2004 (ACT), as amended to insert new Pt 5A, and the Charter of Human Rights and Responsibilities Act 2006 (Vic) s.4(1). Like the Human Rights Act 1998 (UK), these statutes impose certain obligations with respect to human rights on "public authorities". Unlike the UK Act, the ACT and Victorian legislation defines "public authorities" by way of an itemised list: specific examples and entities whose functions are or include functions of a public nature, when it is exercising those functions for the state or territory or a public authority (whether under contract or otherwise). Courts are excluded except when exercising an administrative function, as is the Parliament.

No case in Victoria has directly considered the test to determine what are "functions of a public nature" under s.4(1) of the Victorian Charter. However, a number of cases have considered the extent to which the judiciary is bound by the Charter. Section 4(1)(j) excludes "a court or tribunal except when it is acting in an administrative capacity". In *Sabet v Medical Practitioners Board* [2008] V.S.C. 346, the parties agreed that "administrative capacity" is equivalent to "administrative power" at common law, thus invoking well-known, if still unclear, distinctions between judicial and administrative power. This approach thus requires consideration and classification of a body's functions into those that are administrative and those that are judicial. Applying that approach, Hollingworth J. held that the Medical Practitioners Board, in suspending Dr Sabet, was acting administratively and was thus subject to the Charter obligations.

This approach has recently been criticised by a Mental Health Review Board. The Board "noted that the potential complexities resulting from the *Sabet* analysis may have arisen from an interpretation which is contrary to the logical and purposive analysis originally intended by the Victorian Parliament in passing the Charter in its current form" (09–085 [2009] VMHRB (February 23, 2009).The characterisation of different functions as administrative or judicial was described as "complex, convoluted and somewhat arbitrary" and that "it defies both common sense and logic to assume that such a[n approach] was ever part of the Parliamentary intention in enacting the Charter in its current form". Recently, Bell J., President of the Victorian Civil and Administrative Tribunal clarified the meaning of s.6(2)(b), which provides that the Charter applies to courts and tribunals "to the extent that they have functions under Part 2 and Division 3 of Part 3" of the Charter. His Honour held that courts and tribunals must act consistently with all the specified human rights when acting in their administrative capacity (*Kracke v Mental Health Review Board* [2009] VCAT 646 at [282]. When acting in their judicial capacity, courts and tribunals must still act consistently with those rights that relate to court or tribunal proceedings (at [254]).

Canada

[Add at end of para.3–109]   **3–109**

In *Greater Vancouver Transportation Authority v Canadian Federation of Students—British Columbia Component*, 2009 SCC 31 at para.16, the Supreme Court summarised the impact of *McKinney, Eldridge*, and other earlier case law. For the purposes of the Canadian Charter of Rights and Freedoms, an entity could be "government" because of its "very nature or because the government exercises substantial control over it". A non-governmental entity could also be subject to the Charter to the extent that it "performs governmental functions". In this instance, the court held that a transportation service that was controlled by a statutorily constituted regional municipal authority itself constituted a government entity.

[Add new para.3–109A after para.3–109]

Amenability of functions relating to pre-contractual and contractual powers

In *Irving Shipbuilding Inc v Canada (Attorney General)*, 2009 F.C.A. 116, the **3–109A** Federal Court of Appeal accepted that government procurement decisions made on the basis of statutory authority and having public interest dimensions were appropriate targets of applications for judicial review. However, it went on to find that the sub-contractor of a disappointed bidder could not assert an entitlement to procedural fairness in the contract tendering process. The court also acknowledged that, to the extent that the government awarded contracts on the basis of residual executive power, the less likely it was that judicial review was available to challenge the process.

In *Dunsmuir v New Brunswick*, 2008 SCC 9; [2008] 1 S.C.R. 190, the Supreme Court of Canada rejected the application of the principles of procedural fairness to the dismissal of a Justice Department functionary who served at pleasure and whose relationship with the Crown was statutorily defined by reference to the normal rules of contract. The court held that, in such cases, the law of contract, not public law principles applied. The court also took pains to emphasise that its holding reached beyond the particular arrangements under which Dunsmuir served. After referring to the difficulties of distinguishing between public office holders and those who have a contractual employment relationship with the Crown, the court went on to state that, where a contractual relationship existed between a public employee and the Crown, the law of contract governed irrespective of that person's status as a public office holder. To the extent that *Knight v Indian Head School Division No. 19* [1990] 1 S.C.R. 653 held otherwise, it was no longer the law. The only exceptions where a public servant could rely on the public law principles of procedural fairness were situations where a public employee had no contract of employment or where the terms of the relationship between the Crown and a public servant either permitted summary dismissal or was silent on the matter. Read in the light of the facts of *Dunsmuir*, this suggests that, so long as the relevant legislation includes some form of grievance procedure or provides the normal contractual protections of access to damages in the event of wrongful dismissal or without adequate notice, a public employee, even if clearly an office holder, will not have any entitlement to public law procedural fairness or the protection of public law remedies.

In stark contrast, the court held very shortly after *Dunsmuir*, in *Société de l'assurance automobile du Québec v Cyr*, 2008 SCC 13; [2008] 1 S.C.R. 338, that an employee of a company licensed by the province to carry out motor vehicle inspections was entitled to procedural fairness before the state removed his certification as an accredited mechanic for vehicle inspection purposes: as the consequence of the loss of accreditation, the employee was no longer able to carry out inspections on behalf of his employer. This state action was sufficiently public in nature as to carry with it an entitlement to public law relief on the basis of procedural fairness. It did not matter that the relationship between the state and the company was a contractual one. The employee was not a party to that contract.

India

3–110   *[Add at end of para.3–110]*

A body is performing a "public function" when it seeks to achieve some collective benefit for the public or a section of the public and is accepted by the public or that section of the public as having authority to do so. Bodies therefore exercise public functions when they intervene or participate in social or economic affairs in the public interest. There cannot be any general definition of public authority or public function. The facts of each case decide the point: see *Binny Ltd v V. Sadasivan*, 2005 (6) S.C.C. 657.

New Zealand

3–113   *[Add at end of para.3–113]*

In *Air Nelson Ltd v Minister of Transport* [2008] N.Z.A.R. 139 (CA) the Court of Appeal rejected submissions on behalf of the Minister that decisions to increase landing charges at Hawke's Bay airport, which is part owned by the Crown, were of a purely commercial nature and thus not subject to review. It held that the Minister's price-setting power had a public law aspect, having a dual commercial and regulatory focus.

Two recent decisions illustrate the importance of the availability of alternative relief to the court's decision whether to exercise its supervisory powers on review. In *Macaskill v Ogden* [2009] N.Z.A.R. 111 (HC) Wild J.

held that customers of an energy trust could not review certain decisions made by the trustees pursuant to the trust deed. Key to this decision was the existence of equitable obligations similar or identical to those that would be imposed by judicial review, which indicated that it was neither necessary nor appropriate for the court to extend its review power to cover the trustees' conduct. In *Stratford Racing Club Inc v Adlam* [2008] N.Z.A.R. 329 (CA) the Court of Appeal said that part of the courts' traditional reluctance to intervene in the running of clubs by way of judicial review was that members had a contractual remedy against the club for rule breaches. However those refused membership did not have a contractual remedy, meaning their only recourse was judicial review. Decisions refusing memberships were considered amenable to review.

Falun Dafa Association of New Zealand Inc v Auckland Children's Christmas Parade Trust Board [2009] N.Z.A.R. 122 (HC) concerned an application for judicial review by the Falun Dafa Association of the trust board's decision to decline their application to participate in an annual Christmas parade run by the board. The proceedings were interlocutory and the association sought interim relief. The board was incorporated under the Charitable Trusts Act 1957, and its relevant decision was considered an exercise of statutory power. Randerson J. cited the 6th edition of *De Smith's Judicial Review* for the proposition that charities are not necessarily immune from judicial review. However, he said that judicial review would only be available where "it is clearly established that the body in question is exercising significant public functions or with substantial public effects which warrant intervention on public law grounds" (at [33]). He was not persuaded that there was a seriously arguable case that the trust board had exercised public powers in rejecting the association's application. While the parade was staged for the benefit of the public and occurs in a public place (downtown Auckland) it did not follow that the powers being exercised were of a public nature.

South Africa

Private powers of public bodies

[Add to end of para.3–117]

3–117

In *Government of the Republic of South Africa v Thabiso Chemicals (Pty) Ltd*, 2009 (1) S.A. 163 (SCA), Brand J.A. stated that he did not believe that the principles of administrative law have any role to play in the cancellation of a tender award. After a tender has been awarded, he went on, the case is governed by the principles of contract law. "The fact that the tender board relied on authority derived from a statutory provision to cancel the contract on behalf of the government, does not detract from this principle. Nor does the fact that the grounds of cancellation on which the tender board relied were inter alia, reflected in the regulation" (at para.18).

"Purely contractual" reasoning has proved attractive to the Constitutional Court as well. In *Chirwa v Transnet Ltd*, 2008 (4) S.A. 367 (CC) a majority of the Constitutional Court held that the High Court had no jurisdiction to deal with labour disputes: for a critique, see C. Hoexter "Clearing the Intersection? Administrative Law and Labour Law in the Constitutional Court" (2008) 1 Constitutional Court Review 209. The Constitutional Court also dealt with the question whether the public-sector dismissal amounted to administrative action and was thus reviewable under the Promotion of Administrative Justice Act 2000, the majority holding that dismissal by a public authority did entail the exercise of a public power.

CHAPTER 4

CONCEPTS OF JURISDICTION AND LAWFUL ADMINISTRATION

STATUTORY RESTRICTION OF JUDICIAL REVIEW

[Add new para.4–027A after para.4–027]   4–027

Transfer of "judicial review" functions away from the Administrative Court

A statute may stipulate a forum other than the Administrative Court as the   4–027A
one where judicial review proceedings should be determined. In *A v B
(Investigatory Powers Tribunal: jurisdiction)* [2008] EWHC 1512 (Admin);
[2008] 4 All E.R. 511 the Administrative Court considered whether
s.65(2)(a) or (b) of the Regulation of Investigatory Powers Act 2000,
specifying the investigatory powers tribunals as the "only appropriate
tribunal" for the purposes of s.7 of the Human Rights Act 1998, ousted the
jurisdiction of the Administrative Court. Collins J. held that they did not,
as the words were insufficiently clear. The question whether the tribunal
was an adequate alternative remedy to judicial review, such that the
Administrative Court should decline jurisdiction, was a separate question.
Where claims raised matters of "surveillance, interception of communications and use of material obtained thereby, the use of covert services, the
acquisition of means whereby protected electronic data can be decrypted",
those should be dealt with by the tribunal. The claimant, a former member
of the Security Service, challenged a decision of his former employer
refusing him consent to publish a book including descriptions of his work:
the Administrative Court appeared to be an appropriate forum for such a
challenge.

JURISDICTION AND VIRES TODAY

[Add to end of n.130]   4–041

And see now R. Williams, "When is an error not an error? Reform of
jurisdictional review of error of law and fact" [2007] P.L. 793

FROM "VOID AND VOIDABLE" TO "LAWFUL AND UNLAWFUL"

The situation today

Residual categories

4–063   *[Add to end of para.4–063 new para.4–063A]*

4–063A   The concept of "nullity" was also invoked by the majority in *Re JJ* [2007] UKHL 45; [2008] 1 A.C. 385 in relation to the role of courts viewing decisions of the Secretary of State to make "control orders" against individuals suspected of involvement in terrorism. The Prevention of Terrorism Act 2005 makes a distinction between "derogating control orders" (imposing obligations incompatible with the right to liberty under art.5 ECHR) which may be made by a court and "non-derogating control orders" which may be made by the Home Secretary with the permission of a court. In respect of non-derogating orders, the function of a court is to decide, applying "the principles applicable on an application for judicial review", whether any relevant decision of the Secretary of State was "obviously flawed" (s.3). The court's powers are to quash the order, to quash one or more obligations imposed by the order, or to give directions to the Secretary of State for the revocation of the order or for the modification of the obligations it imposes. In a series of cases, courts held that obligations the Home Secretary sought to impose in non-derogating orders—including 18-hour curfews and restrictions on visitors—were contrary to art.5 ECHR and quashed each order in its entirety (rather than giving directions to the Secretary of State for the modification of the orders in question).

On appeal to the House of Lords, Lord Bingham of Cornhill, for the majority, held (at [27]):

> ". . . the Secretary of State has no power to make an order that imposes any obligation incompatible with art.5. An administrative order made without power to make it is, on well-known principles, a nullity: see the recent decision of the Privy Council in *Dr Astley McLaughlin v A-G of the Cayman Islands* [2007] UKPC 50. The defects in the orders cannot be cured by amending specific obligations, since what the Secretary of State made was a series of orders, applicable to the individuals named, and these are what he had no power to make. It is true that, because public law remedies are generally discretionary, the court may in special circumstances decline to quash an order, despite finding it to be a nullity: ibid, para 16. But no such circumstances exist here, and it would be contrary to principle to decline to quash an order, made without power to make it, which had unlawfully deprived a person of his liberty."

Lord Hoffmann, dissenting, took a different view (at [53]):

> "If the order of the Secretary of State is found to be flawed on principles of judicial review, that means that it was not lawfully made. I do not

understand how some unlawful orders can be more lawful than others or that it makes sense to invoke distinctions which English law abandoned forty years ago in order to create different categories of unlawfulness. The power to direct the Secretary of State to revoke or modify the order does not imply that the order was lawfully made. On the contrary, the power arises only if the order is found to have been flawed, that is to say, not lawfully made. Thus the grounds on which the judge refused to consider the exercise of the powers conferred by s.3(12)(b) and (c) would simply write them out of the statute. But there seems to me no conceptual reason why Parliament should not say that if the exercise of a power is found to have been unlawful, the court shall have power to modify the order or direct the Secretary of State to modify it so as to make it lawful. The judge's failure to accept that he had these powers means that in my opinion he did not properly exercise his discretion."

COMPARATIVE PERSPECTIVES

Canada

[Add to end of para.4–087] 4–087

In *Dunsmuir v New Brunswick*, 2008 SCC 9; [2008] 1 S.C.R. 190, the Supreme Court of Canada revisited its entire approach to judicial review of the substantive decisions of statutory and prerogative authorities. In the course of doing so, the court emphasised that the concepts of jurisdiction and vires remained part of Canadian judicial review law. On such issues, the standard of review was that of correctness. However, the court cautioned that it was not signalling a return to the broad conceptions of jurisdiction and vires that had proved so problematic in earlier Canadian decisions. Jurisdiction was "intended in the narrow sense of whether or not the tribunal had the authority to make the inquiry" (at para.59). How lower courts will interpret this message remains to be seen. What is clear, however, is that the court has implicitly abandoned its previous position that the term "jurisdiction" was nothing more than a description of any category of question on which, after a standard of review analysis, the statutory or prerogative authority had to be correct: *Pushpanathan v Canada (Minister of Citizenship and Immigration)* [1998] 1 S.C.R. 982. Instead, the court identified three specific categories of question that were jurisdictional in character or raised issues of vires: constitutional issues, the jurisdictional lines between competing tribunals, and the limits of the authority of municipalities to enact byelaws.

[Add to end of para.4–088] 4–088

In *Dunsmuir* (above), the Supreme Court also reaffirmed that privative or preclusive ("ouster") clauses remain a significant element in the standard of review analysis. They provide "a strong indication" (at para. 52) of what is now the only deferential standard under Canadian common law judicial review: unreasonableness.

[Add new para.4–088A after para.4–088]

India

4–088A Finality clauses do not exclude jurisdiction of the courts particularly on grounds of lack of jurisdiction, nullity, illegality, irrationality, natural justice and perversity: *Raja Ram Pal v Honourable Speaker, Lok Sabha*, 2007 (3) S.C.C. 184. Judicial review is part of the basic structure of the Constitution and cannot be excluded: *IR Coelho v State of TN* 2007 (2) S.C.C. 1.

South Africa

4–092 *[Add to end of para.4–092]*

It is very clear now that all material errors of law are reviewable, as indicated by the wording of s.6(2)(d) of the Promotion of Administrative Justice Act 2000. *Tantoush v Refugee Appeal Board*, 2008 (1) S.A. 232 (T) illustrates the distinction between an error that is material and one that is not: the board had misconstrued its appellate functions and had gone on to insist on the presence of a "real risk" of persecution rather than a "reasonable possibility" of persecution. The first error was found not to be material as it had not distorted the board's discretion (at para.93), while the second was held to be material (at paras 97–99).

Part II
GROUNDS OF JUDICIAL REVIEW

CHAPTER 5

ILLEGALITY

STATUTORY INTERPRETATION

[Add to end of n.56]   5-020

And see *Waltham Forest LBC v Maloba* [2007] EWCA Civ 1281; [2008] 2
All E.R. 701 (interpretation of "A person shall not be treated as having
accommodation unless it is accommodation which it would be reasonable
for him to continue to occupy"). The Court of Appeal held that good sense
could be made of s.175(3) of the Housing Act 1996 by construing the
words "reasonable for him to continue to occupy" as synonymous with
"reasonable for him to occupy for a continuing period", meaning for the
future, whether or not he was in occupation at the moment of the
application or the decision. *Begum (Nipa) v Tower Hamlets LBC* [2000] 1
W.L.R. 306 CA, was not followed.

[In para.5–021, add new sentence before "Although in judicial review. . ."] 5-021

Assessing the purpose for which legislation was enacted may require the
court to consider the "premise of the legislation". In *Wells v Parole Board*
[2008] EWCA Civ 30; [2008] 3 All E.R. 104, the Court of Appeal held
that the legislative framework governing indeterminate sentences for public
protection (ISPPs) in the Criminal Justice Act 2003 was enacted on the
assumption that prisoners serving ISPPs would be able to take part in the
courses necessary for them to demonstrate to the Parole Board that they
were no longer a risk to public safety. Instead, there had been "a systemic
failure on the part of the Secretary of State to put in place the resources
necessary to implement the scheme of rehabilitation necessary to enable the
relevant provisions of the 2003 Act to function as intended" (at [72]).

Non-statutory sources of power and the Ram Doctrine

[Add new para.5–025A after para.5–025]   5-025

The Court of Appeal has recently considered the extent of the Crown's 5-025A
common law powers and their relationship with statutory powers. In *R.
(on the application of Shrewsbury and Atcham BC) v Secretary of State for
Communities and Local Government* [2008] EWCA Civ 148; [2008] 3 All

E.R. 548 local authorities challenged actions of the Secretary of State in developing and implementing a policy of local government reorganisation. A statutory framework, in the form of the Local Government Act 1992, existed for carrying out local government reorganisation but the Secretary of State decided not to use this. Instead, her department published a White Paper and consulted with a view to introducing a bill to give effect to what was finally decided (which eventually happened in the form of Pt 1 of the Local Government and Public Involvement in Health Act 2007). The claimants argued that the Secretary of State had no power to consult without statutory authority and the 1992 Act regime covered the same field. All three Lords Justice agreed that the claimants' appeal should be dismissed but they expressed differing views on the scope and significance of the concept of a "third source" of power (beyond statutory and prerogative powers).

Carnwath L.J held at [48]:

"Unlike a local authority, the Crown is not a creature of statute. As a matter of capacity, no doubt, it has power to do whatever a private person can do. But as an organ of government, it can only exercise those powers for the public benefit, and for identifiably 'governmental' purposes within limits set by the law. Apart from authority, I would be inclined respectfully to share the view of the editors of de Smith that 'The extension of the Ram doctrine beyond its modest initial purpose of achieving incidental powers should be resisted in the interest of the rule of law' (de Smith's Judicial Review (6th edn) para 5–025)".

It was however unnecessary to invoke the concept of a "third source" of power to explain the Secretary of State's powers to prepare and publish a White Paper; that was "simply a necessary and incidental part of the ordinary business of central government" (at [49]). Dismissing the appeal, Carnwath L.J. held that it was "a constitutional principle of some importance that local authorities should be able to rely on the safeguards of a statutory framework for the processes leading to decisions of this importance", however it was "impossible to avoid the conclusion that Parliament has (if only retrospectively) given its stamp of approval to the procedure in this case, and there is no evidence that the authorities have been prejudiced in presenting their opposition" (at [70]).

Richards L.J. did not share Carnwath L.J.'s "reservations about the extent of the common law powers of the Crown":

"it is still necessary to explain the basis on which that ordinary business of government is conducted, and the simple and satisfactory explanation is that it depends heavily on the 'third source' of powers, i.e. powers that have not been conferred by statute and are not prerogative powers in the narrow sense but are the normal powers (or capacities and freedoms) of a corporation with legal personality" (at [73]).

It would be wrong to introduce qualifications to their exercise such as that they are only "for the public benefit" or for "identifiably 'governmental' purposes"; "any limiting principle would have to be so wide as to be of no practical utility or would risk imposing an artificial and inappropriate restriction upon the work of government" (at [74]). Waller L.J. said that he instinctively favoured "some constraint on the powers by reference to the duty to act only for the public benefit" (at [81]).

[Add to end of n.80]

In *R. (on the application of Child Poverty Action Group) v Secretary of State for Work and Pensions* [2009] EWHC 341 (Admin) the claimants challenged the defendant's practices of seeking to recover overpaid social security benefits other than under the Social Security Administration Act 1992 s.71. It was held that s.71 neither expressly nor by necessary implication removed the defendant's powers to claim repayment at common law of money paid by mistake of fact or law— "the court ought not to infer the exclusion of common law rights unless Parliament has covered the same ground, by legislating specifically in relation to the circumstances which have arisen in the instant case" (at [29]).

The discovery of Parliament's intent and use of Hansard

[Add to n.85 after second sentence] 5–026

[. . .meet those criteria.] In 2007 a new system for correcting errors in *Hansard* was introduced: see D. Greenberg, "Hansard, the whole Hansard and nothing but the Hansard" (2008) 124 L.Q.R. 181. For a recent and relatively rare example of a case in which regard was had to *Hansard*, see *R. v JTB; R. v B* [2009] UKHL 20; [2009] 2 W.L.R. 1088 (not a judicial review claim). And for consideration of the use of other parliamentary records—ministerial evidence to the select committee—see *R. (on the application of Federation of Tour Operators) v HM Revenue & Customs* [2007] EWHC 2062 (Admin) at [108]–[125] (Stanley Burnton J.: "it is necessary to consider whether this material would otherwise be admissible on or relevant to the determination of the Claimants' substantive claims, before deciding whether its origin precludes their adducing it in evidence"). And see also *Toussaint v Attorney General of St Vincent and the Grenadines* [2007] UKPC 48; [2007] 1 W.L.R. 2825 (proper of a claimant to rely on evidence of what was said by a minister in Parliament to show the motivation for the government's actions outside Parliament).

Always-speaking statutes

[Add new n.93a after ". . . may be of limited value,"] 5–032

93a Cf. *R. v Clarke (Ronald Augustus)* [2008] UKHL 8; [2008] 1 W.L.R. 338, where the issue was whether a failure to sign an indictment had deprived a trial court of its jurisdiction. Lord Bingham of Cornhill held that in interpreting the Administration of Justice (Miscellaneous Provisions) Act 1933, "The 'always speaking' principle has no application. The answer to the question now is the same as should have been given then. It is inescapable: Parliament intended that the bill should not become an indictment unless and until it was duly signed by the proper officer" (at [18]).

[Add to end of n.97]

For an example, see *R. (on the application of Blackpool Council) v Howitt and Secretary Of State for Culture Media and Sport* [2008] EWHC 3300 (Admin); [2009] L.L.R. 325 (the term "crime and disorder" in the Licensing Act 2003 s.4 included breaches of the smoking ban introduced by the Health Act 2006).

Interpretation in relation to constitution principles and constitutional rights

5–036 *[Add to end of n.108]*

For an example of Parliament countermanding the assertion of a constitutional right, see *R. v Davis (Iain)* [2008] UKHL 36; [2008] 1 A.C. 1128 (Lord Bingham of Cornhill at [5]: "a long-established principle of the English common law that, subject to certain exceptions and statutory qualifications, the Defendant in a criminal trial should be confronted by his accusers in order that he may cross-examine them and challenge their evidence") and the Criminal Evidence (Witness Anonymity) Act 2008 (introducing witness anonymity orders).

[Add to end of para.5.036]

That approach was continued in *R. (on the application of Morgan Grenfell & Co Ltd) v Special Commissioners of Income Tax* [2002] UKHL 21; [2003] 1 A.C. 563, where the House of Lords considered whether a statute authorised disclosure by the bank of its instructions to and advice of counsel in relation to a tax avoidance scheme. Lord Hoffmann considered that the words in the statute could not be read as necessarily implying that the long-established common law right to legal professional privilege could be overridden. In other cases, although the principle of legality has been applied, it has been held that the words of the statute were sufficiently clear and precise to infringe the human right *R. (on the application of Gillan) v Commissioner of Police of the Metropolis* [2006] UKHL 12; [2006] 2 A.C. 307—stop and search powers of police upheld; and *M v Chief Constable of Northern Ireland; C v Chief Constable of Northern*

Ireland; McE v Prison Service of Northern Ireland [2009] UKHL 15; [2009] 2 W.L.R. 782 (powers of covert surveillance of persons in custody with their legal and medical advisers upheld despite the infringement of professional privilege). However, in *Secretary of State for the Home Department v GG* [2009] EWCA Civ 786, the Court of Appeal held that the Prevention of Terrorism Act 2005 was not sufficiently clear to permit the search of the appellant's person under a control order issued under that Act.

[Add to end of n.111]   5–037

See also *A v HM Treasury* [2008] EWCA Civ 1187; [2009] 2 All E.R. 747, which concerned orders putting in place draconic powers to freeze assets of people thought to be involved in terrorism under the United Nations Act 1946 s.1 which empowers the UK Government to "make such provision as appears . . . necessary or expedient" for implementing UN Security Council measures. Sedley L.J. held that "absent a manifest delegation by Parliament to the executive of a power which it alone possesses (and which few constitutional theorists now regard as unlimited), no words of general delegation will allow the executive to encroach on rights and freedoms of which the rule of law is the source and the courts are the guarantor" (at [129]); and see Sir Anthony Clarke at [43]–[46]. See also *R. (on the application of Hay) v HM Treasury* [2009] EWHC 1677 (Admin), in which Owen J. quashed the Al Qaida and Taliban (United Nations Measures) Order 2006 (SI 2006/2952) insofar as it related to the claimant. The United Nations Act 1946 s.1 neither expressly nor by necessary implication empowered the executive to remove the right of access to the courts. The claimant contended that the 2006 Order was made "in such a way that even if the claimant should not be on the Consolidated List, there is no UK public authority which has the power of preventing him being a designated person under the order, and that in consequence he is deprived of the right effectively to challenge the fundamental interference with his basic rights, the result of the economic measures imposed by the Security Council" (at [41]), a submission that was accepted by the court. Owen J. held that as neither the claimant nor the UK Government knew the full basis on which the claimant had been designated by the "1267 Committee" of the UN Security Council (a decision which had automatically led to his designation in the United Kingdom under the 2006 Order), "there cannot be an effective merits review of his designation by the court" —the practical effect of the 2006 Order "is to preclude access to the court for protection against what the claimant contends to be wrongful interference with his basic rights. To hold otherwise would be tokenism"(at [45]). And see too *A v B (Investigatory Powers Tribunal: jurisdiction)* [2008] EWHC 1512 (Admin); [2008] 4 All E.R. 511 at [12] (Collins J.: "The courts of this country have always recognised that the right of a citizen to access a court is a right of the highest constitutional importance and that legislation removing that right is prima facie contrary to the rule of law"). The right of access to a court was also considered in *Seal v Chief Constable of South Wales* [2007] UKHL 31; [2007] 1 W.L.R. 1910.

5–038 *[Add to end of n.116]*

And see *Revenue and Customs Commissioners v Total Network SL; Total Network SL v Revenue and Customs Commissioners* [2008] UKHL 19; [2008] 1 A.C. 1174 at [21]–[33] (Lord Hope of Craighead).

5–039 *[Add to end of n.125]*

See *R. (on the application of Juncal) v Secretary of State for the Home Department* [2007] EWHC 3024 (Admin). The claimant, who had been detained in various hospitals for over 10 years following a finding of unfitness to be tried on a charge of unlawful wounding, advanced arguments based on the principle of legality. For the claimant it was said that there was an "established common law right of freedom from arbitrary detention". For the defendant it was said that it was "not sufficient to speak in terms such that there is a general principle or presumption in favour of the liberty of the subject". Wyn Williams J. held that "the citizens of this country do enjoy a fundamental or constitutional right not to be detained arbitrarily at common law. That conclusion is not capable of much elaboration" (at [47]). See also *Secretary of State for the Home Department v GG (proceedings under the Prevention of Terrorism Act 2005)* [2009] EWCA Civ 786 at [12] (Sedley L.J.: "It is in my judgment axiomatic that the common law rights of personal security and personal liberty prevent any official search of an individual's clothing or person without explicit statutory authority. That these are rights customarily defined by correlative wrongs rather than by affirmative declarations is an artefact of our constitutional history; but it makes them no less real and the courts' vigilance in defence of them no less necessary".

[Add to end of n.133]

But see now *R. (on the application of Bancoult) v Secretary of State for Foreign and Commonwealth Affairs* [2008] UKHL 61; [2008] 3 W.L.R. 955.

Interpretation and international law

5–043 *[Add to end of n.146]*

And see P. Sales and J. Clements, "International law in domestic courts: the developing framework" (2008) 124 L.Q.R. 388.

Unincorporated treaties

[Add to end of n.163]   **5–046**

In *R. (on the application of Corner House Research) v Director of the Serious Fraud Office* [2008] UKHL 60; [2008] 3 W.L.R. 568, the House of Lords considered the OECD Convention on Combating Bribery of Foreign Public Officials in International Business Transactions (1997).

[Add to end of n.164]

And see the discussion in *R. v Asfaw (Fregenet)* [2008] UKHL 31; [2008] 1 A.C. 1061 (a criminal appeal raising issues on the UN Convention relating to the Status of Refugees 1951 (United Nations), art.31 and domestic statutes).

Customary international law

[Add to end of n.166]   **5–047**

But see *R. (on the application of Al-Haq) v Secretary of State for Foreign and Commonwealth Affairs* [2009] EWHC 1910 (Admin), [40] (Pill L.J.: "The issue of the incorporation of customary international law into domestic law is not susceptible to a simple or general answer . . ."). And see further P. Sales and J. Clements, "International law in domestic courts: the developing framework" (2008) 124 L.Q.R. 388.

[Add to end of para.5–047]

Additional illustrations of reference by the courts to customary international law norms include the following. In *R. (on the application of Al-Saadoon) v Secretary of State for Defence* [2009] EWCA Civ 7; [2009] U.K.H.R.R. 638 at [70], the Court of Appeal held that it was "in no position whatever to arrive at any overall conclusion as to the effects of hanging for the purpose of making an assessment of its compatibility or otherwise with norms of customary international law"). The Court of Appeal rejected an argument that customary international law recognised de facto adoption of children, which the claimants contended was important in relation to a country where formal adoption was unlikely to take place because institutions of the state were depleted and for religious reasons (*MK (Somalia) v Entry Clearance Officer* [2008] EWCA Civ 1453; [2009] 2 F.L.R. 138). In *BE (Iran) v Secretary of State for the Home Department* [2008] EWCA Civ 540; [2009] I.N.L.R. 1 at [29] the Court of Appeal held that it was right to describe the outlawing of anti-personnel mines "as an emerging norm of international law": accordingly, the claimant, who had deserted from the Iraqi army in order to avoid involvement in the laying of unmarked anti-personnel mines in roads used by civilians, was entitled to asylum.

5–048 *[Add to end of n.169]*

Immunity applies equally to a foreign head of state in his personal capacity as it applies to his public capacity: see *Aziz v Aziz* [2007] EWCA Civ 712; [2008] 2 All E.R. 501.

Mandatory and Directory Duties and Powers

5–056 *[Add to end of para.5–056]*

In *R. v Clarke (Ronald Augustus)* [2008] UKHL 8; [2008] 1 W.L.R. 338, the House of Lords held that Administration of Justice (Miscellaneous Provisions) Act 1933, ss.1–2 required a bill of indictment to be signed by a proper officer; there could be no valid trial on indictment if there was no indictment. Many errors pertaining to indictments fell into the category of procedural error but the failure to sign the indictment deprived the court of jurisdiction. And in *Seal v Chief Constable of South Wales* [2007] UKHL 31; [2007] 1 W.L.R. 1910, the House of Lords held (Lord Woolf and Baroness Hale of Richmond dissenting) that the omission of a claimant to seek the permission of a High Court judge under s.136 of the Mental Health Act 1983 before making a damages claim (shortly before the expiry of the limitation period) resulted in the proceedings being a complete nullity.

5–059 *[Add to n.194]*

For an example of the application of Jeyeanthan, see *R. (on the application of London Borough of Waltham Forest) v Waltham Forest Magistrates' Court* [2008] EWHC 3579 (Admin): the requirement under the Non Domestic Rating (Collection and Enforcement) (Local Lists) Regulations 1989 (SI 1989/1058) reg.5(1) that a demand for business rates "shall be served as soon as practicable" was a directory rather than a mandatory requirement. It was held that the requirement was satisfied by substantial compliance.

5–060 *[Add to end of para.5–060]*

For further examples, see the following cases. In *R. (on the application of JJB Sports Plc) v Telford and Wrekin BC* [2008] EWHC 2870 (Admin); [2009] R.A. 33, it was held that a local authority was not prevented by reason of serving the demand notice 56 days late from proceeding to seek a liability order enforcing payment of business rates. In *R. (on the application of P) v Haringey LBC* [2008] EWHC 2357 (Admin); [2009] E.L.R. 49, school governors in a decision letter had specified the wrong date for lodging an appeal against their determination that a pupil should be permanently excluded; applying a flexible approach, the court held that the notice was not for that reason invalid (but the local authority had acted unlawfully in not recognising that the appeal had indeed been lodged on the due date—an email had arrived after school closing time but before midnight on that day). See also *R. (on the application of Winchester College) v Hampshire CC* [2008] EWCA Civ 431; [2009] 1 W.L.R. 138.

[Add to n.200]

The case was the subject of a judgment of the European Court of Human Rights as *Bullen v United Kingdom* (3383/06) [2009] Lloyd's Rep. F.C. 210 (where it was held that the periods of delay in the proceedings for confiscation of assets were in breach of the reasonable time under art.6 EHCR).

Target duties: "directory" rather than "mandatory"

[Add to end of para.5–064]   5–064

- National Health Service Act 2006 s.1 ("The Secretary of State must continue the promotion in England of a comprehensive health service. . ."): see *R. (on the application of YA) v Secretary of State for Health* [2009] EWCA Civ 225 at [69].

[Add to end of n.214]

See also *Friends of the Earth v Secretary of State for Business Enterprise and Regulatory Reform* [2009] EWCA Civ 810 at [20] (an obligation to implement a strategy to ensure that "as far as reasonably practicable persons do not live in fuel poverty" was an obligation "correctly described in terms of effort or endeavour").

[Add to end of n.215]   5–065

Baroness Hale of Richmond has said that "there is a fundamental difference in public law between a duty to provide benefits or services for a particular individual and a general or target duty which is owed to a whole population": *R. (on the application of Ahmad) v Newham LBC* [2009] UKHL 14; (2009) 153(9) S.J.L.B. 29 at [13]

[Add to end of para.5–067]   5–067

This approach was followed by the Northern Ireland Court of Appeal in relation to a challenge to the minister for failing to issue advice or guidance to women and clinicians on the availability of termination of pregnancy services (*Family Planning Association of Northern Ireland v The Minister for Health, Social Services and Public Safety* [2004] NICA 39. The relevant Order—the Health and Personal Social Services Order (Northern Ireland) 1972— provided a general duty to provide "integrated health services" and "personal social services designed to promote the social welfare of the people and to secure effective co-ordination of Health and Personal Social Services". At first instance these provisions were held by Kerr J. to be mere target duties with which the court could not interfere, but Nicholson L.J. in the Court of Appeal held that, although there was a degree of tolerance and elasticity with which the courts should be slow to intervene, the courts would be well within their competence to indicate to the public body that they should consider what steps they should take to fulfil the target duty, even though they would not necessarily order the body concerned to perform a specific act.

Discretionary power in the context of law enforcement

5–071 *[Add to end of n.239]*

And see *R. (on the application of Corner House Research) v Director of the Serious Fraud Office* [2008] UKHL 60; [2008] 3 W.L.R. 568 at [30].

5–072 *[Add to end of n.240]*

In *R. (on the application of Corner House Research) v Director of the Serious Fraud Office* [2008] UKHL 60; [2008] 3 W.L.R. 568 the House of Lords declined to hold that a decision to stop investigations into allegedly corrupt payments, following threats from the Saudi officials to cease co-operation on counter-terrorism, was unlawful. *Phoenix Aviation* was distinguished on the ground that the DSFO had given careful thought to the implications for the rule of law in stopping the investigation whereas the council in *Phoenix* had not (see Lord Brown of Eaton-Under-Heywood at [58]). See R. Hopkins and C. Yeginsu, "Storm in a Teacup: Domestic and International Conservatism from the Corner House Case" (2008) 13 J.R. 267; J. Jowell, "Caving In: Threats and the Rule of Law" (2008) 13 J.R. 273.

[Add to end of n.241]

And a prosecutor may be under a legal duty to publish a policy as to how the public interest element of prosecutorial decisions in relation to a specific offence will be approached: *R. (on the application of Purdy) v DPP* [2009] UKHL 45; [2009] 3 W.L.R. 403.

THE INTERPRETATION OF POLICIES

[Add to end of n.247]   5–074

In *R. (on the application of Vale of White Horse DC) v Secretary of State for Communities and Local Government* [2009] EWHC 1847 (Admin) at [23] Robin Purchas Q.C., sitting as a Deputy High Court judge, held that there was nothing in *R. (on the application of Raissi) v Secretary of State for the Home Department* [2008] EWCA Civ 72; [2008] 3 W.L.R. 375 (see below) "which purports to overrule the general approach to planning policies in planning cases to which I have referred above and in my judgment the proper approach should remain as set out in *Woods*".

[Add at end of para.5–074]

In *R. (on the application of Raissi) v Secretary of State for the Home Department* [2008] EWCA Civ 72; [2008] 3 W.L.R. 375 the Court of Appeal had to consider whether the Home Secretary's ex gratia compensation scheme—set out in a policy statement—for those imprisoned following a wrongful conviction also applied to a person detained pursuant to extradition proceedings. The court, acknowledging that in different contexts different approaches had been adopted, held at [122] that they had:

> "some difficulty with the reasonable meaning approach. One presumes that, if the minister has applied a meaning to some part of the policy, then the minister, without announcing any change in the policy, could not in a later case adopt another meaning, arguing that both meanings are reasonable and it is up to him or her to choose which meaning to use in any particular case. If that is right, then the reasonable meaning approach would only benefit the minister when interpreting the meaning of a particular part of the policy for the first time".

Nothing said in *Re McFarland* [2004] UKHL 17; [2004] 1 W.L.R. 1289 prevented the Court of Appeal from deciding what the policy means.

DECISIONS BASED UPON IRRELEVANT CONSIDERATIONS OR FAILURE TO TAKE ACCOUNT OF RELEVANT CONSIDERATIONS

[Insert at end of para.5–119]   5–119

In *R. (on the application of Gulliver) v Parole Board* [2007] EWCA Civ 1386; [2008] 1 W.L.R. 1116 the claimant challenged a decision by the Parole Board not to direct his re-release from prison, following his recall to prison by the Secretary of State for Justice. The claimant was required to wear a satellite tracking unit to monitor his whereabouts and the reason for his recall was that he failed to recharge the battery. The question for the Court of Appeal was whether the Parole Board, having held that there was in fact no breach of the appellant's licence conditions, was entitled to consider all the evidence available at the date of the oral hearing, and to hold that the appellant's risk to the public was such that he should not have been released. The court held that the Parole Board:

"is to have regard to all the circumstances of the case, including, of course, the circumstances of the recall, but in the end to decide whether to recommend the release of the prisoner having made an assessment of risk to the public, on the basis of all the material available to it when it makes its decision. One of those considerations will, of course, be whether appropriate licence conditions could be devised. The Parole Board considered the available licence conditions in this case and plainly decided that, in all the circumstances, they could not" (per Sir Anthony Clarke M.R. at [35]).

Government policy as a relevant consideration

5–120 *[Add at end of para.5–120]*

A further question that may arise is whether a minister has acted lawfully in issuing policy guidance: see *R. (on the application of BAPIO Action Ltd) v Secretary of State for the Home Department* [2008] UKHL 27; [2008] 1 A.C. 1003.

International law and relevancy

5–123 *[Add end of n.385]*

And see P. Sales and J. Clements, "International law in domestic courts: the developing framework" (2008) 124 L.Q.R. 388.

PARTIAL ILLEGALITY AND SEVERANCE

5–136 *[Add to n.434]*

See e.g. *A v HM Treasury* [2008] EWCA Civ 1187; [2009] 2 All E.R. 747 at [104] (the words "or may be" were severed from a statutory instrument).

DELEGATION OF POWERS

Delegation of "Judicial" Powers

[Add to n.445]   5–140

In *Heald v Brent LBC* [2009] EWCA Civ 930 the Court of Appeal considered the practice adopted by some local authorities of contracting-out the reviews they are required to conduct under s.202 of the Housing Act 1996 where an applicant for housing assistance requests a review. It was held that the Local Authorities (Contracting Out of Allocation of Housing and Homelessness Functions) Order 1996 clearly permits such practices, notwithstanding doubts expressed in several speeches in *Runa Begum v Tower Hamlets LBC* [2003] UKHL 5; [2003] 2 A.C. 430 about the difficulties that would be associated with contracting out such a function. See also *R. (on the application of Gilboy) v Liverpool City Council* [2008] EWCA Civ 751; [2008] 4 All E.R. 127 (not cited in *Heald*) which concerned a "demoted tenancies" scheme (reference at [47] to the "good sense of non-delegation" of review functions to officers *in another local authority*). And see *Morina v Secretary of State for Work and Pensions; Borrowdale v Secretary of State for Work and Pensions* [2007] EWCA Civ 749; [2007] 1 W.L.R. 3033 (legally qualified panel members of the Social Security Appeal Tribunal).

General principles of delegation

Named officers

[Add to n.487]   5–153

In *R. (on the application of Queen Mary, University of London) v Higher Education Funding Council for England* [2008] EWHC 1472 (Admin); [2008] E.L.R. 540 at [39] a decision of HEFCE was unlawful "because Chief Executive did not make the decision as he should have done within the scheme of delegation" made in accordance with the Further and Higher Education Act 1992 Sch.1 para.10; it had been made by an auditor. And see *R. (on the application of Blow Up Media UK Ltd) v Lambeth LBC* [2008] EWHC 1912 (Admin); [2009] 1 P. & C.R. 10 (interpretation of local authority's scheme of delegation—court looked at the substance rather than the form of the matter).

The *Carltona* principle

5–162 *[Add to end of n.510]*

And see *Somerville v Scottish Ministers* [2007] UKHL 44; [2007] 1 W.L.R. 2734, in which one of the issues was whether a prison governor making an order under the Prisons and Young Offenders (Scotland) Rules 1994 r.80(1)—on the removal of association— should be regarded as a member of the Scottish Executive. The House held the *Carltona* principle did not apply in these circumstances.

5–166 *[Add to end of n.530]*

Although it did not arise for decision in the case, in *DPP v Haw* [2007] EWHC 1931 (Admin) Lord Phillips C.J. suggested (at [29]) that there was scope for further refinement of the *Carltona* principle, and devolution of a minister's powers should be subject to a requirement that the seniority of the official exercising a power should be of an appropriate level having regard to the nature of the power in question.

5–169 *[Add to end of n.545]*

But see *DPP v Haw* [2007] EWHC 1931 (Admin); [2008] 1 W.L.R. 379 at [33] (Lord Phillips C.J. holding that where a statutory power is conferred on an officer, who is himself a creature of statute, the question of whether that officer has the power to delegate is dependent upon the interpretation of the relevant statute). Where the responsibilities of the office are such that delegation is inevitable, there will be an implied power to delegate unless the statute, expressly or by implication, provides to the contrary. These principles are indistinguishable from the *Carltona* principle, and thus, whether Sedley L.J. was correct to hold in *R. (on the application of Chief Constable of the West Midlands) v Birmingham Justices* [2002] EWHC 1087; [2002] Po. L.R. 157 that the Carltona principle applied to a Chief Constable's statutory functions, was "of only academic significance".

CHAPTER 6

PROCEDURAL FAIRNESS: INTRODUCTION, HISTORY AND COMPARATIVE PERSPECTIVES

HISTORICAL DEVELOPMENT AFTER THE FIRST WORLD WAR

The rise of statutory procedures and the demise of the audi alteram partem principle

[Note 99] 6–027

Delete "Compulsory Purchase by Non-Ministerial Acquiring Authorities (Inquiries Procedure) Rules 1990 (SI 1990/512)" and substitute "Compulsory Purchase (Inquiries Procedure) Rules 2007 (SI 2007/3617)".

The impact of the distinctions

[Note 157] 6–040

Delete "Compulsory Purchase by Non-Ministerial Acquiring Authorities (Inquiries Procedure) Rules 1990 (SI 1990/512)" and "Compulsory Purchase by Ministers (Inquiries Procedure) Rules 1994 (SI 1994/3264)" and substitute "Compulsory Purchase (Inquiries Procedure) Rules 2007 (SI 2007/3617)".

HISTORICAL DEVELOPMENT SINCE THE 1960s

The duty to act fairly

[Add to end of n.168] 6–045

See *R. (on the application of Lewis) v Redcar and Cleveland BC* [2008] EWCA Civ 746; [2009] 1 W.L.R. 83 and *R. (on the application of Fraser) v National Institute for Health and Clinical Excellence* [2009] EWHC 452 (Admin) for examples of the application, post-*Ridge v Baldwin*, of the duty to act fairly to bodies that are not judicial or quasi-judicial, with a modification of content of the duty to suit the context.

COMPARATIVE PERSPECTIVES

Historical comparisons

6–050   *[Add to end of n.193]*

For a discussion of the evolution of procedural fairness in Canadian law, see *Dunsmuir v New Brunswick (Board of Management)* 2008 SCC 9; [2008] 1 S.C.R. 1 at paras 85–90 ("procedural fairness has grown to become a central principle of Canadian administrative law. Its overarching purpose is not difficult to discern: administrative decision-makers, in the exercise of public powers, should act fairly in coming to decisions that affect the interests of individuals": at para.90). In terms of entitlement to judicial review, the *Dunsmuir* case also establishes that, in the public employment context, if there is a contract of employment, the public law duty of fairness will not apply: at paras 102–103; see also 7–003.

[Add to end of n.194]

The duty to act fairly has been described as "a requirement of the rule of law which requires that the exercise of public power should not be arbitrary": *Masetlha v President of South Africa*, 2008 (1) S.A. 566 at para.189.

Contemporary comparisons

6–052   *[Note 197]*

Delete "Delany (2001), pp.236-238" and substitute "H. Delany, *Judicial Review of Administrative Action*, 2nd edn. (2009), pp.327–330".

6–053   *[Add to n.200 after ". . . 161 D.L.R. (4th) 112, 119"]*

But see *Dunsmuir v New Brunswick (Board of Management)* 2008 SCC 9; [2008] 1 S.C.R. 190 at [102]–[103] (holding that a civil servant, holding office "at pleasure" but also pursuant to contract, was not entitled to public law procedural fairness and commenting that dismissing an office holder and contractual employee both involved the private employer "merely exercising its private law rights as an employer").

6–054   *[Add to end of n.205]*

There has, however, been some discussion in the courts as to whether s.27 is narrower in its scope than the common law. This has arisen from comments of the Supreme Court in the case of *Taunoa v Attorney-General* [2007] NZSC 70; [2008] 1 N.Z.L.R. 429 at para.221 (to the effect that visits by a superintendent and medical officer to prisoners did not engage s.27(1) because they did not involve "an adjudicative function"). The comments have subsequently been interpreted by the Court of Appeal not to indicate that s.27(1) is narrower than the common law: *Combined Beneficiaries Union Incorporated v Auckland City COGS Committee* [2008] NZCA 423 at para.38 (see also para.15, where it is noted that the term "determination" in s.27(1) is "open-ended" and para.50 where it is held that the content of s.27(1) is "coincident with that at common law").

[Add to end of n.227]   6–058

; *R. v M* [2008] 3 S.C.R. 3 at paras 14, 19–20 (criminal trial judges, although the trial judge need not expound on matters that are well-settled, uncontroversial, understood and accepted by the parties, nor detail his or her finding on each piece of evidence, so long as the findings linking the evidence to the verdict can be logically discerned). For an interesting discussion of the rationale for a duty to give reasons and the sufficiency of reasons, see paras 8–26 and 35. See also *Dunsmuir v New Brunswick (Board of Management) v Dunsmuir*, 2008 SCC 9; [2008] 1 S.C.R. 190 at para.47 (the Supreme Court noting that reasonableness is concerned mostly with the existence of "justification, transparency and intelligibility within the decision-making process").

[Add to end of n.228]

The Freedom of Information Act 1997 in Ireland has been described as causing a "transformation" in this context: H. Delany, *Judicial Review of Administrative Action*, 2nd edn. (2009), p.316.

[Add to n.235 after ". . . [54]–[69] (Buchanan J.A.)"]

; *International Finance Trust Company Ltd v New South Wales Crime Commission* [2008] NSWCA 291 at para.46 (duty on judge to give reasons for an order freezing property given the "utmost gravity" and "drastic" nature of the power).

[Add to n.240 after ". . . natural justice rules"]   6–059

It has subsequently been held that this formulation was effective to exclude common law procedural fairness: *Saeed v Minister for Immigration and Citizenship* (2009) 176 F.C.R. 53 (affirming *Minister for Immigration and Multicultural and Indigenous Affairs v Lat* (2006) 151 F.C.R. 214).

[Add to end of n.240]

See also *Minister for Immigration and Citizenship v SZIZO* [2009] HCA Trans 71 (Gummow J., April 23, 2009).

[Add to end of n.242]

However, where it is held that the legislation has effectively excluded common law procedural fairness, any "subversion" of the statutory procedures has "the immediate consequence of stultifying the operation of the legislative scheme to afford natural justice": *SZFDE v Minister for Immigration and Citizenship* (2007) 232 C.L.R. 189 at 201 and 206. There is necessarily a failure to accord procedural fairness, even where common law procedural fairness rules may not have been breached: see G. Weeks, "The Expanding Role of Process in Judicial Review" (2008) 15 Australian J. of Administrative L. 100.

CHAPTER 7

PROCEDURAL FAIRNESS: ENTITLEMENT AND CONTENT

ENTITLEMENT TO PROCEDURAL FAIRNESS: OVERVIEW

From "natural justice" to "the duty to act fairly"

[Add to n.16 after ". . . to put it") 7–003

See also *Odelola v Secretary of State for the Home Department* [2009] 1 W.L.R. 1230; [2009] UKHL 25 at [33] ("simple fairness"). For recent use of the term "natural justice", see *R. (on the application of D) v Independent Education Appeal Panel of Bromley LBC* [2007] EWCA Civ 1010; [2008] B.L.G.R. 267 at [6].

[Add to end of n.17]

; *R. (on the application of Murungaru) v Secretary of State for the Home Department* [2008] EWCA Civ 1015; [2009] I.N.L.R. 180 at [39] ("a common law due process claim").

[Note 23]

Delete "P. Craig, *Administrative Law*, 5th edn. (2003), pp.415–418" and substitute "P. Craig, *Administrative Law*, 6th edn. (2008), paras 12–009— 12–010".

Attempts to categorise boundaries of procedural fairness

[Add to n.28] 7–005

The reference to *R. (on the application of Murungaru) v Secretary of State for the Home Department* [2006] EWHC 2416 must now be read in light of *R. (on the application of Murungaru) v Secretary of State for the Home Department* [2008] EWCA Civ 1015; [2009] I.N.L.R. 180.

[Note 30]

Delete "Export of Goods, Transfer of Technology and Provision of Technical Assistance (Control) Order 2003 (SI 2003/2764) Art.15" and substitute "Export Control Order 2008 (SI 2008/3231) art.33".

The recognition of a general duty of fairness

7–009   *[Add to n.41 after ". . . [2007] EWHC 199 at [47]"*

(see now R. *(on the application of BAPIO Action Ltd) v Secretary of State for the Home Department* [2008] UKHL 27; [2008] 1 A.C. 1003).

[Add to n.47 after ". . . tablets of stone"]

; R. *(on the application of H) v Secretary of State for Justice* [2008] EWHC 2590 (Admin) at [1] ("It is clear that procedural fairness does not impose the straightjacket of a quasi-judicial process and more informal procedures than what one expects before the courts or even tribunals may be acceptable. An oral hearing does not necessarily imply the adversarial process").

STATUTORY REQUIREMENTS OF FAIR PROCEDURES

Express statutory requirements

7–011   *[Note 55]*

Delete "Town and Country Planning (Appeals) (Written Representations Procedure) (England) Regulations (SI 2000/1628)" and substitute "Town and Country Planning (Appeals) (Written Representations Procedure) (England) Regulations 2009 (SI 2009/452)".

Supplementing statutory procedures

7–013   *[Add to end of n.59]*

; *Belfast City Council v Miss Behavin' Ltd* [2007] UKHL 19; [2007] 1 W.L.R. 1420 at [8] (discretion to consider late objections supplementary to the statutory scheme to ensure fair and workable).

[Add to n.60 after ". . . type of decision);"]

R. *(on the application of Hillingdon LBC, Leeds City Council, Liverpool City Council, Norfolk City Council) v Lord Chancellor, Secretary of State for Communities and Local Government* [2008] EWHC 2683 (Admin); [2009] C.P. Rep. 13 (where Parliament had prescribed the nature and extent of consultation which the Lord Chancellor was required to undertake before exercising his power to prescribe court fees no wider duty of consultation existed at common law (in the absence of a clear promise to consult more widely or any clear established practice of wider consultation by the decision-maker) (at [38]); the courts should not add a burden of consultation which the democratically elected body decided not to impose (at [39])). See also *R. (on the application of Edwards) v Environment Agency* [2008] UKHL 22; [2008] 1 W.L.R. 1587 (the relevant EC Directive specified what information should be made available to the public and the Regulations effected and extended those requirements; it was not for the courts to impose a broader duty); *easyJet Airline Company Ltd v The Civil Aviation Authority, Gatwick Airport Ltd* [2009] EWHC 1422 (Admin).

[Add to end of n.63]

; *R. (on the application of BAPIO Action Ltd) v Secretary of State for the Home Department)* [2007] EWCA Civ 1139 at [35] ("where there is a want of fairness in procedures laid down by Parliament, the common law will supply it").

[Add to para.7–015 after ". . . of other functions.⁶⁷"]   7–015

Similarly, where a statutory provision conferred a degree of flexibility as to how consultation should be conducted in framing the obligation as an obligation to "take such steps as [the decision makers] consider sufficient", "the court should not place them in a rigid straightjacket beyond that which the statute necessitates".⁶⁷ᵃ

[Insert new n.67a]

⁶⁷ᵃ *R. (on the application of Breckland DC) v The Boundary Committee* [2009] EWCA Civ 239 at [43].

FAIRNESS NEEDED TO SAFEGUARD RIGHTS AND INTERESTS

Licences and similar benefits

[Add to end of n.71]   7–019

; see also *R. (on the application of Hodgson) v South Wales Police Authority* [2008] EWHC 1183 (Admin); *R. (on the application of Abbey Mine Ltd) v The Coal Authority* [2008] EWCA Civ 353; (2008) 152(16) S.J.L.B. 28 (procedural fairness applied where the applicant was applying for an underground coal mining licence and demise of coal).

The scope of interests protected by fair procedures

Legislative decisions

7–026 *[Add to end of n.98]*

; *R. (on the application of BAPIO Action Ltd) v Home Secretary* [2007] EWCA Civ 1139 at [47] (there was no obligation to consult those affected or their representatives before introducing the material changes to the Immigration Rules, but Sedley L.J. did not want to "elevate this to a general rule that fairness can never require consultation as a condition of the exercise of a statutory function"). The point was not considered in the House of Lords: ([2008] UKHL 27; [2008] 1 A.C. 1003). See also *R. (on the application of C) v Secretary of State for Justice* [2008] EWHC 171 (Admin); [2008] A.C.D. 32.

[Add to n.100 after ". . . which the duty relates"]

See also *R. (on the application of C (A Minor)) v Secretary of State for Justice* [2008] EWCA Civ 882; [2009] 2 W.L.R. 1039 at [45] ("The legal obligation to take certain steps before laying legislation before Parliament is that of the executive. It is not Parliament's role to control that obligation: that is the function of the courts.")

Legitimate expectations

7–031 *[Add to end of n.110]*

See also *R. (on the application of Niazi) v The Independent Assessor* [2008] EWCA Civ 755 at [50] (if an authority has distinctly promised to consult those affected or potentially affected, then ordinarily it must consult); *R. (on the application of Actis SA) v Secretary of State for Communities and Local Government* [2007] EWHC 2417 (Admin) at [136], [155]. Contrast *R. (on the application of Bhatt Murphy) v Independent Assessor* [2008] EWCA Civ 755 (no legitimate expectation or exceptional circumstance to require consultation regarding changes to scheme for compensation).

[Note 112]

Delete "P. Craig, *Administrative Law*, 5th edn. (2003), pp.419–421" and substitute "P. Craig, *Administrative Law*, 6th edn. (2008), paras 12–016—12–017".

Fair Procedures under ECHR Art.6: Threshold Issues

[Add to end of n.115]   7–033

See also *K v Secretary of State for the Home Department* [2009] EWHC
3452 (Admin) and *HH (Iran) v Secretary of State for the Home Department*
[2008] EWCA Civ 504 (that assessment of refugee status did not amount
to art.6 civil proceedings has not been changed by the implementation of
Council Directive 2005/85/EC of December 1, 2005 on minimum standards on procedures in Member States for granting and withdrawing refugee
status [2005] OJ L326/13); *R. (on the application of Murungaru) v
Secretary of State for the Home Department* [2008] EWCA Civ 1015;
[2009] I.N.L.R. 180 (a challenge to the withdrawal of a visa was a
challenge to immigration controls and could not be disguised as an
assertion of property rights); *R. (on the application of Mdlovu) v Secretary
of State for the Home Department* [2008] EWHC 2089 (Admin) at [13].

[Add to the end of n.120]   7–034

; *R. (on the application of Wright) v Secretary of State for Health* [2009]
UKHL 3; [2009] 1 A.C. 739 at [20].

[Add to end of n.121]

; see also *R. (on the application of Wright) v Secretary of State for Health*
[2009] UKHL 3; [2009] 1 A.C. 739 (a provisional listing of a care worker
as unsuitable to work with vulnerable adults could result in possibly
irreparable damage to a person's employment or prospects of employment
in the care sector and engaged art.6(1) ECHR notwithstanding that it was
only an interim measure); *Jain v Trent Strategic Health Authority* [2009]
UKHL 4; [2009] 1 A.C. 739; *BM v Secretary of State for the Home
Department* [2009] EWHC 1572 (Admin) at [8] (art.6 ECHR was engaged
by an appeal against the modification of a control order as the interference
with the civil right would be for an "uncertain, but finite, period").

7–035

[Add to end of n.126]

; *R. (on the application of Wright) v Secretary of State for Health* [2009]
UKHL 3; [2009] 1 A.C. 739.

[Add to end of n.130]

; *L v Law Society* [2008] EWCA Civ 811; see also *Re Solicitor No 13 of
2007* [2008] EWCA Civ 411 (assumed although not determined that
imposing conditions on a practising certificate determines a civil right).

[Add to end of n.138]

But see *Ladbrokes Worldwide Betting v Sweden* (2008) 47 E.H.R.R. SE10 (application for a permit to provide betting and gaming services in Sweden did not engage art.6 where the grant of the permit was entirely within the discretion of the government and there were no clear criteria).

[Add to end of n.140]

; see also *Primary Health Investment Properties Ltd v Secretary of State for Health* [2009] EWHC 519 (Admin) (where a trust had discretion to deny financial assistance a civil right for the purpose of art.6 did not arise).

[Add to end of n.141]

; *R. (on the application of M) v Lambeth LBC* [2008] EWHC 1364 (Admin).

[Insert new n.143a in para.7–035 after ". . . applications,"[143]]

deportation[143a]

[143a] *RB (Algeria) v Secretary of State for the Home Department* [2009] UKHL 10; [2009] 2 W.L.R. 512.

[Add to para.7–035 after ". . . generally do not engage Art.6."]

In a tendering process, where a contracting committee was obliged to recommend tenders which ensured the best value for money at the lowest possible cost, this did not mean that the least expensive bid had to be chosen, and there was no expectation, even less so a right, that the lowest offer would be awarded the tender.[144a]

[144a] *ITC Ltd v Malta* (2008) 46 E.H.R.R. SE13 at para.41.

[add to end of n.147]

For recent comparative perspective on this question, see *Dunsmuir v New Brunswick (Board of Management)* 2008 SCC 9; [2008] 1 S.C.R. 190; *Société de l'assurance automobile du Quebec v Cyr* [2008] S.C.C. 13.

[In para.7–035]

The last sentence must be read in the light of *Vilho Eskelinen v Finland* (2007) 45 E.H.R.R. 43 ECtHR at para.62 where it was held that in order to prevent civil servants relying on art.6 ECHR, the state must show (a) that national law had expressly excluded access to a court for the post or category of staff in question; and (b) that the exclusion was justified on objective grounds in the state's interest.

[Add to end of n.150]   7–036

; *Galstyan v Armenia*, App.No.26986/03, Judgment of November 15, 2007, ECtHR at paras 56–60; *Secretary of State for the Home Department v MB* [2007] UKHL 46; [2008] 1 A.C. 440 (control orders civil and not criminal).

[Add to para.7–036 after ". . . detrimental".[150]]

The imposition of a control order under the Prevention of Terrorism Act 2005 has not been considered to involve the determination of a criminal charge.[150a]

[150a] *Secretary of State v MB and AF* [2007] UKHL 46; [2008] 1 A.C. 440.

Fair Procedures Required by ECHR Art.2: Threshold Issues

[Add to end of n.158]   7–037

See also *R. (on the application of Allen) v HM Coroner for Inner North London* [2009] EWCA Civ 623 (art.2 ECHR is not only engaged in cases where there were fundamental failures that caused the condition itself that caused the death, and where a mental patient had been detained in a hospital and died during the detention, it was possible that the medical authorities failed in their obligation to take general measures to save her from dying, which was sufficient to trigger an art.2 investigation).

[Add to para.7–037 after ". . . surrounding the death.[157]"]

This is because the object of an art.2 investigation is not limited to securing the accountability of state agents, but extends to opening up the circumstances, correcting mistakes, identifying good practice and learning lessons for the future.[157a]

[157a] *R. (on the application of Gentle) v Prime Minister* [2008] UKHL 20; [2008] 1 A.C. 1356 at [5]–[7]; *R. (on the application of L (A Patient)) v Secretary of State for Justice (Equality and Human Rights Commission intervening)* [2008] UKHL 68; [2009] 1 A.C. 588 at [24], [29], [40].

[Add to para.7–037 after ". . . of its obligation,[158]"]

and the obligation will not just arise where individuals are in the custody of the state, such as is the case with prisoners or mental health patients, but extends to soldiers of the territorial army.[158a]

158a *R. (on the application of Smith) v Oxfordshire Assistant Deputy Coroner (Equality and Human Rights Commission intervening)* [2009] EWCA Civ 441.

[Add new para.7–037A after para.7–037]

7–037A It has also been held that the art.2 obligation to conduct an investigation can be triggered in the context of a near-suicide of a prisoner. This is because prisoners as a class present a particular risk of suicide, and art.2 requires prison authorities to put in place systemic precautions to prevent suicide and to take operational measures when they know or ought to know of a real and immediate risk that a prisoner might commit suicide.[158a] Thus, the obligation to hold an art.2 investigation arises not only where there has arguably been a breach of the substantive duty to protect life but is triggered automatically by an attempted suicide which resulted in long-term injury.[158b]

158a *R. (on the application of L (A Patient)) v Secretary of State for Justice (Equality and Human Rights Commission intervening)* [2008] UKHL 68; [2009] 1 A.C. 588 at [39], [57].
158b *R. (on the application of L (A Patient)) v Secretary of State for Justice (Equality and Human Rights Commission intervening)* [2008] UKHL 68; [2009] 1 A.C. 588 at [37].

PRIOR NOTICE OF THE DECISION

The importance of prior notice

7–043 *[Add to end of n.182]*

See, e.g. *R. (on the application of Elliott) v First Secretary of State* [2007] EWHC 3492 (Admin).

The degree of notice required

7–047 *[Add to end of n.202]*

See also *R. (on the application of Cameroon) v Asylum and Immigration Tribunal* [2008] EWCA Civ 100; [2008] 1 W.L.R. 2062 at [10]; *Powell v Secretary of State for Environment, Food and Rural Affairs* [2009] EWHC 643 (Admin) at [31] (refusal of an application for an adjournment amounted to a breach of the rules of natural justice as it was not inevitable that the planning inspector's decision would have been the same had the claimant been given the opportunity to prepare his case); *R. (on the application of H) v Secretary of State for Justice* [2008] EWHC 2590 (Admin) at [20].

Statutory requirements for notice

[Add new para.7–050A]   7–050

A claimant's action need not be founded on a duty to consult the claimant   7–050A
himself and can be based on the decision-maker's duty to consult a third party.[224a]

[224a] *R. (on the application of C (A Minor)) v Secretary of State for Justice* [2008] EWCA Civ 882; [2009] 2 W.L.R. 1039.

CONSULTATION AND WRITTEN REPRESENTATIONS

Standards of consultation

7–053

[Add to end of n.233]

; *R. (on the application of Enfield BC) v Secretary of State for Health, Barnet Primary Care Trust* [2009] EWHC 743 (Admin) at [15]; *R. (on the application of Royal Borough of Windsor and Maidenhead) v Royal Berkshire Fire Authority* [2009] EWHC 354 (Admin) at [34].

[Add to n.234 after ". . . [90]–[94], [102]–[106]"]   7–054

(affirmed [2008] UKHL 22; [2008] 1 W.L.R. 1587).

[Add to end of n.234]

; *R. (on the application of O'Callaghan) v The Charity Commission for England and Wales* [2007] EWHC 2491 (Admin) at [26] (it was a "nonsense" to hold a consultation on a lease without disclosing the terms of the lease).

[Add to end of n.235]

; *R. (on the application of Greenpeace Ltd) v Secretary of State for Trade and Industry* [2007] EWHC 311 (Admin) (necessary to consult on new nuclear build where the Government had created a legitimate expectation that it would not consider this option).

[Add to para.7–054 after ". . . phased²³⁶]

, but if it is phased, the full package has to be sufficiently identified as part of the final stage of publication, and there has to be adequate time after the publication of the final part of the package for the package to be considered as a whole and for representations to be made.²³⁶ᵃ

²³⁶ᵃ *R. (on the application of Breckland DC) v The Boundary Committee* [2009] EWCA Civ 239 at [49].

[Add to end of n.237]

There had been no breach of the duty to consult where there had been consultation of representative organisations that had expertise and representatives of affected junior doctors: *R. (on the application of Legal Remedy UK Ltd) v Secretary of State for Health* [2007] EWHC 1252 (Admin) at [135].

Add to para.7–054 after ". . . bland generality."]

There may be cases where consultation on alternatives is required in order to ensure fairness, for example, where there is a legitimate expectation that consultation will include alternatives²⁴¹ᵃ; however there is no duty to consult on non-viable options.²⁴¹ᵇ

²⁴¹ᵃ*The Bard Campaign v Secretary of State for Communities and Local Government* [2009] EWHC 308 (Admin) at [90].
²⁴¹ᵇ[2009] EWHC 308 (Admin) at [90].

[Add to end of n.242]

(affirmed [2008] UKHL 22; [2008] 1 W.L.R. 1587).

[Add to para.7–054 after ". . . consultation process.²⁴²"]

However, the mere fact that information is "significant" does not mean that fairness necessarily requires its disclosure, although the degree of significance of the undisclosed material is a "highly material factor".²⁴²ᵃ Where there is doubt over whether a document is a consultation paper or merely an issues paper, the court should resolve this by asking whether those consultees who took the document at face value could reasonably foresee that following consideration of their responses, the issue of principle would be decided.²⁴²ᵇ

²⁴²ᵃ *R. (on the application of Eisai Ltd) v National Institute for Health and Clinical Excellence* [2008] EWCA Civ 438 at [26].
²⁴²ᵇ *R. (on the application of Greenpeace Ltd) v Secretary of State for Trade and Industry* [2007] EWHC 311 (Admin); [2007] N.P.C. 21; *R. (on the*

application of The Bard Campaign) v Secretary of State for Communities and Local Government [2009] EWHC 308 (Admin) at [74]–[75].

[Add to para.7–054 after ". . . to adopt,[244]*"]*

[. . .to adopt,[244]]—defined as a change of such a kind that it would be conspicuously unfair for the decision-maker to proceed without having given consultees a further opportunity to make representations about the proposal as so changed[244a]—

[244a] *R. (on the application of Elphinstone) v Westminster City Council* [2008] EWHC 1289 (Admin) at [62]: see also [2008] EWCA Civ 1069; [2009] B.L.G.R. 158 at [62].

[Add to n.245 after ". . . at [103]"]

(affirmed [2008] UKHL 22; [2008] 1 W.L.R. 1587).

[Add to n.246 after ". . . attend a meeting"]

, *R. (on the application of Eisiai Ltd) v National Institute for Health and Clinical Excellence* [2008] EWCA Civ 438.

[Add to n.246 after ". . . out of date)"]

(affirmed [2008] UKHL 22; [2008] 1 W.L.R. 1587).

[Add to para.7–054 after ". . . or the advisor.[246]*"]*

[. . . or the advisor.[246]] Whether or not consultation is a legal requirement, if it is embarked upon it must be carried out properly.[246a]

[246a] *R. (on the application of Eisai Ltd) v National Institute for Health and Clinical Excellence* [2008] EWCA Civ 438 at [24].

DUTY OF ADEQUATE DISCLOSURE BEFORE A DECISION IS TAKEN

The level of disclosure required

[Add to end of n.255]   7–057

; *R. (on the application of D) v Independent Education Appeal Panel of Bromley LBC* [2007] EWCA Civ 1010; [2008] B.L.G.R. 267 (parents entitled to be told, case to be met on reinstatement); *R. (on the application* of *Oyeyi-Effiong*) *v Bridge NDC Seven Sisters Partnership* [2007] EWHC 606 (Admin); [2007] B.L.G.R. 669 at [55] (given importance of the outcome of the investigation, namely the possible removal of elected members from a body entrusted with considerable public funds, more information should have been given); *R. (on the application of Benson) v Secretary of State for Justice* [2007] EWHC (Admin) 2055 (recalled prisoner is entitled to information regarding alleged licence breach such as to know "what the allegations against him are in sufficiently detailed form so that he can make meaningful objections or put forward meaningful representations": at para.22). But see *R. (on the application of O) v Independent Appeal Panel for Tower Hamlets LBC* [2007] EWHC 1455 (Admin) (no general duty to draw attention to every provision that might be relevant to the conduct of an appeal).

[Add to end of n.256]

; *R. (on the application of Breckland DC) v The Boundary Committee* [2009] EWCA Civ 239 at [44], [46] (important to enable "effective representations" to be made and to publish enough material to enable all those interested to respond intelligently).

[Add to end of n.257]

; *R. (on the application of Eisai Ltd) v National Institute for Health and Clinical Excellence* [2008] EWCA Civ 438 at [59] (even if disclosure were prima facie a breach of confidence, the public authority would have a public interest defence available to it if disclosure were necessary in order to meet the requirements of procedural fairness); *R. (on the application of Centro) v Secretary of State for Transport, West Midlands Travel ("TWM")* [2007] EWHC 2729 (Admin) (not unfair not to disclose internal advice received from employees as it was not suggested that the material on which advice was received related to matters that had not been raised or considered by the parties).

[Add to end of n.258]

; *Primary Health Investment Properties Ltd v Secretary of State for Health* [2009] EWHC 519 (Admin) (unfairness where a district valuer, instructed on behalf of a trust, obtained one party's expert file and only disclosed to the other party the fact that he had that file and would only disclose any material derived from it if he saw fit). But see *R. (on the application of Abbey Mine Ltd) v Coal Authority* [2008] EWCA Civ 353 at [31]–[32] (licence bidder entitled to be told concerns regarding bid, but not details of rival bidder's case).

[Add to end of n.259]

See also *MH v Secretary of State for the Home Department* [2009] EWCA Civ 287; [2009] 1 W.L.R. 2049 at [17].

[Add to end of n.261]

See also *R. (on the application of Cameroon) v Asylum and Immigration Tribunal* [2008] EWCA Civ 100; [2008] 1 W.L.R. 2062.

Failure to make adequate disclosure

[Add to para.7–058 after ". . . interviews with witnesses.[265]*"]*   **7–058**

Where public interest immunity is asserted, the onus is on the court to determine whether sufficient reasons have been provided by the person asserting immunity for withholding documents.[265a]

[265a] *Sommerville v Scottish Ministers* [2007] UKHL 44; [2007] 1 W.L.R. 2734. See also *R. (on the application of Al-Sweady) v Secretary of State for Defence* [2009] EWHC 1687 (Admin) at [45] (the "complete integrity" of any public interest immunity certificates and the schedules attached to them, signed by Ministers of the Crown, is absolutely essential as the courts must be able to have "complete confidence in the credibility and reliability" of such certificates and schedules.)

HEARINGS

[Add to end of para.7–062]   **7–062**

It has been observed that where an oral hearing is required, "[t]he interests at stake are such as to trump other factors in the balance such as cost and perhaps efficiency".[294a] Whether an oral hearing is necessary in any given case will depend on the facts of the particular case and it will be preferable to have an oral hearing where, for instance, on the evidence, there are facts which are in dispute.[294b] In the context of re-categorisation of prisoners, it has been suggested that factors which may "tip the balance" in favour of holding an oral hearing include being a Category A prisoner, having a tariff which has expired, and recommendations by the local prison for re-categorisation. In any case, if there is a failure to request an oral hearing, it may be fatal to a judicial review challenge on this ground.[294c]

[294a] *R. (on the application of H) v Secretary of State for Justice* [2008] EWHC 2590 (Admin) at [1].
[294b] *Hopkins v Parole Board* [2008] EWHC 2312 (Admin) at [33]. See also *R. (on the application of H) v Secretary of State for Justice* [2008] EWHC 2590 (Admin) (inconsistency between the approach of local prison and the Director of High Security Prisons was a factor which favoured an oral hearing); *R. (on the application of Wilkinson) v Secretary of State for Justice*

[2009] EWHC 878 (Admin). But see *R. (on the application of Moor & Edgecomb Ltd) v Financial Ombudsman Service* [2008] EWCA Civ 642 at [65] (oral hearing sought for purposes of cross-examination which was unnecessary especially given that the Ombudsman was intended to provide a system of resolving disputes quickly); *R. (on the application of Storm) v Secretary of State for Justice* [2009] EWHC 2168 (Admin); *R. (on the application of O'Connell) v Parole Board* [2007] EWHC 2591 (Admin); [2008] 1 W.L.R. 979 at [24] (the board's decision was not one which could have been affected by anything the claimant could have said beyond that which he had set out in his written representation, although the Parole Board should be predisposed to hold an oral hearing when making a decision as to whether a prisoner poses a relevant risk and should certainly do so where there is any dispute of fact or any need to examine the prisoner's motives or state of mind) (overruled on the application of art.5(4) ECHR to determinate sentences: *R. (on the application of Black) v Secretary of State for the Home Department* [2009] UKHL 1; [2009] 2 W.L.R. 282 and reversed on same issue by *R. (on the application of O'Connell) v Parole Board* [2009] EWCA Civ 575).
294c *Re Solicitor (No.13 of 2007)* [2008] EWCA Civ 411 at [27].

[Add to end of n.294]

; *R. (on the application of Moor and Edgecomb Ltd v Financial Ombudsman Service and Simon Lodge* [2008] EWCA Civ 642 (a fair determination of the dispute required that there should be an oral hearing but one that was limited to those officers of the applicant and the complainant who had been directly involved).

Requirements at an oral hearing

7–064   *[Add to n.301 after ". . . a criminal offence)."]*

Where there is a general rule that a hearing is conducted in public, even if the applicant requests a hearing in private, the general rule should not be departed from unless there is "good reason": *Re A Solicitor No. 18 of 2008* [2008] EWCA Civ 1358 at [3]; *L v The Law Society (No 13 of 2008)* [2008] EWCA Civ 811.

RIGHT TO CROSS-EXAMINATION

7–083   *[Add to end of n.377]*

; *Johnson Brothers v Secretary of State for Communities and Local Government* [2009] EWHC 580 (Admin) at [29] (nothing to suggest that the claimant was not given an opportunity to ventilate issues freely).

[Add to end of n.378]

See also *Johnson Brothers v Secretary of State for Communities and Local Government* [2009] EWHC 580 (Admin).

RIGHT TO REASONS

Reasons as an aspect of procedural fairness

[Add to end of n.391]   7–090

; *R. (on the application of Nottingham Healthcare NHS Trust) v Mental Health Review Tribunal* [2008] EWHC 2445 (Admin) at [18] (referring to "the general duty in courts to give their reasons"); *EE & Brian Smith (1928) Ltd v Hodson* [2007] EWCA Civ 1210 at [28] (it is sometimes possible to announce a decision at the conclusion of the hearing but to reserve the reasons for it but if that is done, the reasons should follow without undue delay).

[Add to para.7–090 after ". . . appellate capacity;[399]*"]*

in respect of applications for citizenship[399a];

[399a] *MH v Secretary of State for the Home Department* [2009] EWCA Civ 287; [2009] 1 W.L.R. 2049.

[Add to end of n.404]   7–091

; *Mubarak v General Medical Council* [2008] EWHC 2830 (Admin) at [36] ("The duty to give reasons is a facet of the obligation to deal fairly with the parties.")

[Add to end of n.405]

But the absence of a general duty to give reasons was recently affirmed in *R. (on the application of Hasan) v Secretary of State for Trade and Industry* [2008] EWCA Civ 1312; [2009] 3 All E.R. 539 at [8].

Circumstances in which reasons will be required

Required by statute

[Add to end of n.436]   7–098

; Mental Health Review Tribunal Rules 1983 r.23(2) and *R. (on the application of Nottingham Healthcare NHS Trust) v Mental Health Review Tribunal* [2008] EWHC 2445 (Admin).

[Add to end of n.437]

; For another example in the planning context, see *R. (on the application Midcounties Co-operative Ltd) v Forest of Dean DC* [2007] EWHC 714 (Admin) (planning permissions were quashed for failure to give summary reasons as required by the Town and Country Planning (General Development Procedure) Order 1995 (SI 1995/419)).

Brief survey of case law on reason giving

7–103   *[Add to end of n.462]*

The Criminal Injuries Compensation Appeals Panel should also give sufficiently full and clear reasons to indicate not only how and why the discretion has been exercised, but in particular, if submissions as to why it should be exercised in favour of the applicant are rejected, the reasons for rejecting those submissions: *R. (on the application of Green) v Criminal Injuries Compensation Appeals Panel* [2008] EWHC 3501 (Admin) at [32].

[Add to para.7–103 after ". . . supply reasons.[471]"]

- A coroner should have given reasons for her conclusion that there was no evidence on which the jury could have returned an unlawful killing verdict.[471a]

  [471a] *R. (on the application of Cash) v Northamptonshire Coroner* [2007] EWHC 1354 (Admin); [2007] 4 All ER 903 at [45].

- Reasons were not required, however, for arms export decisions.[471b]

[471b] *R. (on the application of Hasan) v Secretary of State for Trade & Industry* [2007] EWHC 2630 (Admin); affirmed *R. (on the application of Hasan) v Secretary of State for Trade and Industry* [2008] EWCA Civ 1312 at [8].

The standard of reasons required

7–104   *[Add to end of n.472]*

; *EE & Brian Smith (1928) Ltd v Hodson* [2007] EWCA Civ 1210 at [30].

[Add to the end of n.473]

; *R. (on the application of Wheeler) v Assistant Commissioner of the Metropolitan Police* [2008] EWHC 439 (Admin).

[Add to end of n.474]

; *R. (on the application of London Fire and Emergency Planning Authority) v Secretary of State for Communities and Local Government* [2007] EWHC 1176 (Admin) at [64].

[Add to end of n.475]

; *R. (on the application of Sivanesan) v Secretary of State for the Home Department* [2008] EWHC 1146 (Admin); *R. (on the application of S) v Secretary of State for the Home Department* [2009] EWCA Civ 688 at [8] (absence in the decision letter of any indication that the Secretary of State had considered ill-treatment at the hands of Sri Lankan authorities, which constituted a failure to apply anxious scrutiny); *R. (on the application of SS (Sri Lanka)) v Secretary of State for the Home Department* [2009] EWHC 223 (Admin).

[Add to end of n.476]

; *R. (on the application of London Fire and Emergency Planning Authority) v Board of Medical Referees* [2007] EWHC 2805 (Admin) at [41] (accepting that it was "wrong to be too critical of the reasons given by a board that is not chaired by a lawyer", but nonetheless the reasons given were inadequate as they did not set out the legal test, the standard of proof, why the injury was a qualifying one within the rules, why the board's views differed from a medical opinion).

[Add to para.7–104 after ". . . express themselves".[476]]

Where the issues dealt with by the tribunal or administrative actor are "extremely important", the duty to give reasons may be equated with the general duty in courts to give their reasons, rather than the "less exacting standard applied to ordinary administrative decision-making".[476a]

[476a] *R. (on the application of Nottingham Healthcare NHS Trust) v Mental Health Review Tribunal* [2008] EWHC 2445 (Admin) [18].

[Add to end of n.478]

; *Consistent Group Ltd v Kalwak, Welsh Country Foods Ltd* [2008] EWCA Civ 430; [2008] I.R.L.R. 505 at [46] ("it was basic that the Chairman had to provide a proper explanation as to why, given the evidential conflicts, he was preferring one side's evidence to that of the other").

[Add to end of n.480]

Reasons should also be read from the standpoint of an "informed party": *R. (on the application of Roberts) v Secretary of State for Communities and*

Local Government [2008] EWHC 677 (Admin); [2009] J.P.L. 81. For useful summary of the standard of reasons required, see *Proctor & Gamble UK v Revenue and Customs Commissioners* [2009] EWCA Civ 407 at [19].

[Add to end of n.481]

; *Mubarak v General Medical Council* [2008] EWHC 2830 (Admin) at [35] (a "short initial explanation" was "more than adequate" to enable the appellant to know why the Panel had found against the claimant); *R. (on the application of Nottingham Healthcare NHS Trust) v Mental Health Review Tribunal* [2008] EWHC 2445 (Admin) at [15] ("the length of reasons . . . is not itself necessarily a reflection of their quality. Short reasons can be adequate.").

7–108   *[Add to end of n.496]*

See also *R. (on the application of Martin) v Legal Services Commission* [2007] EWHC 1786 (Admin) at [60].

Remedy for lack or insufficiency of reasons

7–114   *[Add to the end of n.514]*

; *EE & Brian Smith (1928) Ltd v Hodson* [2007] EWCA Civ 1210 at [38]; *R. (on the application of Bancoult) v Secretary of State for Foreign & Commonwealth Affairs* [2007] EWCA Civ 498; [2008] Q.B. 365 at [70]: reversed on other grounds [2008] UKHL 61; [2009] 1 A.C. 453. See also *R. (on the application of London Fire and Emergency Planning Authority) v Secretary of State for Communities and Local Government* [2007] EWHC 1176 (Admin); [2007] L.G.R. 591 at [66]; *R. (on the application of C) v Secretary of State for Justice* [2008] EWCA Civ 882 at [49].

[Note 515]

Delete "4th edn. (2004)" and substitute "5th edn. (2008) para.62.5".

7–115   *[Add to end of n.518]*

; *R. (on the application of Bancoult) v Secretary of State for Foreign & Commonwealth Affairs* [2007] EWCA Civ 498; [2008] Q.B. 365 at [70] ("in principle a decision-maker who gives one set of reasons cannot, when challenged, come up with another set") reversed on other grounds [2008] UKHL 61; [2009] 1 A.C. 453. See also *R. (on the application of London Fire and Emergency Planning Authority) v Secretary of State for Communities and Local Government* [2007] EWHC 1176 (Admin); [2007] L.G.R. 591 at [66].

[Add new n.520a after ". . . with the original reasons;" to para.7–115]

[520a] See, e.g. *R. (on the application of T) v Independent Appeal Panel for Devon County Council* [2007] EWHC 763 (Admin); [2007] E.L.R. 499 at [42].

[Add to end of n.521]

; *W v The Independent Appeal Panel of Bexley LBC* [2008] EWHC 758 (Admin) at [36] (clerk's notes did not amount to "contradiction, but simply a clarification or supplementation, of the decision letter"); *Swords v Secretary of State for Communities and Local Government* [2007] EWCA Civ 795; [2007] B.L.G.R. 757 at [47].

ECHR Article 6: Content

Fair hearing

[Add to end of n.538]   7–121

; *Battista v Bassano* [2007] EWCA Civ 370.

Public hearing and public pronouncement of judgment

[Add to end of n.546]   7–122

; *Hellborg v Sweden* (2007) 45 E.H.R.R. 3 ECtHR, at para.56.

[Add to para.7–122 after ". . . in public.[546]"]

An oral hearing is not required if an accused or a party has waived his right to such a hearing, if the waiver is unequivocal and there is no important public interest consideration that calls for the public to have the opportunity to be present.[546a]

[546a] *Warren v Random House Group Ltd* [2008] EWCA Civ 834; [2009] 2 W.L.R. 314.

[Add to end of n.553]   7–123

; *Hermi v Italy* (2008) 46 E.H.R.R. 46 ECtHR (Grand Chamber) at para.58.

[Add to end of n.557]   7–124

; *Aziz v Aziz* [2007] EWCA Civ 712; [2008] 2 All E.R. 501 (redactions should be refused where not strictly necessary and justified and where the judgment could not be understood without the relevant parts sought to be redacted).

Hearing within a reasonable time

7–125 *[Add to end of n.560]*

For an example of "culpable and undue" delay giving rise to "conspicuous unfairness" at common law, see *FH (Bangladesh) v Secretary of State for the Home Department* [2009] EWCA Civ 385 at [15].

[Add to end of n.563]

; *Vilho Eskelinen v Finland* (2007) 45 E.H.R.R. 43 ECtHR, at para.67.

ECHR ART.2: CONTENT

7–128 *[Add to para.7–128 after ". . . events.[572]"]*

An investigation may be inadequate and ineffective if "appropriate steps" are not taken to reduce the risk of collusion.[572a]

[572a] *R. (on the application of Saunders) v Independent Police Complaint Commissioner; R. (on the application of Tucker) v Independent Police Complaints Commission* [2008] EWHC 2372 (Admin); [2009] 1 All E.R. 379 at [40].

[Add to end of n.573]

; *SP v Secretary of State for Justice* [2009] EWHC 13 (Admin) (an investigation into the claimant's detention while in young offender institutions was not sufficiently independent to make the report compliant with art.2 ECHR because an investigator for the report had worked for the prison service for 30 years on issues relevant to the investigation and had a social acquaintance with the governor of one of the institutions investigated).

[Add to end of n.575]

; *Dodov v Bulgaria* (2008) 47 E.H.R.R. 41 ECtHR.

[Add to end of n.582]

However, where the incident results in near-suicide, rather than death, a public inquiry will not necessarily be required, although an "enhanced investigation" (not an internal investigation) will be necessary: *R. (on the application of L (A Patient)) v Secretary of State for Justice (Equality and Human Rights Commission intervening)* [2008] UKHL 68; [2009] 1 A.C. 588 at [41].

[Add to para.7–128 ". . . witness is at risk.[583]"]

It is not necessary for the investigator to investigate and state his conclusion in relation to every issue raised; what is required is that the investigation is focused on the central issue or issues in the case.[583a]

[583a] *R. (on the application of Allen) v Inner North London Coroner* [2009] EWCA Civ 623.

Inquests

[Add to para.7–129 after ". . . inquest is conducted.[584]"]   **7–129**

There are two types of inquest: the traditional inquest and the art.2 inquest. The essential difference between them is twofold.[584a] First, the permissible verdict or verdicts in a traditional inquest is significantly narrower than in an art.2 inquest, which requires an expression, however brief, of the jury's conclusion on the disputed factual issues at the heart of the case.[584b] Secondly the scope of the investigation is or is likely to be narrower at a traditional inquest.[584c]

[584a] *R. (on the application of Smith) v Oxfordshire Assistant Deputy Coroner (Equality and Human Rights Commission intervening)* [2009] EWCA Civ 441 at [64].
[584b] *R. (on the application of Smith) v Oxfordshire Assistant Deputy Coroner (Equality and Human Rights Commission intervening)* [2009] EWCA Civ 441 at [64] and [71]–[76].
[584c] *R. (on the application of Smith) v Oxfordshire Assistant Deputy Coroner (Equality and Human Rights Commission intervening)* [2009] EWCA Civ 441 at [64].

CHAPTER 8

PROCEDURAL FAIRNESS: EXCEPTIONS

RISK TO THE PUBLIC INTEREST

National security and terrorism

[Add to end of n.36]   8–007

For discussion see T. Poole "Courts and Conditions of Uncertainty in 'Times of Crisis'" [2008] P.L. 234.

[Add n.36a after ". . . of the decision." to para.8–007]

[36a] *R. (on the application of Mohamed) v Secretary of State for Foreign and Commonwealth Affairs (4)* [2009] EWHC 152 (Admin) at [18] (referring to the balancing of the public interest in national security and the public interest in open justice, the rule of law and democratic accountability).

[Add new para.8–009A]   8–009

Where the government certifies that information cannot be disclosed in the   8–009A
interests of national security, the "complete integrity" of any public interest immunity certificates and the schedules attached to them, signed by Ministers of the Crown, is absolutely essential as the courts must be able to have "complete confidence in the credibility and reliability" of such certificates and schedules.[50a]

[50a] *R. (on the application of Al-Sweady) v Secretary of State for Defence* [2009] EWHC 1687 (Admin) at [45] (also deploring the "lamentable history" of systemic and individual failures underpinning the certificates and schedules under consideration).

Counter-terrorism measures

[Add to end of n.52]   8–012

See generally M. Chamberlain "Special Advocates and Procedural Fairness in Closed Proceedings" (2009) 28 C.J.Q. 314; J. Ip, "The Rise and Spread of the Special Advocate" [2008] P.L. 717.

8–013 *[Add to para.8–013 after ". . . the rule of law."]*

In *Secretary of State for the Home Department v AF (No.3)*, Lord Phillips noted that there were strong policy considerations that supported a rule that a trial procedure could never be considered fair if a party to it was kept in ignorance of the case against him. The first was that there would be many cases where it was impossible for the court to be confident that disclosure would make no difference. Further, there would be feelings of resentment if a party to legal proceedings was placed in a position where it was impossible for him to influence the result. Indeed, if the wider public were to have confidence in the justice system, they needed to be able to see that justice was done rather than being asked to take it on trust.[52a]

[52a] *Secretary of State for the Home Department v AF (No.3)* [2009] UKHL 28; [2009] 3 W.L.R. 74 at [63]–[64]. For discussion generally on the risks of secret evidence, see G. Van Harten "Weaknesses of Adjudication in the Face of Secret Evidence" (2009) 13 Evidence and Procedure 1.

[Add to para.8–013 after ". . . trial".[53a]]

In the case of *A v United Kingdom*,[53b] the Grand Chamber of the European Court of Human Rights made it clear that non-disclosure could not go so far as to deny a party knowledge of the essence of the case against him, at least where he is at risk of consequences as severe as those normally imposed under a control order. That decision established that the "controlee" had to be given sufficient information about the allegations against him to enable him to give effective instructions in relation to those allegations. Provided that this requirement was satisfied, there could be a fair trial notwithstanding that the controlee was not provided with the detail or the sources of the evidence forming the basis of the allegations. Where, however, the open material consisted purely of general assertions and the case against the controlee was based solely or to a decisive degree on closed materials, the requirements of a fair trial will not be satisfied, however cogent the case based on the closed materials might be. The Strasbourg Court accepted that the judge is in the best position to form a judgment about the extent to which the controlled person is disadvantaged by the lack of disclosure—or to put it the other way, the proceedings over which he is presiding afford a sufficient measure of procedural protection.[53c]

[Add to end of n.53a]

The reading down of the Prevention of Terrorism Act 2005 in *MB* was upheld in *Secretary of State for the Home Department v AF (No. 3)* [2009] UKHL 28; [2009] 3 W.L.R. 74 at [67].

[53b] App.No.3455/05, 26 B.H.R.C. 1 (Grand Chamber).

[53c] 26 B.H.R.C. 1 at [220]. See also *Secretary of State for the Home Department v AF (No. 3)* [2009] UKHL 28; [2009] 3 W.L.R. 74 (Lord Phillips noting that "with the assistance of the dedicated special advocates that are available and the input of judges with the ability and experience of those who hear these cases, the approach approved by this House in *MB*, including the 'makes no difference' principle, could have been applied without significant risk of producing unjust results": at [62]); *BM v Secretary of State for the Home Department* [2009] EWHC 1572 (Admin); *Secretary of State for the Home Department v N* [2009] EWHC 1966 (Admin) at [3] (art.6 was violated where non-disclosure went so far as to deny N of the "essence" of the case against him)

[Add new para.8–013A after para.8–013]

The use of special advocates will vary according to context.[53d] For example, in citizenship cases, where an individual is refused citizenship on the ground that he is not of "good character" and the Secretary of State refuses to give full reasons or to disclose relevant material which he took into account in reaching his decision, it is not the case that a special advocate must always be appointed. Rather, a special advocate should be appointed where it is just to do so, having regard to the requirement that proceedings must be fair to the claimant and to the Secretary of State.[53e] In such cases the Secretary of State should consider with counsel, who should consider the issue dispassionately, whether it was appropriate for the trial judge to have the assistance of a special advocate. A special advocate should be appointed where it was just, and therefore necessary, to do so in order for the issues to be determined fairly. Where the material was not to be disclosed, or full reasons were not to be given to the claimant, there were only two possibilities, namely that the judge would determine the issues by looking at the documents himself, or that he would do so with the assistance of a special advocate. The appointment of a special advocate was likely to be just where there might be significant issues or a significant number of documents. Everything depended on the circumstances of the particular case, but it was important to have in mind the importance of the decision from the claimant's point of view, the difficulties facing the claimant in effectively challenging the case against him in open court and whether the assistance of a special advocate would or might assist him in meeting the case against him and assist the court in arriving at a fair conclusion. If the judge decided to read the documents, in order to consider whether or not a special advocate should be appointed, the Secretary of State should not make oral or written submissions but should include a short note merely identifying the key pages or documents in order to direct the judge to the relevant material and briefly stating the grounds upon which it was said that the material should not be disclosed. The judge should then decide how to proceed in the light of all the circumstances of the case and after hearing oral open submissions.[53f]

8–013A

107

[53d] *MH v Secretary of State for the Home Department* [2009] EWCA Civ 287; [2009] 1 W.L.R. 2049 at [45]–[47].
[53e] *MH v Secretary of State for the Home Department* [2009] EWCA Civ 287; [2009] 1 W.L.R. 2049 at [35].
[53f] *MH v Secretary of State for the Home Department* [2009] EWCA Civ 287; [2009] 1 W.L.R. 2049 at [37].

8–013B *[Add new para.8–013B]*

In the deportation context, it has been held that where safety on return is in issue, it is not likely to be critically important for the special advocate advancing the case of the deportee to obtain input from him in relation to the evidence which the receiving state wished to remain closed. Unlike in the control order context, it is not the case that the deportee does not know the case against him; rather the deportee will normally be aware of the facts which create the risk of a violation of his human rights on return to his own country, and indeed he will be relying on them to establish the risk that he faces on his return. His situation is not that of an individual who is unaware of the case that is made against him.[53f]

[53f] *RB (Algeria) v Secretary of State for the Home Department* [2009] UKHL 10; [2009] 2 W.L.R. 512.

FAIR PROCEDURES WOULD HINDER PROMPT ACTION

Statutory relaxation of procedural propriety

8–016 *[Add to n.72 after "... ss.17, 37"]*

; see also, e.g. Health and Social Care Act 2008 s.30.

Common law exclusion of procedural propriety for urgency

8–019 *[Add to end of n.81]*

However, see now Legal Services Act 2007 Sch.14 (requiring a minimum of eight days notice).

[Add to para.8–019 after "... holding operation".[82]"]

There may also be circumstances where an injunction has to be granted as a matter of urgency without it being possible to give full reasons on the same day.[82a]

[82a] *EE & Brian Smith (1928) Ltd v Hodson* [2007] EWCA Civ 1210 at [30] (although not relevant in this case as judgment had been reserved for almost four weeks).

IMPRACTICABLE TO PROVIDE FAIR PROCEDURE

[Add to n.85 after ". . . 199 at [47];"]   8–020

(point not considered in the House of Lords: [2008] UKHL 27; [2008] 1 A.C. 1003)

SUBSEQUENT FAIR HEARING OR APPEAL

ECHR art.6 and subsequent hearings

Limits of curative effect

[Add new para.8–031A after para.8–031]   8–031

Thus, it is clear from *Tsfayo* that in deciding whether a breach of art.6 at   8–031A
the first stage of the process can be cured by a later stage of the process, it
is necessary to have regard to the nature of the first stage breach.[153a] The
more serious the breach in the first stage of the process, the more likely it is
that a breach in the first stage of the process cannot be cured at the second
stage; where the breach involves "denial of one of the fundamental
elements of the right to a fair determination of a person's civil rights,
namely the right to be heard", judicial review does not afford full
jurisdiction, since it cannot make good the consequences of the denial of
the opportunity to make representations at the earlier stage.[153b]

[153a] *R. (on the application of Wright) v Secretary of State for Health* [2007] EWCA Civ 999; [2008] Q.B. 422 at [105]) (upheld [2009] UKHL 3; [2009] 1 A.C. 739).
[153b] *R. (on the application of Wright) v Secretary of State for Health* [2007] EWCA Civ 999; [2008] Q.B. 422 at [106] (holding that a failure to afford a worker the opportunity to make representations before being included in a list of those deemed unsuitable to work with vulnerable adults could not be cured by judicial review) (upheld [2009] UKHL 3; [2009] 1 A.C. 739).

PRELIMINARY DECISIONS

Proximity between investigation and act or decision

8–035 *[Add to end of para.8–035]*

The exercise of the court's power of judicial review is less rare in the case of a decision not to prosecute than a decision to prosecute because the former is final whereas the latter leaves the defendant free to challenge the prosecution's case in the usual way through the criminal court.[164a]

[164a] *R. (on the application of FB) v Director of Public Prosecutions* [2009] 1 Cr. App. R. 38; [2009] EWHC 106 (Admin) at [52].

LACK OF FAIR PROCEDURE MADE NO DIFFERENCE OR CAUSED NO HARM

8–044 *[Add to end of n.189]*

; *W v The Independent Appeal Panel of Bexley LBC* [2008] EWHC 758 (Admin) at [38]; *R. (on the application of Edwards) v Environment Agency (No. 2)* [2008] UKHL 22; [2008] 1 W.L.R. 158 at [65] (pointless to quash a permit simply to enable the public to be consulted on out-of-date data).

Statutory applications to quash

8–046 *[Add to end of n.199]*

; *R. (on the application of Midcounties Co-operative Ltd) v Wyre Forest DC* [2009] EWHC 964 (Admin) at [96].

8–048 *[Add to end of n.204]*

See also *R. (on the application of C) v Secretary of State for Justice* [2008] EWCA Civ 882 at [49] (regulations were quashed where a race equality impact assessment had been carried out subsequently even though it validated the decision as refusing relief would have sent the "wrong message" to public authorities).

8–049 *[Add to n.206]*

R. (on the Application of Midcounties Co-Operative Ltd) v Wyre Forest DC [2009] EWHC 964 (Admin) (Ouseley J.) (even though a legitimate expectation to consultation had been breached, no prejudice had been caused to the claimant and therefore the planning permission under challenge would not be quashed).

Illustrations

[Add to end of n.207]   8–050

; *R. (on the application of Siborurema) v Office of the Independent Adjudicator* [2007] EWCA Civ 1365 at [66] (there was "no real possibility" that disclosure of the information for comment would have affected the decision).

CHAPTER 9

PROCEDURAL FAIRNESS: FETTERING OF DISCRETION

FETTERING OF DISCRETION BY SELF-CREATED RULES OR POLICY

[Add to end of n.2] 9–003

This terminology is retained in H.W.R. Wade and C. Forsyth, *Administrative Law*, 10th edn. (2006), Ch.10.

Application of the no-fettering principle

[Add to end of n.9] 9–006

See also *R. (on the application of S) v Secretary of State for the Home Department* [2007] EWCA Civ 546 at [50] ("A public authority may not adopt a policy which precludes it from considering individual cases on their merits, nor may it allow its treatment of applications to be dictated by agreement with another government body").

Illustrations

[Add to end of n.22] 9–007

; *P v Hackney LBC* [2007] EWHC 1365 (Admin).

[Add to para.9–007 after ". . . therefore unlawful.[38]"]

- Likewise, where a prisoner had received a consecutive sentence in default of payment of a confiscation order and applied for temporary release while serving her first sentence, to refuse her pursuant to a blanket policy which provided that release could only be considered during the second period of imprisonment amounted to an unlawful fettering of discretion.[38a]

[38a] *Adelana v Governor of HMP Downview* [2008] EWHC 2612 (Admin) at [43].

- A local authority could not fetter its discretion by a term in a secure tenancy agreement to the effect that it would not use its statutory power to vary tenancy agreements by notice without approval of the tenants' representatives.[38b]

- In the context of asylum applications, it was unlawful for the Secretary of State to defer dealing with a whole class of applications, older applications, in order to meet targets set for consideration of more recent applications; this amounted to "a textbook case" of unlawful fettering of discretion.[38c] The court noted that although the principle is normally applied to substantive decisions on applications, there was no reason why it should not apply equally to "a procedural decision to defer a whole class of applications without good reasons and without consideration of the effects on the applicants".[38d]

- Where a statute granted to the courts a wide discretion to consider what is equitable having regard to all the circumstances, it was not desirable to fetter that discretion by rules.[38e]

[38b] *R. (on the application of Kilby) v Basildon DC* [2007] EWCA Civ 479.

[38c] *R. (on the application of S) v Secretary of State for the Home Department* [2007] EWCA Civ 546 at [50].

[38d] [2007] EWCA Civ 546. See also *R. (on the application of AK) v Secretary of State for Foreign and Commonwealth Affairs* [2008] EWHC 2227 (Admin) at [32] (Blake J. observing obiter that it would "probably be unlawful for a Secretary of State to fetter her statutory discretion about the admission of people who are subject to immigration control").

[38e] *Dunn v Parole Board* [2008] EWCA Civ 374; [2090] 1 W.L.R. 728 at [31], [43].

Power to articulate rules or policy

9–010   *[Add to end of n.49]*

; *A v Croydon LBC, Secretary of State for the Home Department* [2009] EWHC 939 (Admin) (a policy of giving prominence to a particular assessment in determining whether an immigrant was a child did not constitute an unlawful fetter provided that the Home Office was satisfied that there had been a proper assessment and that the reasons given and observations made had been satisfactory); *R. (on the application of Banks) v The Mayor and Burgess of Tower Hamlets LBC* [2009] EWHC 242 (Admin) (a local authority had not abdicated the exercise of its discretion by adopting a policy generally not to prosecute for over-sized market stalls as it had brought a small number of prosecutions); *R. (on the application of Siborurema) v Office of the Independent Adjudicator* [2007] EWCA Civ 1365 (where there was nothing in the facts of the case to require the OIA to carry out a review otherwise than in accordance with its standard practice, it would not be a fetter of its discretion to do so).

Do exceptions have to be specified in the rule or policy?

[Add to end of para.9–013] 9–013

How the exceptions are defined is important: a trust which required an application for funding to be refused where a patient was "representative of a group of patients" did not in fact allow for exceptional cases, but actually required patients to demonstrate uniqueness rather than exceptionality to qualify for funding.[69a]

[69a] *R. (on the application of Ross) v West Sussex Primary Care Trust* [2008] EWHC 2252 (Admin) at [78]–[79].

Undertaking not to Exercise a Discretion

Discretion in relation to land

[Add to end of n.105] 9–024

R. (on the application of Kilby) v Basildon DC [2007] EWCA Civ 479 (where a statute specifically stated that the local authority's contractual tenancies could be varied by unilateral notice, a system which circumscribed that power by giving to tenants' representatives an absolute veto was incompatible with the statute).

Discretion and contract

[Add to end of n.109] 9–025

See also *R. (on the application of Kilby) v Basildon DC* [2007] EWCA Civ 479.

[Note 119] 9–028

Delete "P. Craig, *Administrative Law*, 5th edn. (2003), pp.547–548; H.W.R. Wade and C. Forsyth, *Administrative Law*, 9th edn. (2004) pp.332–333" and substitute: "A.C.L. Davies, *The Public Law of Government Contracts* (2008) pp.176–183; P. Craig, *Administrative Law*, 6th edn. (2008), paras 16–021—16–033; H.W.R. Wade and C.F. Forsyth, *Administrative Law*, 10th edn. (2009) pp.276–281".

CHAPTER 10

PROCEDURAL FAIRNESS: BIAS AND CONFLICT OF INTEREST

INTRODUCTION

[Add to end of n.7]   **10–005**

See also *R. v Abdroikov* [2007] UKHL 37; [2007] 1 W.L.R. 2679 at [17].

THE TEST OF BIAS

[Add to para.10–012 new n.39a after ". . . appearance of bias"]   **10–012**

[39a] For discussion, see J. Goudkamp, "The Rule against Bias and the Doctrine of Waiver" (2007) 26 C.J.Q. 310.

Gough adjusted: "real possibility"

[Add to end of n.57]   **10–017**

; *R. v Abdroikov* [2007] UKHL 37; [2007] 1 W.L.R. 2679 at [15]; *Howell v Lee Millais* [2007] EWCA Civ 720 at [4].

[Add to end of n.59]

For consideration of the attributes of the "fair-minded and informed observer" see *Helow v Secretary of State for the Home Department* [2008] UKHL 62; [2008] 1 W.L.R. 2416 at [1]–[3].

AUTOMATIC DISQUALIFICATION FOR BIAS

Can automatic disqualification be justified?

[Add to end of n.105]   **10–036**

But see *Re Duffy (FC) (Northern Ireland)* [2008] UKHL 4; [2008] N.I. 152 (finding unlawful the appointment of members of the Orange Order to the Northern Ireland Parades Commission).

Other Situations in which Bias May Occur

Participation in subsequent decisions

10–038 *[Add to end of n.107]*

R. (on the application of AB) v X [2009] EWHC 1149 (Admin) (a Crown Court judge who has presided over the discharge of a jury in a fraud trial, should have recused himself from hearing a wasted costs order against the claimant barrister who had made misleading closing remarks, where the claimant intended to directly challenge the reasonableness of the judge's decision to discharge the jury). But see *Bolkiah v Brunei Darussalam* [2007] UKPC 62 PC (Bru) (fanciful that the Chief Justice of Brunei would break his judicial oath and jeopardise his reputation in order to please the Sultan. Despite the fact that legislative amendments made by the Sultan of Brunei, which included provision for in camera hearings, were not unconnected to the particular proceedings that had been brought, the Chief Justice was a judge of unblemished reputation, nearing the end of a long and distinguished judicial career in more than one jurisdiction. Furthermore there had been a complete absence of any evidence of intervention by the executive in the matter of the court's listing arrangements in respect of the instant proceedings). For examples of the application of this principle in the art.6 ECHR context see *Kyprianou v Cyprus* (2007) 44 E.H.R.R. 27 ECtHR (a want of impartiality where the same judges of the court in respect of which the applicant had allegedly committed contempt had tried, convicted and sentenced him for that contempt); *Ekeberg v Norway*, App.No.11106/04 July 31, 2007, ECtHR, para.42 (there was only a "tenuous" difference between the issue to be decided and the issue previously decided against the applicant, which gave rise to a breach of art.6); *Chmelir v The Czech Republic* (2007) 44 E.H.R.R. 20 ECtHR (breach of art.6 where separate proceeding had previously been brought by the applicant against the judge personally). Cf. *Lindon v France* (2008) 46 E.H.R.R. 35, ECtHR (Grand Chamber) (no lack of impartiality where two out of the three judges had previously ruled against two of the applicants in closely-related matters where the facts were different in material respects and the "accused" was not the same: paras 78–79); *Elezi v Germany* (2008) 47 E.H.R.R. 53 ECtHR (no violation of art.6 where judges trying the applicant had seen material relating to the pre-trial investigation and to the confession of his sister).

Relationships

Family and kinship

[Add to end of n.131]   **10–044**

See also *R. (on the application of Compton) v Wiltshire Primary Care Trust* [2009] EWHC 1824 (Admin).

Professional and vocational relationships

[Add to end of n.133]   **10–045**

; *R. v Abdroikov* [2007] UKHL 37; [2007] 1 W.L.R. 2679.

[Add to end of n.135]

In the art.6 ECHR context, see *Eggertsdottir v Iceland* (2009) 48 E.H.R.R. 32 ECtHR, paras 53–54 (violations of impartiality where certain members of the special expert body which advised the Supreme Court on medical matters were closely associated with one of the parties).

[Add to end of para.10–045]

However, all the surrounding circumstances should be considered in evaluating the relevance of the relationship in question.[137a]

[137a] *R. (on the application of Lewis) v Redcar and Cleveland BC* [2008] EWCA Civ 746, [2009] 1 W.L.R. 83 at [62] (elected members of a planning committee would be entitled, and indeed expected, to have, and to have expressed, views on planning issues and the test to be applied was very different from that which applied in a judicial or quasi-judicial position). See also *R. (on the application of Gardner) v Harrogate BC* [2008] EWHC 2942 (Admin) (it was held that the number of complaints made about the relationship between the chair of a planning committee and a fellow Conservative councillor who was granted planning permission by the committee was relevant to the question of bias).

[Add to end of para.10–046]   **10–046**

Where a deputy coroner of the Queen's household determined that she had jurisdiction to conduct an inquest into the death of Princess Diana without a jury, there was a risk of an impression that the coroner was on the side of the royal family.[142a]

[142a] *R. (on the application of Paul) v Coroner of the Queen's Household* [2007] EWHC 408 (Admin); [2008] Q.B. 172 at [60].

10–047 *[Add to end of n.144]*

In the art.6 ECHR context, see *Chmelir v The Czech Republic* (2007) 44 E.H.R.R. 20 ECtHR (breach of art.6 where separate proceeding had previously been brought by the applicant against the judge personally).

10–047A *[Add new para.10–047A]*

Where there was no conflict between the evidence of the police and the evidence of the defendant, and there was no particular link between the trial court and the station where the police officer on the jury served or between the police witnesses and the juror, it would not appear to the fair minded and informed observer that there was a possibility that the jury was biased due to the inclusion of the police officer on the jury. However, where there was a crucial dispute on the evidence between the defendant and a police sergeant who, although not known to the police officer on the jury, shared the same local service background, justice was not seen to be done; likewise, where a member of the jury was a full-time, salaried employee of the prosecuting authority.[144a]

[144a] *R. v Abdroikov* [2007] UKHL 37; [2007] 1 W.L.R. 2679 (the requirement for impartiality had been breached where a police officer sat as a juror in a case which turned on a dispute on the evidence between the defendant and a police sergeant with the same local policing background as the juror and where a Crown prosecutor sat as a juror); *R. v I (Alan)* [2007] EWCA Crim 2999 at [33] (there was a real possibility of bias arising from the presence on the jury of a police officer who knew the police witnesses and who might be likely to accept the words of his colleagues, irrespective of the dispute between the parties).

10–048 *[Add new para.10–048A]*

10–048A Similarly, in *Helow v Secretary of State for the Home Department*,[145a] the fact that Lady Cosgrove was a member of the International Association of Jewish Lawyers and Jurists was insufficient to establish bias in her hearing an appeal by a Palestinian woman in an asylum case. It was argued that there was a real possibility of bias either by virtue of Lady Cosgrove's membership of the association or because she might have been influenced by the views expressed in its publications. While certain statements in the association's publications would, if they had been made by the judge herself, have led to a conclusion of bias, there was no basis on which it could be concluded that there was a real possibility of bias. It was "possible to conceive of circumstances involving words or conduct so extreme that members might be expected to become aware of them and dissociate themselves by resignation if they did not approve or wish to be thought to approve of them"[145b] but the material at issue fell far short of this. The suggestion that "mere membership" would give rise in the eyes of a fair-minded observer to "a real possibility of unconscious influence, through some form of osmosis,"[145c] was easily rejected. However in *Re Duffy's Application for Judicial Review*,[145d] the appointment of two members of the Orange Order to the Northern Ireland Parades Commission was held to be unlawful. The appointees had both been prominent and committed proponents of the loyalist parade along the Garvaghy Road to Portadown and, when appointed, neither had resigned from the bodies to which they belonged.

[145a] [2008] UKHL 62; [2008] 1 W.L.R. 2416. For comment on *Helow* see J. Goudkamp, "Apparent Bias: *Helow v Secretary of State for the Home Department*" (2009) 28 C.J.Q. 183.
[145b] [2008] UKHL 62; [2008] 1 W.L.R. 2416 at [55] (Lord Mance).
[145c] [2008] 1 W.L.R. 2416 at [56] (Lord Mance).
[145d] [2008] UKHL 4; [2008] N.I. 152.

Employer and employee

[Add to end of n.146]   10–049

; *R. v Abdroikov* [2007] UKHL 37; [2007] 1 W.L.R. 2679 (jury member was a full-time, salaried employee of the prosecuting authority); *R. (on the application of Primary Health Investment Properties Ltd) v Secretary of State for Health* [2009] EWHC 519 (Admin) (assistance given by CEO of a valuation office to a body determining a rent dispute led to apparent bias where an employee of the same valuation office had assisted one of the parties to the dispute); *Amritpal Singh Virdi v The Law Society* [2009] EWHC 918 (Admin) (the fact that the clerk to the Solicitors Disciplinary Tribunal was an employee of the Law Society, which was a party to proceedings against a suspended solicitor, did not result in bias as the clerk's employment was technical employment for remuneration purposes and she was not the decision-maker); *SP v Secretary of State for Justice* [2009] EWHC 13 (Admin) (an investigation into the claimant's detention while in young offender institutions was not sufficiently independent to make the report compliant with art.2 ECHR because an investigator for the report had worked for the prison service for 30 years on issues relevant to the investigation and had a social acquaintance lunch with the governor of one of the institutions investigated); and *R. (on the application of Reynolds) v Chief Constable of Sussex* [2008] EWHC 1240 (Admin) (a decision to make use of officers from the force under investigation in an inquiry by the Independent Police Complaints Commission ("IPCC") would not make the investigation lack independence provided that the IPCC remained in control and could dictate what was and was not to be done).

Personal hostility

10–051 *[Add to para.10–051 after ". . . come to blows.*[151]*"]*

Where a judge had been involved in unsuccessful negotiations to join a firm and had indicated that he was very unimpressed with the firm, he should have recused himself from a case in which the partners of the firm were involved.[151a]

[151a] *Howell v Lees Millais* [2007] EWCA Civ 720.

[Add to end of n.152]

Howell v Lees Millais [2007] EWCA Civ 720 at [26] (the Court of Appeal describing the judge's contribution to the exchange between the judge and counsel for the firm as "intemperate").

[Add new n.154a after ". . . have not acted as a disqualification."]

[154a] See, e.g. *C v Crown Prosecution Service* [2008] EWHC 148 (Admin) (the appellant had been convicted of harassment and it was considered whether a reference by the Crown Court to "generously" taking into account the appellant's culture amounted to subconsciously stereotyping him, but this "subconscious bias" argument could not withstand scrutiny in the light of the finding that the appellant had acted completely out of character, a character that the Crown Court had found to be impeccable).

[Add to end of n.158]

; and see *Stanley Muscat v Health Professions Council* [2008] EWHC 2798 (QB) (suggestion by a member of the tribunal that the appellant had been misleading did not give rise to bias; criminal cases argued by analogy, in which the judge had asked too many questions and was taking over role of prosecutor, distinguished).

[Add to para.10–051 after ". . . should be reopened.[160]*"]*

A judge who joked about whether respondent who was an Arab Sheikh would disappear on his flying carpet, that an affidavit was "a bit like Turkish delight", and about a "relatively fast-free time of the year ", was found to have used language which was mocking and disparaging of the respondent for his status as a Sheikh and/or his Saudi nationality and/or his ethnic origins and/or his Muslim faith. It was concluded therefore that there was an appearance to the fair-minded and informed observer that there was a real possibility that the judge would carry into his judgment the scorn and contempt his words conveyed.[160a]

[160a] *El-Farargy v El Farargy* [2007] EWCA Civ 1149 at [30]–[31].

[Add to end of n.161]

See also *R. (on the application of Bates) v Parole Board* [2008] EWHC 2653 (Admin) where remarks by the chairman of the parole board expressing scepticism that the claimant would be honest with his supervisors may have meant that the chair had been somewhat brisk in his manner of dealing with the claimant but that was a long way short of being able to establish a claim of potential bias.

[Add new para.10–054A]   10–054A

Pre-determination

Apparent bias can arise where the decision-maker is judged to have pre-determined the issue. Where the context is the decision of a body whose members may be expected to have prior views, such as a planning decision by a local authority, the requirement is that the members approach the issue fairly and on the merits:

> "So the test would be whether there is an appearance of predetermina-tion, in the sense of a mind closed to the planning decision in question . . . [what needs to be shown is] something which goes to the appearance of a predetermined, closed mind in the decision-making itself."[171a]

A showing of prior views is insufficient. There must at least be a pre-determination, a closed mind at an early stage and this is a difficult test to satisfy.[171b] This test was not satisfied in *R. (on the application of Fraser) v National Institute for Health and Clinical Excellence*,[171c] involving a challenge that the constitution and membership of an expert body propo-sing guidelines for treatment of a medical condition gave rise to an appearance of pre-determination because of the alleged prior preference of members of the body in favour of a particular treatment. As well as the lack of sufficient evidence to make out a case, the recommendation was a decision of a large group and the public interest in the need for clinical guidance also had to be considered.

[171a] *R. (on the application of Lewis) v Redcar and Cleveland BC* [2008] EWCA Civ 746; [2009] 1 W.L.R. 83 at [96] (Rix L.J.); *Chandler v Camden LBC* [2009] EWHC 219 (Admin). See also *Secretary of State for the Home Department v AF* [2008] EWCA Civ 117; [2008] 1 W.L.R. 2528 to the effect that in a hearing under s.3(1) of the Prevention of Terrorism Act 2005, findings made by the court in a previous hearing under the same subsection were not binding or even the starting point for second or subsequent control orders but that the judge was to have such regard to those findings, as a factor to be taken into account, as was appropriate in all the circumstances of the particular case.

[171b] See *R. (on the application of Lewis v Redcar and Cleveland BC* [2008] EWCA Civ 746; [2009] 1 W.L.R. 83 at [109] (Longmore L.J.).
[171c] [2009] EWHC 452 (Admin); (2009) 107 B.M.L.R. 178.

SITUATIONS WHERE BIAS WILL NOT APPLY

Waiver

[Add to the end of n.172]

For discussion, see J. Goudkamp, "The Rule against Bias and the Doctrine of Waiver" (2007) 26 C.J.Q. 310.

10–055 *[Add to end of n.173]*

; *R. (on the application of B) v South Region Mental Health Review Tribunal, Broadmoor Special Hospital, The Secretary of State for the Home Department* [2008] EWHC 2356 (Admin) at [19] (the High Court suggested that if a tribunal was so obviously biased as had been asserted, one would have expected some submissions to that effect to have been made to the tribunal at the time of the hearing); *Steadman-Byrne v Amjad* [2007] EWCA Civ 625; [2007] 1 W.L.R. 2484 at [17] (appellate and reviewing courts tend not to look favourably on complaints of vitiating bias made only after the complainant has taken his chance on the outcome and found it unwelcome).

Necessity

10–060 *[Add to end of para.10–060]*

Illustrations

- Evidence of political affiliation or of the adoption of policies towards a planning proposal will not for these purposes by itself amount to an appearance of the real possibility of predetermination or what counts as bias for these purposes on the part of councillors on a planning committee.[191a]

[191a] *R. (on the application of Lewis) v Redcar and Cleveland BC* [2008] EWCA Civ 746; [2009] 1 W.L.R. 83.

[Delete the following words in para.10–064]

". . .), or perhaps even exercise their power to decide the matter themselves.[199]""

The explanation for this deletion is that CPR r.54.19(3) has been revoked by the Civil Procedure (Amendment No.2) Rules 2007 (SI 2007/3543).

Policy and bias

[Add to end of para.10–066] **10–066**

Councillors were entitled to be predisposed to determine a planning application in accordance with their political views and policies provided that they had regard to all material considerations and gave fair consideration to relevant points raised with them.[203a]

[203a] *R. (on the application of Lewis) v Redcar and Cleveland BC* [2008] EWCA Civ 746; [2009] 1 W.L.R. 83.

ARTICLE 6 ECHR

[Add to para.10–077 after ". . . politicians, discussed above"] **10–077**

More generally, a decision-maker who exercises legislative as well as judicial functions may not meet the art.6 test. In *R. (on the application of Barclay) v Lord Chancellor and Secretary of State for Justice*,[229a] it was held that the combination in Sark of the judicial with the other functions of the Seneschal was inconsistent with the art.6 requirement to establish by law an independent and impartial tribunal.

[229a] [2008] EWCA Civ 1319.

[Add to para.10–077 new n.229b after ". . . judicial-style tribunal,"]

[229b] There is no requirement under art.6 that prosecutors in criminal cases be independent and impartial: *R. (on the application of Haase) v Independent Adjudicator* [2008] EWCA Civ 1089.

[Add to end of n.236] **10–080**

Cf. *R. (on the application of M) v Lambeth LBC* [2008] EWHC 1364 (Admin) where it was held that the right to be provided with accommodation under s.20 of the Children Act 1989 did not equate to a civil right within art.6(1) ECHR; and *R. (on the application of Gilboy) v Liverpool City Council* [2008] EWCA Civ 751; [2008] 4 All E.R. 127, holding that the demoted tenancies scheme was compatible with art.6, one of the reasons being the possibility of seeking judicial review of an authority's decision to terminate a demoted tenancy.

10–083 *[Add to end of n.244]*

See also the position under art.5(4) ECHR. In *R. (on the application of Brooke) v Parole Board* [2008] EWCA Civ 29; [2008] 1 W.L.R. 1950 it was held that the Parole Board did not meet the requirements of the common law and of art.5(4) ECHR for a court to have demonstrated objective independence of the executive and the parties, with the funding of the Parole Board (by the Ministry of Justice and previously by the Home Office) creating the impression that the Board was either part of the Home Office or the Prison Service.

COMPARATIVE PERSPECTIVES

New Zealand

10–091
and
10–092
Paragraphs 10–091 and 10–092 must now be read in light of *Muir v Commissioner of Inland Revenue* [2007] 3 N.Z.L.R. 495 which has adopted the *Porter v Magill* test. This means that the law in New Zealand is now the same as that in England and Australia.

CHAPTER 11

SUBSTANTIVE REVIEW AND JUSTIFICATION

THE CONSTITUTIONAL CONTEXT OF SUBSTANTIVE REVIEW

[Add to end of n.32]   11–013

And see J. Jowell, "What Decisions Should Judges Not Take?" in M. Andenas and D. Fairgrieve (eds), *Tom Bingham and the Transformation of the Law*, 2009 (Oxford: OUP), Ch.9; A. Kavanagh, "Judging Judges under the Human Rights Act: Deference, Disillusionment and the 'War on Terror'" [2009] P.L. 287.

Constitutional and institutional limits on the court's role

[Add to n.35]   11–014

And see *R. (on the application of Bancoult) v Secretary of State for Foreign and Commonwealth Affairs* [2008] UKHL 61; [2008] 3 W.L.R. 955 at [132] (Lord Carswell: "Decisions about how far to accommodate such concerns and wishes are very much a matter for ministers, who have access to a range of information not available to the courts and are accountable to Parliament for their actions. I think that courts should be more than a little slow to pin that butterfly to the wheel"—about the possibility of a policy for resettlement of the Chagos Islands).

Courts' secondary function of testing quality of reasoning and justification

[Substitute in n.39]   11–015

T.R.S. Allan, "Human Rights and Judicial Review: a Critique of 'Due Deference'" (2006) 65 C.L.J. 671 at 693.

Political mandate

[Add to end of para.11–017]   11–017

The notion of political mandate has been used as an explanatory justification for the non-justiciability of foreign policy: see *R. (on the application of*

Al-Haq) v Secretary of State for Foreign and Commonwealth Affairs [2009] EWHC 1910 (Admin) at [59] (Cranston J.: "Constitutionally the overall conduct of foreign policy is entrusted to those with a democratic mandate, the government, in particular the Prime Minister and Foreign Secretary. They are accountable to Parliament, to public opinion and ultimately to the electorate through the ballot box. The basal principle of our system of representative democracy is that the people of the United Kingdom entrust the conduct of the country's foreign policy to their elected representatives, not to the courts").

UNREASONABLE PROCESS

Uncertainty

Inadequate Evidence and Mistake of Fact

11–041 *[Add to end of n.113]*

It should not be assumed—as it has been on occasion in the past—that the judicial review procedure is inherently unsuited to dealing with disputes of fact. In *Birmingham City Council v Doherty* [2008] UKHL 57; [2008] 3 W.L.R. 636 (an appeal in relation to an eviction from a caravan site after 17 years), Lord Scott of Foscote observed that "traditional features of judicial review challenges to decisions taken by public authorities are that they must be brought in the High Court, that they cannot be brought unless permission to bring them is first obtained and that that permission is not usually given where the challenge raises and depends upon disputed issues of fact. I am not clear whether permission is invariably, or merely usually, refused in these disputed fact cases. Nor am I clear why normal judicial review procedure should not be adjusted so as to enable issues of fact to be judicially resolved where such resolution is necessary in order to enable the challenge to the decision in question to be fairly disposed of. But it does appear to be the case that permission to bring judicial review proceedings is sometimes, or perhaps usually, refused where the challenge, if it is to succeed, has to dispute facts on which the local authority relies in justification of its decision"—"the perceived procedural deficiencies are surely curable by a simple procedural adjustment enabling a challenge to the public authority's decision to terminate the occupier's tenancy or licence to be part of the occupier's defence to the possession claim (i.e. gateway (b) and see Winder), thus enabling any factual disputes that needed to be resolved to be dealt with in the ordinary way in the course of the proceedings" (at [68]). Lord Mance agree with Lord Scott about "the possibility of adjusting judicial review procedure in appropriate circumstances to cover any necessary factual investigation and determination" (at [138]). See also *R. (on the application of Lunt) v Liverpool City Council* [2009] All E.R. (D) 07 (Aug) (Blake J. judicial review procedure was appropriate even where there was a dispute as to facts). Cf. *E (A Child) v Chief Constable of Ulster* [2008] UKHL 66; [2008] 3 W.L.R. 1208 at [31] (in judicial review challenge to the way the police had handled incidents of loyalist violence in 2001, acknowledging that factual disputes about what was said at meetings "cannot readily be resolved in judicial review proceedings").

Fact and law distinguished

[Add to end of n.118]   11–043

For an example of rival submissions as to whether a step in a decision-making process involves a question of law or of fact, see *RB (Algeria) v Secretary of State for the Home Department* [2009] UKHL 10; [2009] 2 W.L.R. 512 at [62]. An appeal lay from a tribunal (the Special Immigration Appeals Commission) to the Court of Appeal on questions of law only. The tribunal's determination involved the following steps in relation to the issue whether the appellants would face a real risk of ill-treatment, contrary to art.3 ECHR, if they were returned to their home nations: (1) the tribunal had to direct themselves as to the appropriate test for a breach of the relevant article—a question of law; (2) the tribunal had to determine the relevant primary facts—obviously, a question of fact; (3) the tribunal had to determine whether those facts satisfied the appropriate test—was this law or fact? The House of Lords held that the assessment carried out at step (3) is a question of fact (see Lord Phillips of Worth Matravers at [73], Lord Hoffmann at [187], and Lord Hope of Craighead (at [214]). SIAC's conclusions that the facts it had found did not amount to a real risk of a flagrant breach of the relevant Convention rights could only be attacked if they were conclusions that no reasonable tribunal, properly directed, could have reached. It is however "now recognised that questions of proportionality which necessarily arise when striking the balance between private and public interests in cases involving qualified Convention rights cannot be regarded as pure questions of fact" ; but the "most critical question raised in each appeal is whether the proposed deportees would face a real risk of art.3 ill-treatment on return. *Par excellence* this is a question of fact calling for an evaluation of all the evidence and ultimately a single factual judgment" (Lord Brown at [253]–[254]).

Situations where review of fact permitted

Misdirection or mistake of material fact

11–051 *[Add to end of n.141]*

The approach adopted in the *E* case has also been followed in the following cases: *R. (on the application of Lunt) v Liverpool City Council* [2009] EWHC 2356 (Admin); [2009] All E.R. (D) 07 (Aug) (Blake J. held authority responsible for approving design of taxis had fundamentally misunderstood documentary evidence about accessibility for wheelchair users); *R. (on the application of McDougal) v Liverpool City Council* [2009] EWHC 1821 (Admin) (officers of the council had made the proper inquiries of central government and they had received answers and the understanding of them was duly communicated to the members of the council who were the decision-makers. In other words, this was not a case of "unfairness resulting from misunderstanding or ignorance of established and relevant fact"); *Phelps v First Secretary of State* [2009] EWHC 1676 at [17] (*E* described as "the leading authority on the law as it currently stands in relation to errors of fact amounting to errors of law"—but the case did not fall within the principles articulated in *E*); *VH (Malawi) v Secretary of State for the Home Department* [2009] EWCA Civ 645 at [48] (Longmore L.J.: "It may well be that mistake as to an established fact which was uncontentious and objectively verifiable can constitute an error of law as stated in *E v SSHD* . . .. But the weight which is to be accorded to evidence properly before a tribunal cannot, to my mind, fall within that category"); *Eley v Secretary of State for Communities and Local Government* [2009] EWHC 660 (QB); [2009] All E.R. (D) 28 (Apr), [51] ("a mistake of fact by an inspector who is determining a planning appeal which gives rise to unfairness is now established as a head of challenge in an appeal" under Town and Country Planning Act 1990 s.288).

Evidence not before the decision-maker

11–053 *[Add to end of n.149]*

It was not necessary to imply the *Ladd v Marshall* test, designed to place restrictions on the admission of fresh evidence in the Court of Appeal, into the disciplinary procedure of an academic institution: see *R. (on the application of Peng Hu Shi) v King's College London* [2008] EWHC 857 (Admin); [2008] E.L.R. 414 at [33] ("All that is necessary is that there should have been new evidence which was not put before or heard by the Committee, and which was for good reason not made available at the time of the hearing").

VIOLATION OF CONSTITUTIONAL PRINCIPLE

The principle of equality

Illustrations of application of substantive inequality principle in common law

[Add to text at end of paragraph on "location-related factors"]   11–069

A common law principle of equality was accepted in *R. (on the application of Limbu) v Secretary of State for the Home Department* [2008] EWHC 2261 (Admin); [2008] H.R.L.R. 48, a case in which Gurkhas challenged a change of policy in relation to the grant of indefinite leave to remain in the United Kingdom at the conclusion of military service; different policies applied according to whether discharge took place before or after July 1997. Blake J. held at [50]:

> "Even if art.14 [ECHR] was not engaged, the common law principle of equal treatment certainly would be. Moreover, for the reasons explained by McCombe J. in *Gurung* [[2002] EWHC 2463 (Admin)], that I gratefully adopt, the common law principle is an important instrument whereby it can be determined whether a discretionary public law decision is rational. It is also clear from *AL and Rudi* [*AL (Serbia) v Secretary of State for the Home Department* [2008] UKHL 42; [2008] UKHL 42; [2008] 1 W.L.R. 1434] at [5] [42] and [51] that the common law and Convention principle essentially walk hand in hand together, although the common law principle has to be applied through the public law doctrine of rationality. Thus even if art.14 was not in play the court should enquire: 'Was it open to a reasonable SSHD properly directing herself to conclude that the differences in treatment between Gurkhas and other non UK nationals was justified by reasons of differences of distinction in their situation so as not to infringe the common law principle of equality?'".

Blake J. held that there was no discrimination: the position of Gurkhas discharged before 1997 was not sufficiently similar to non-British soldiers to have required equal treatment. (The policy was, however, held to be irrational). In *AL (Serbia)*, it was held that:

> "the justification advanced for a difference in treatment covered by art.14 must be 'objective and reasonable', it is difficult to see what the common law adds to the Convention in a case where it is accepted that art.14 is engaged" (Baroness Hale of Richmond at [42]).

[Add to end of n.252]   11–072

And see now T. Hickman, "The substance and structure of proportionality" [2008] P.L. 694 (concluding "We are at a crossroads, and there is a choice: proportionality can either become the fig leaf for unstructured judicial decision-making or it can become a powerful normative and predictive tool in public law").

DISPROPORTIONATE DECISIONS

Proportionality as a structured test of justifiability

Structured proportionality in Convention rights

11–079 *[Add new para.11–079A after 11–079]*

11–079A In *Wood v Commissioner of Police of the Metropolis* [2009] EWCA Civ 414; (2009) 106(22) L.S.G. 24, the Court of Appeal held (Laws L.J. dissenting on this issue) that the police had failed to justify as proportionate the interference with art.8 ECHR when they took and retained photographs of a shareholder (a person of good character and no previous convictions and who the police had no reason to believe was guilty of any misconduct) leaving a hotel where the company's AGM was taking place; the shareholder was a campaigner against the arms trade and the company was involved in organising an arms trade fair. Dyson L.J. held (at [83]–[84]):

> "In deciding whether the interference is necessary, the court must have regard to the nature of the Convention right in issue, its importance for the individual, the nature of the interference and the object pursued by the interference: see *Marper v United Kingdom* [ECtHR, December 4, [2008] at [102]. At [103], the court went on to say that the protection of personal data is of fundamental importance to a person's enjoyment of his or her art.8 rights and the domestic law must afford appropriate safeguards to prevent any such use of personal data as may be inconsistent with the guarantees of art.8. The need for such safeguards is all the greater where the protection of personal data undergoing automatic processing is concerned, not least when such data are used for police purposes.
>
> In other words, the court is required to carry out a careful exercise of weighing the legitimate aim to be pursued, the importance of the right which is the subject of the interference and the extent of the interference. Thus an interference whose object is to protect the community from the danger of terrorism is more readily justified as proportionate than an interference whose object is to protect the community from the risk of low level crime and disorder. The importance of the former was emphasised by the House of Lords in *R. (on the application of Gillan) v Commissioner of Police of the Metropolis* [2006] UKHL 12, [2006] 2

A.C. 307: see per Lord Bingham of Cornhill at [29] and Lord Scott of Foscote at [62]."

Dyson L.J. concluded at [86]

"The retention by the police of photographs of a person must be justified and the justification must be the more compelling where the interference with a person's rights is, as in the present case, in pursuit of the protection of the community from the risk of public disorder or low level crime, as opposed, for example, to protection against the danger of terrorism or really serious criminal activity."

Structured proportionality in English law

[Add to end of para.11–083]   **11–083**

In *Somerville v Scottish Ministers* [2007] UKHL 44; [2007] 1 W.L.R. 2734 the issue arose whether "want of proportionality is a relevant complaint of unlawfulness at common law" (in a case where prisoners complained that their segregation from other prisoners was unlawful). Both the Lord Ordinary and the First Division held that the common law did not recognise proportionality as an independent ground for judicial review. On appeal to the House of Lords, Lord Hope of Craighead held that "it would not be appropriate for your Lordships to seek to reach a decision on this issue in the circumstances of this case" (at [56]) as proportionality would be considered in relation to the art.8 ECHR ground of challenge advanced by the prisoners. Lord Scott of Foscote (at [82]), Rodger of Earlsferry (at [147]), and Lord Mance (at [198]) all took a similar view. The question of the status of proportionality as a freestanding ground of review in the common law therefore remains to be decided at the highest level.

INTENSITY OF REVIEW

Variable intensity unreasonableness review

Heightened scrutiny unreasonableness review

[Add to end of para.11–093]   **11–093**

And in *R. (on the application of Bancoult) v Secretary of State for Foreign and Commonwealth Affairs (No.2)* [2008] UKHL 61; [2008] 3 W.L.R. 955 at [53] Lord Hoffmann rejected the proposition that the court should adopt a "light touch" approach to review (as submitted by the Crown on the basis that it was "acting in the interests of the defence of the realm, diplomatic relations with the United States and the use of public funds in supporting any settlement on the islands") and preferred the view that the court should adopt an "anxious degree of scrutiny"—but adding "However, I think it is very important that in deciding whether a measure affects fundamental rights or has 'profoundly intrusive effects', one should consider what those rights and effects actually are". He suggested that the right in issue "should be seen for what it is, as a right to protest in a particular way and not as a right to the security of one's home or to live in one's homeland". See also Lord Mance, dissenting, at [172] and Lord Carswell at [131].

COMPARATIVE PERSPECTIVES

Australia

11–103   *[Add to n.349]*

See K. Stern, "Substantive Unfairness in UK and Australian Law" (2007) 29 Aust. Bar Rev. 266.

Canada

11–108   *[Add to end of para.11–108]*

In *Dunsmuir v New Brunswick*, 2008 SCC 9; [2008] 1 S.C.R. 190, the Supreme Court of Canada revisited its approach to determining whether courts should show deference to the decisions or actions of a statutory or prerogative authority. It determined that there should no longer be three possible standards of review at common law but just two, correctness and unreasonableness. It jettisoned the previously most deferential standard, that of "patent unreasonableness." The court also abandoned the language of "pragmatic and functional" used to describe the approach that courts should adopt in determining the appropriate standard of review. Rather, the process is now called simply "standard of review analysis." However, despite the reduction in the number of standards and the name change, the four factors that form part of this inquiry remain the same: the presence or absence of a privative or preclusive clause, the purpose of the tribunal as indicated by its constitutive legislation, the nature of the question at issue, and the tribunal's expertise.

In an endeavour to minimise the attention paid in applications for judicial review and statutory appeals to the determination of an appropriate standard of review, the court also identified a number of presumptions intended to serve as signposts as to whether the standard in any particular case should be that of correctness or unreasonableness. Aside from an admonition to courts to accept precedents where the standard of review has already been determined satisfactorily and a continuing emphasis that a privative or preclusive clause provides a strong indicator of the need for deference, the court identified two situations where unreasonableness review is generally required: (i) issues of fact, discretion or policy; and (ii) interpretations of the statutory authority's "own statute or statutes closely connected to its function, with which it will have particular familiarity" (at para.54).

Deference might also be justified with respect to the application of common and civil law rules with which the statutory authority has developed a particular expertise or familiarity.

In contrast, correctness should be the standard where issues of jurisdiction or vires arise, as, for example, constitutional issues, the jurisdictional lines between competing tribunals, and the limits of the authority of municipalities to enact byelaws. As well, the courts should assess on a correctness basis determinations of questions of general law that are "both of central importance to the legal system as a whole and outside the adjudicator's special area of expertise" (at para.59).

Given the comprehensive framework within which the court articulated the new approach in *Dunsmuir*, it seemed clear that it would apply not just to judicial review of tribunals but all forms of statutory or prerogative authority as well as statutory appeals. Thereafter, in *Canada (Citizenship and Immigration) v Khosa*, 2009 SCC 12, the court not only reiterated the application of the standard of review methodology to statutory appeals but also held that it constituted an overlay on the codified grounds of review in the Federal Courts Act. Thus, for example, an unqualified statutory specification of error of law review did not amount to a direction that the Federal Court and Court of Appeal should review all questions of law on a correctness basis.

However, this judgment does not affect those statutory provisions (such as found in the British Columbia Administrative Tribunals Act, S.B.C. 2004. c.45, ss.58–59) that actually specify a standard of review, and now most relevantly, patent unreasonableness. In *Manz v British Columbia (Workers' Compensation Appeal Tribunal)*, 2009 BCCA 92, the British Columbia Court of Appeal rejected a challenge to the constitutionality of those provisions. The constitutional guarantee of access to judicial review did not extend to a proscription on legislative designation of the standard of review.

[Add to end of para.11–112]   11–112

In *Dunsmuir*, the Court (at para.47) provided a template for the conduct of reasonableness review and linked it with the common law or statutory duty to provide reasons to which most statutory authorities are now subject. In conducting reasonableness review, the courts are to have regard "both to the process of articulating the reasons and to outcomes." For the most part, reasonableness review should focus on the presence of "justification, transparency and intelligibility within the decision-making process." However, the decision reached is also relevant in the sense that it must fall "within a range of possible, acceptable outcomes which are defensible in respect of the facts and the law."

New Zealand

Proportionality and unreasonableness

11–114 *[Add to end of para.11–114]*

Since 2007, a growing consensus has emerged among commentators that the structured proportionality test should be adopted in New Zealand. Taggart has observed that the methodology is already applied where NZBORA rights are at stake, and he opines that proportionality methodology is more or less the same methodology as is used in variable reasonableness review where "rights" are at stake (see M. Taggart, "Proportionality, Deference, Wednesbury" [2008] N.Z. L. Rev. at 423, 448–449). The main debate in New Zealand now concerns whether proportionality should be limited to cases involving NZBORA rights, or also be applied in cases involving fundamental common law rights thus subsuming variable reasonableness review where "rights" are at stake (favoured by Taggart), or be applied more generally and beyond the area of fundamental rights, potentially supplanting reasonableness review altogether—favoured by Joseph (see P.A. Joseph, *Constitutional and Administrative Law in New Zealand*, 2008 (3rd edn) at [21.7.5], [23.5.2]) and Chief Justice Dame Sian Elias speaking extra-judicially (see S. Elias, "Righting Administrative Law" in D. Dyzenhaus, M. Hunt and G. Huscroft (eds), *A Simple Common Lawyer: Essays in Honour of Michael Taggart*, 2009, pp.55, 72, supporting the argument made by Paul Craig that the proportionality methodology is appropriate to administrative law more generally: P. Craig, *Administrative Law*, 2003 (5th edn) p.630).

This difference of academic opinion was recently discussed in *Mihos v Attorney-General* [2008] N.Z.A.R. 177 (HC) where Baragwanath J. considered the possibility of proportionality applying outside the NZBORA context (at [87]–[98]). In the process he discussed the distinction made in the 6th edition of *de Smith* between the structured proportionality test and proportionality as a test of fair balance (at [11–074]), while also noting the discussion in *de Smith* of the historical origins of proportionality (at [11–073]). On the facts he did not feel it necessary to resolve this issue and preferred to opt for "the familiar tool" of variable intensity review (at [98]). Two recent decisions of the Court of Appeal discussed whether proportionality should be applied in the context of decisions not to cancel orders for the removal of individuals unlawfully in New Zealand, where their children had been born in New Zealand and granted New Zealand citizenship. The statutory context examined in both cases was identical. Glazebrook J. in a separate judgment in *Ye v Minister of Immigration* [2009] 2 N.Z.L.R. 596 (CA) noted the academic commentary on proportionality, showing some sympathy for Taggart's argument that proportionality should be applied outside the NZBORA context where fundamental rights are at stake (at [304]). She did not need to resolve this question as the case could be decided on established administrative law grounds. However, she did opine that a case involving the fundamental rights of the child and the potential break-up of a family unit should attract anxious scrutiny, and she doubted whether upholding immigration policy could ever be proportionate to breaking up a family without there being some other public interest factors. In *Huang v Minister of Immigration* [2009] 2 N.Z.L.R. 700 (CA) the Court of Appeal considered Glazebrook J.'s dicta, and were firm in their rejection of the proportionality methodology, grounding this conclusion in the statutory context and established precedent. Although proportionality was applied to immigration decisions in the United Kingdom, the court observed the UK courts operate in a "legislative and human rights environment which is very much influenced by s.6 of the Human Rights Act 1998 (UK) and the European Convention on Human Rights" and that New Zealand courts operate in a different environment. Furthermore, the court thought it would be difficult to apply an "undiluted" proportionality test given the weighting to be apportioned to various considerations was implicit in the words of the relevant statutory provision, which set out the circumstances in which a person illegally in New Zealand may be able to avoid removal on humanitarian grounds. The court further said that engaging in a balancing approach would be inconsistent with precedent which provided for an approach based on orthodox administrative law grounds in the relevant statutory context. Also, the interests of the family and the children had already been subject to consideration by the Removal Review Authority, and there had been no appeal from or timely application for review of the Authority's decision. The court thus fell back on previous precedent which held that a court should ensure that the children's interests are genuinely taken into account as a primary consideration, but that how the final balance is struck between competing relevant considerations is for the decision-maker and not the court, unless the decision is so unreasonable that no reasonable decision-maker could have come to it. Both of these decisions, *Ye* and *Huang*, were appealed to the Supreme Court however in neither case did the court consider the proportionality issue. It found that the cases turned on "relatively straightforward principles of judicial review", namely error of law: *Ye v Minister of Immigration* [2009] NZSC 76 at [11]; *Huang v Minister for Immigration* [2009] NZSC 77.

Taggart draws a distinction between administrative law cases involving "rights" (NZBORA and common law) and those involving "public wrongs" (see "Proportionality, Deference, *Wednesbury*" [2008] N.Z. L. Rev. 423). He argues that proportionality should only be applied in rights

137

cases since the presence of rights is crucial to the workability of the proportionality methodology and to its normative justification. Taggart expresses the concern that application of proportionality outside the rights area could tempt greater judicial intervention in administrative decision making. Furthermore, New Zealand, not being subject to the same European imperatives as the United Kingdom, should feel free to chart its own indigenous public law path. In cases not involving rights he believes a traditional *Wednesbury* standard should be used as a safety-net to catch those cases of administrative unlawfulness not covered by the other heads of review. He does not consider variable intensity of reasonableness review to be necessary given the expansion and refinement of existing substantive grounds that has occurred, and he argues that the general application of proportionality would subvert the doctrinal approach of carefully going through the established grounds of review. He therefore opposes variable intensity reasonableness review in cases of public wrongs, and supports a "bifurcated" public law; he believed that this approach will in the end lead to greater clarity and certainty in the law (cf. M. Hunt "Against Bifurcation" in D. Dyzenhaus, M. Hunt and G. Huscroft (eds), *A Simple Common Lawyer: Essays in Honour of Michael Taggart*, 2009, p.99).

Intensity of review

11–115 *[Add to end of n.377]*

And see M. Taggart, "Proportionality, Deference, Wednesbury" [2008] N.Z. L. Rev. 423; P.A. Joseph, *Constitutional and Administrative Law in New Zealand*, 2008 (3rd edn) at [21.7.4]–[21.7.5], [23.1]–[23.4]; D.R. Knight, "A Murky Methodology: Standards of Review in Administrative Law" (2008) 6 N.Z.J.P.I.L. 117.

Review for mistake of fact

11–120 *[Add to end of para.120]*

In *Zafirov v Minister of Immigration* [2009] N.Z.A.R. 457 (HC) Mallon J. considered the question "whether evidence of fact that was not before the decision maker can be relevant to an appeal confined to questions of law" (at [76]). She answered this question in the affirmative and adopted the approach of the English Court of Appeal in *E v Secretary of State for the Home Department* [2004] Q.B. 1044 at [66], that "mistake of fact giving rise to unfairness" should be accepted as "a separate head of challenge in an appeal on a point of law". Mallon J. also adopted the English Court of Appeal's four requirements for a finding of unfairness (*E* at [66]). On the facts of the case she held that the Deportation Review Tribunal's failure to consider certain available evidence as to the applicant's future risk of criminal offending gave rise to unfairness based on her application of the four-point test set down in *E*. She opined that she could have alternatively decided the case on the basis of more traditional review grounds including failure to take into account relevant considerations and general unreasonableness.

How Mallon J.'s decision marries up with the previous decision of the Supreme Court in *Bryson v Three Foot Six Ltd* [2005] 3 N.Z.L.R. 721 (SC) is an open question. In that case the Supreme Court examined the circumstances in which an error of fact can constitute an "error of law" in the context of an appeal on a point of law. The court held

"Provided that the [Employment] Court has not overlooked any relevant matter or taken account of some matter which is irrelevant to the proper application of the law, the conclusion is a matter for the fact-finding Court, unless it is clearly unsupportable" (at [25]).

As to what was "unsupportable" the court adopted the test set out by Lord Radcliffe in *Edwards v Bairstow* [1956] A.C. 14 at 36: that there exist a state of affairs "in which there is no evidence to support the determination" or "one in which the evidence is inconsistent with and contradictory of the determination" or "one in which the true and only reasonable conclusion contradicts the determination". Mallon J. took the view that the Supreme Court had not considered the specific point whether uncontentious or material facts which ought to have been before the decision-maker but were not could constitute an error of law, thus leaving the door open for her to adopt the approach in *E*. However, the Supreme Court's dicta that decision-making authorities not overlook relevant matters would appear directly relevant to the facts of *Zafirov*, especially given Mallon J. took the view that the case could have been resolved on the basis of failure to take into account relevant considerations.

South Africa

Mistake of fact

[Delete text of para.11–127 and substitute the following]   **11–127**

At common law, mistakes of (non-jurisdictional) fact were not reviewable in themselves but only on certain grounds—*mala fides*, ulterior motive, failure to apply the mind and breach of an express statutory provision. However, the position is quite different now as a result of the important decision of *Pepcor Retirement Fund v Financial Services Board*, 2003 (6) S.A. 38 (SCA). The Promotion of Administrative Justice Act 2000 (PAJA) does not expressly include mistake of fact as a ground of review, but the Supreme Court of Appeal held in *Pepcor* that s.33(1) of the Constitution and the constitutional principle of legality demanded the recognition of mistake of fact as such a ground. While the PAJA was not of application in this case, the court also suggested that the ground of mistake of fact could be read into s.6(2)(e)(iii) of the statute, which allows for review where "irrelevant considerations were taken into account or relevant considerations were not considered".

In the *Pepcor* case, certificates had been issued by the Registrar of Pension Funds on the basis of what turned out to be incorrect actuarial information supplied to him, and a significant sum of money had in turn been transferred to a retirement fund. The court a quo reasoned that the Registrar had been precluded from applying his mind properly to the matter. The Supreme Court of Appeal, however, took inspiration from the *Tameside* case and approached the problem more directly. In the words of Cloete J.A.:

> "[a] material mistake of fact should be a basis on which a Court can review an administrative action. If legislation has empowered a functionary to make a decision, in the public interest, the decision should be made on the material facts which should have been available for the decision properly to have been made. And if a decision has been made in ignorance of facts material to the decision and which therefore should have been before the functionary, the decision should . . . be reviewable . . .. The doctrine of legality . . . requires that the power conferred on a functionary to make decisions in the public interest, should be exercised properly, ie on the basis of the true facts; it should not be confined to cases where the common law would categorise the decision as *ultra vires*."

The *Pepcor* principle has been applied several times since then. In *Government Employees Pension Fund v Buitendag* [2006] S.C.A. 121 (RSA) a decision of the board of a pension fund was set aside on the basis of mistake of fact: the board had been ignorant of the existence of children of the deceased when it decided to award a gratuity to the husband of the deceased. In *Chairpersons' Association v Minister of Arts and Culture*, 2007 (5) S.A. 236 (SCA) the SCA expressly relied upon s.6(2)(e)(iii) in setting aside a Minister's decision to approve the change of a town's name. In this case the Minister had been wrongly informed by his Director-General that proper consultation had taken place about the name change. Farlam J.A. found for a unanimous court that the Minister had been entitled to assume that the facts conveyed to him were correct, and that the misstatement had clearly influenced the Minister's decision (at paras 47–48). Mistake of fact also operated to set aside a zoning decision in *Hangklip Environmental Action Group v MEC for Agriculture, Environmental Affairs and Development Planning, Western Cape*, 2007 (6) S.A. 65 (C).

CHAPTER 12

LEGITIMATE EXPECTATIONS

INTRODUCTION

[Add new n.3a after ". . . in public law."]   12–001

3a The phrase "legitimate expectation" has been described recently as being "much in vogue": *R. (on the application of EB (Kosovo)) v Home Secretary* [2008] UKHL 41; [2008] 3 W.L.R. 178 at [31] (Lord Scott).

[Add to para.12–002 after ". . . expectation to the protection of"]   12–002

what have been described as secondary procedural legitimate expectations and of

Legitimate expectation of procedural fairness

[Add to end of n.4]   12–003

A legitimate expectation that a particular procedure will be followed has recently been described as the "paradigm case" of procedural expectation: *R. (on the application of Niazi) v The Independent Assessor* [2008] EWCA Civ 755 at [29].

GCHQ case defines legitimate expectation

[Add to end of n.13]   12–006

; contrast *R. (on the application of British Medical Association) v General Medical Council* [2008] EWHC 2602 (Admin) at [83] (factor in deciding against legitimate expectation that the GMC had never consulted before when changing fee exemptions).

Statutory fair procedure requirements

[Add to end of n.17]   12–010

; *R. (on the application of Breckland DC) v The Boundary Committee* [2009] EWCA Civ 239 at [43].

12–010a *[Insert new para.12–010A]*

Secondary procedural legitimate expectation

12–010A In the recent case of *R. (on the application of Niazi) v The Independent Assessor*, Laws L.J. suggested a third category of legitimate expectation, namely "a secondary case of procedural expectation". Such an expectation is that an obligation to consult will arise, if, without any promise, a public authority has established a policy distinctly and substantially affecting a specific person or group who in the circumstances was in reason entitled to rely on its continuance and did so. A secondary case of legitimate expectation will not often be established since, where there has been no assurance either of consultation (the paradigm case of procedural expectation) or as to the continuance of the policy (substantive expectation), there will generally be nothing in the case save a decision by the authority in question to effect a change in its approach to one or more of its functions.[17a] Thus, the assurance required to found such a secondary procedural legitimate expectation must be "pressing and focussed".[17b]

[17a] [2008] EWCA Civ 755 at [39].
[17b] *R. (on the application of Niazi) v The Independent Assessor* [2008] EWCA Civ 755 at [46].

Legitimate expectations of substantive benefit

12–012 *[Note 20]*

Delete "P. Craig, *Administrative Law*, 5th edn. (2003) p.641" and substitute "P. Craig, *Administrative Law*, 2008 (6th edn.) at para. 20–004".

Illustrations

12–014 *[Add to end of para.12–014]*

- Those admitted to the Highly Skilled Migrant Programme had a legitimate expectation that they would enjoy the benefits of the programme as they were at the time they joined it.[35a]

  [35a] *R. (on the application of HSMP Forum (UK) Ltd) v Secretary of State for the Home Department* [2009] EWHC 711 (Admin).

THE SOURCE OF A LEGITIMATE EXPECTATION

Express representation

12–016 *[Add to para.12–016 after ". . . authority will follow.[37]"]*

142

The express representation can include a promise made by a junior minister in Parliament,[37a] although not if consideration of the expectation would involve questioning proceedings in Parliament and undermining parliamentary privilege.[37b]

[37a] R. (on the application of O'Callaghan) v Charity Commission for England and Wales [2007] EWHC 2491 (Admin) at [23] ("it is of particular importance that a promise of that kind, given in Parliament, is honoured").
[37b] R. (on the application of Wheeler) v Office of the Prime Minister [2008] EWHC 1409 (Admin) at [49] (alleged expectations in respect of statements on the holding of a referendum on the Constitutional Treaty).

[Add to end of n.37]

; for an unusual example, see R. (on the application of Kinsley) v Barnet Magistrates Court [2009] EWHC 464 (Admin) at [27] and [30] (where a local authority alleged that a taxpayer was liable for council tax on the basis of s.6(2)(a) of the Local Government Finance Act 1992, the taxpayer had a legitimate expectation that he would win his case if the local authority failed to make its case and a valuation tribunal could not proceed to find the taxpayer liable under a different statutory provision).

Implied representation

[Add to para.12–020 after ". . . council's oversight.[45]"]   **12–020**

No legitimate expectation that the council would refuse a planning application could be "spelled out" of previous refusals where those schemes were "materially different" from the present scheme.[45a] A representation did not arise from the fact that a property company had become the local authority's biggest supplier of temporary accommodation to the effect that the arrangements between the property company and the local authority would not be terminated without adequate notice.[45b]

[45a] R. (on the application of Loader) v Poole Borough Council [2009] EWHC 1288 (Admin) at [28].
[45b] First Real Estates (UK) Ltd v Birmingham City Council [2009] EWHC 817 (Admin).

To whom directed—personal or general

12–021 *[Add to n.51 after ". . . [1983] 1 W.L.R. 1337]*

See also *R. (on the application of S) v the Secretary of State* [2009] EWHC 1315 (Admin) [44] (where the Secretary of State had elected to adopt a policy on how to deal with applications pursuant to a statutory discretion, "there must be a procedural legitimate expectation that he will comply with it").

12–022 *[Add to end of para.12–022]*

However, to benefit from an extra-statutory concession, it is necessary for the claimant to have a case "falling clearly within" the terms of the concession.[54a]

[54a] *Accenture Services Ltd v Commissioners of HM Revenue and Customs* [2009] EWHC 857 (Admin) at [35], [53] (Sales J.).

International treaties

12–026 *[Add to end of para.12–026]*

However, it has been held that where a public officer asserts that his decision accords with an unincorporated treaty obligation, the courts will not entertain a challenge to the decision based upon his arguable misunderstanding of that obligation and then itself decide the point of international law at issue.[66a]

[66a] *R. (on the application of Corner House Research) v Director of the Serious Fraud Office (Justice intervening)* [2008] UKHL 60; [2009] 1 A.C. 756 at [67]. For recent discussion of the domestic effect of international law, see P. Sales and J. Clement, "International Law in Domestic Courts: The Developing Framework" (2008) 124 L.Q.R. 388.

LEGITIMACY

12–029 *[Add to para.12–029 before "To qualify as legitimate . . ."]*

It has been said that the term "legitimate expectation" is a "legal term of art"; it has a "normative element", and "a public authority that is the object of a legitimate expectation is under a legal duty, albeit qualified, in relation to the fulfilment of that expectation".[75a]

[75a] *R. (on the application of SRM Global Master Fund LP) v Commissioners of HM Treasury* [2009] EWHC 227 (Admin); [2009] B.C.C. 251 at [129]

(Stanley Burnton L.J.) (commenting also on the contrast with a "reasonable expectation" which denotes "a purely factual expectation, with no normative content"; [135]).

Clear unambiguous and devoid of relevant qualification

[Add to end of n.76]   12–030

See also *R. (on the application of Bancoult) v Secretary of State for Foreign and Commonwealth Affairs* [2008] UKHL 61; [2009] 1 A.C. 453 at [60] and [134] (an undertaking to work "on the feasibility of resettling the Ilois" on the Chagos Island and of change to the law to permit resettlement did not amount to an "unequivocal assurance" that the Ilois could return); *R. (on the application of Misick) v Secretary of State for Foreign and Commonwealth Affairs* [2009] EWHC 1039 (Admin) at [36] (no legitimate expectation that there would be a trial by jury had been created by the establishment of a commission to investigate allegations of corruption on the part of elected members of the legislature); *R. (on the application of Khan-Udtha) v Secretary of State for the Home Department* [2009] EWHC 1287 (Admin) at [41] (where a published guidance made it clear that a review of a decision could result in a new ground for refusing an application for a work permit transfer, the argument that the earlier decision gave rise to a legitimate expectation that no new ground of refusal would be raised was "unsustainable"); *R. (on the application of Stamford Chamber of Trade and Commerce) v Secretary of State for Communities and Local Government* [2009] EWHC 719 (Admin) at [87] (where parties have to "lever" an implied promise out of passages from a range of different documents published at different times, an expectation could not be founded); *NA and AA v Secretary of State for the Home Department* [2009] EWHC 420 (Admin); *R. (on the application of Al-Saadoon) v Secretary of State for Defence* [2008] EWHC 3098 (Admin) at [202] (a policy of strong opposition to the death penalty and a policy to seek assurances that the death penalty will not be imposed did not go so far as to constitute a policy not to transfer a person to another state in the absence of such assurances); *R. (on the application of Domb) v Hammersmith LBC and Fulham LBC* [2008] EWHC 3277 (Admin) (a council minute of "noted and adopted" in relation to a manifesto promise did not give rise to a legitimate expectation); *R. (on the application of SRM Global Master Fund LP) v Commissioners of HM Treasury* [2009] EWHC 227 (Admin): not discussed at [2009] EWCA Civ 788 (no reasonable expectation prior to nationalisation that the Bank of England would provide or continue to provide financial assistance to any bank); *Odelola v Secretary of State for the Home Department* [2009] UKHL 25; [2009] 1 W.L.R. 1230 at [29] (the applicant accepted that there was "no question her being able to invoke the principle of legitimate expectation" in respect of immigration rules which could be changed at any time in such a way as to deprive a current applicant of any entitlement to the leave being sought); *R. (on the application of Coke-Wallis) v Institute of Chartered Accountants of England and Wales* [2008] EWHC 2690 (Admin) at [37] (representation by professional institute that dismissal of a case would bring the matter to an end did not give rise to a legitimate expectation, as it was not a specific representation that a second disciplinary complaint would not be laid but was merely general advice about the disciplinary process). Legitimate expectation argument not considered on appeal: [2009] EWCA Civ 730.

[Add to para.12–030 after ". . . but not determinative.⁷⁷"]

However, a public authority is not entitled to "thwart legitimate expectations by putting a strained or unconventional meaning" on a policy.[77a]

[77a] *Johnson Brothers v Secretary of State for Communities and Local Government* [2009] EWHC 580 (Admin) at [12].

[Add to new n.77b para.12–030 after ". . . of the representation is therefore important."]

[77b] See, e.g. *R. (on the application of Ishtiaq Ahmed) v The Parole Board for England and Wales* [2008] EWHC 3111 (Admin) (a representation did not arise in the context of a prisoner seeking parole, as the Parole Board must always address the question as to whether or not release would be too dangerous on a particular day in question). See also *R. (on the application of Roberts) v Secretary of State for Communities and Local Government* [2008] EWHC 677 (Admin); [2009] J.P.L. 81 at [80] (discussion of the role of legitimate expectations in the planning context where "the most formally expressed planning policies are always susceptible to change"); *R. (on the application of Stamford Chamber of Trade and Commerce) v Secretary of State for Communities and Local Government* [2009] EWHC 719 (Admin) at [92].

[Add to end of para.12–030]

In the context of prosecutions it, has been suggested that it is not likely to constitute an abuse of process to proceed with a prosecution unless (i) there has been an unequivocal representation by those with the conduct of the investigation or prosecution of a case that the defendant will not be prosecuted and (ii) that the defendant has acted on that representation to his detriment. Even then, if facts come to light which were not known when the representation was made, these may justify proceeding with the prosecution despite the representation.[80a]

[80a] *R. v Abu Hamza* [2007] 1 Cr. App. R. 27.

[Add to end of n.82]   **12–031**

; *R. (on the application of Midcounties Co-Operative Ltd) v Wyre Forest DC* [2009] EWHC 964 (Admin) (a circular gave rise to a legitimate expectation).

Induced by the conduct of the decision-maker

[Add to para.12–032 after ". . . actions of the prison service.[87]"]   **12–032**

However, the representation of one minister may bind another minister, as both ministers are "formulating and implementing the policies of a single entity, Her Majesty's Government".[87a]

[87a] *R. (on the application of BAPIO Action Ltd) v Home Secretary* [2008] UKHL 27; [2008] 1 A.C. 1003; M. Elliott, "British Jobs for British Doctors: Legitimate Expectations and Inter-Departmental Decision-making" (2008) 67 C.L.J. 453.

[Add to end of n.88]   **12–033**

See also *R. (on the application of S, H and Q) v Secretary of State for the Home Department* [2009] EWCA Civ 142 at [46] ("[t]here can moreover be no question of intervention by the court on the basis of a generalised and unfocussed idea of fairness; or by consideration of what subsequently may have happened to the individual in question and categorised in broad terms such as prejudice, loss and detriment").

Full disclosure

[Add to para.12–036 after ". . . use intended to be made of it.[103]"]   **12–036**

It has been suggested that where there is no written request for a tax ruling, then in anything other than very exceptional circumstances a tax official will not have been put on proper notice of the desire of the taxpayer to have a fully considered ruling on the point at issue and will not have been put on proper notice of the importance and significance of the ruling which he is being asked to provide.[103a]

[103a] *Corkteck Ltd v HM Revenue and Customs* [2009] EWHC 785 (Admin) (absence of full disclosure).

Is knowledge of the representation necessary?

[Add new n.104a to para.12–038 after ". . . normal consequences of their representations"]   **12–038**

104a *R. (on the application of Bancoult) v Secretary of State for Foreign and Commonwealth Affairs (No. 2)* [2008] UKHL 61; [2009] 1 A.C. 453 at [182] (Lord Mance noting that he had "no difficulty in accepting as the underlying principle a requirement of good administration, by which public bodies ought to deal straightforwardly and consistently with the public").

12–039 *[Add to end of n.110]*

But see *R. (on the application of Midcounties Co-Operative Ltd) v Wyre Forest DC* [2009] EWHC 964 (Admin) at [94]–[97]; *R. (on the application of Dwr Cymru Cyfyngedig (Welsh Water)) v The Environment Agency* [2009] EWHC 435 (Admin); [2009] 2 All E.R. 919 at [53] (the doctrine of legitimate expectation could not be argued because parties who had relied on an initial decision which had subsequently been withdrawn were not involved in the action).

THE STANDARD OF JUDICIAL REVIEW

12–048 *[Add new n.137a to para.12–048 after ". . . of the matter themselves."]*

137a *Corkteck Ltd v HM Revenue and Customs* [2009] EWHC 785 (Admin) (a substantive legitimate expectation claim depended on the true underlying facts as found by the court and did not proceed by reference to a test whether the person said to have given the assurance had acted irrationally in refusing to acknowledge it).

12–052 *[Add to para.12–052 after ". . . the test of proportionality.147"]*

Laws L.J. also proposed the test of proportionality in the *Niazi* case on the basis that:

"the doctrine of legitimate expectation, should be treated as a legal standard which, although not found in terms in the European Convention on Human Rights, takes its place alongside such rights as fair trial, and no punishment without law".147a

147a *R. (on the application of Niazi) v The Independent Assessor* [2008] EWCA Civ 755 at [51].

Detrimental reliance

12–058 *[Add to end of n.164]*

; *R. (on the application of Bancoult) v Secretary of State for Foreign and Commonwealth Affairs* [2008] UKHL 61; [2009] 1 A.C. 453 at [60] and

[135]; *Gokool v Permanent Secretary of the Ministry of Health and Quality of Life* [2008] UKPC 54 at [21].

CAN UNLAWFUL REPRESENTATIONS CREATE LEGITIMATE EXPECTATIONS

[Add to end of n.173]   12–061

; see also *Brown v Government of Rwanda* [2009] EWHC 770 (Admin) at [29] (Laws L.J. noting: "It is elementary that a concrete statutory duty of this kind cannot be overridden by any claim based on legitimate expectation"); *R. (on the application of Sovio Wines Ltd) v The Food Standards Agency (Wine Standards Branch)* [2009] EWHC 382 at [95] (any legitimate expectation must yield to the agency's statutory duties); *R. v Connolly* [2008] EWCA Crim 2643 at [10] (where a prisoner was wrongly informed as to the effect of his sentence, no legitimate expectation arose from the judge's erroneous explanation).

A changing approach

[Note 196]   12–072

Delete "P. Craig, *Administrative Law*, 5th edn. (2003) pp.665 *et seq.*" and substitute "P. Craig, *Administrative Law*, 2008 (6th edn.) paras 20–47–12–051".

COMPARATIVE PERSPECTIVES

Australia

[Add to end of n.212]   12–080

See also *C Incorporated v Australian Crime Commission* [2008] FCA 1806 at [68], [71] (noting that a clear distinction is drawn between decisions affecting a particular person or persons and those affecting the public at large, but that in this case even though the group may be large, each member of the group was affected in a "direct and immediate way").

[Add to end of n.214]

For examples of *Lam* being applied, see, e.g. *Habib v Commonwealth of Australia (No.2)* [2009] FCA 228 at [70] ("it has been held on high authority that Australian law knows no action based on substantive legitimate expectations"); *Village Building Company Ltd v Airservices Australia* 170 FCR 147; [2008] FCAFC 57 at [192]. For discussion see M. Graves, "Substantive Legitimate Expectations in Australian administrative law" (2008) 32 Melbourne U. L. Rev. 470.

12–081 *[Add to end of n.219]*

See now also *Australian Crime Commission v NTD8* [2009] FCAFC 86 at [67] (adoption of an international treaty does not, of itself, create an obligation where it is not part of Australian domestic law).

New Zealand

12–087 *[Add to end of n.233]*

; *Westpac Banking Corporation v Commissioner of Inland Revenue* [2009] NZCA 24 at [56]–[59] (noting that the introduction of the care and management provisions created a legislative context which was more conducive to following the English cases but that nonetheless it was appropriate to continue to apply the established principles).

South Africa

12–092 *[Add to end of n.251]*

On a number of occasions, the Supreme Court of Appeal has indicated that a legitimate expectation cannot be used to give effect to substantive rights: see, e.g. *Gibbs v Minister of Justice and Constitutional Development* [2009] ZASCA 73.

12–093 *[Add to end of n.254]*

; *Van Schalkwyk v The Chief Financial Officer*, Case No.1570/2007, July 5, 2007 (High Court of South Africa).

CHAPTER 13

CONVENTION RIGHTS AS GROUNDS FOR JUDICIAL REVIEW

PROTECTION OF FUNDAMENTAL RIGHTS IN DOMESTIC AND INTERNATIONAL LAW

The Council of Europe

[Add to n.14] 13–006

All 47 current members of the Council of Europe have signed Protocol 14, but it has not yet entered into force as Russia has not yet ratified it. However, under an Addendum to the Rules of Court dated July 1, 2009 with effect on all states which have ratified Protocol 14, a single judge is empowered to reject clearly inadmissible applications and a three-judge committee is entitled to declare admissible and give judgment in cases which are plainly well-founded because the particular issue in the country concerned has already been determined by the court. For a critical review of the role and legitimacy of the European Court of Human Rights, see Lord Hoffmann, "The Universality of Human Rights" (2009) 125 L.Q.R. 416.

[Add to n.16]

See n.14 above.

THE EUROPEAN CONVENTION ON HUMAN RIGHTS

[Note 23] 13–008

Delete reference to Starmer.

[Note 29] 13–011

Delete "see 13–089" add "see 13–098".

ABSOLUTE, LIMITED AND QUALIFIED RIGHTS

Unqualified rights

General limitations on Convention rights

13–016 *[Note 35 Delete last sentence and add]*

They are described in greater detail in Lord Lester of Herne Hill, Lord Pannick and J. Herberg, *Human Rights Law and Practice*, 2009, para.4.16.

Derogations

13–020 *[Add to n.43]*

The ECtHR agreed with the House of Lords' conclusions that there had been a situation of emergency at the time and that the measure was disproportionate (*A v UK* (2009) 26 B.H.R.C. 1 at [181] and [190]).

Interpreting the ECHR

13–028 *[Add to n.56]*

The ECtHR has changed its position on whether denying adoption to a single homosexual person is consistent with art.14 read with art.8 (*EB v France* (2008) 47 E.H.R.R. 21 at [70]–[73] and [91]–[93]).

The Human Rights Act 1998

13–030 *[Note 62]*

Replace reference to Lester and Pannick (2004) with Lester, Pannick and Herberg (2009), n.35 above.
Replace date of Clayton and Tomlinson with (2009)
Replace reference to Grosz et al with J. Beatson, S. Grosz, T. Hickman, R. Singh and S. Palmer, *Human Rights: Judicial Protection in the United Kingdom* (2008).

[Note 63 Delete first sentence and add]

The campaign is described by one of its principal participants (Lord Lester of Herne Hill) in Lester, Pannick and Herberg (2009), paras 1.35–1.46.

The omission of arts 1 and 13

13–033 *[Add to n.73]*

The ECtHR has indicated that over time the consistent practice of giving effect to declarations of incompatibility may crystallise into a binding obligation and that, at that time, applicants would be required to exhaust this national remedy before applying to Strasbourg (except where an effective remedy necessarily required the award of damages) (*Burden and Burden v United Kingdom, FS* (2008) 47 E.H.R.R. 857 at [43]).

The authority of Strasbourg decisions

[*Add to n.75*]   13–034

The House of Lords' decision in *N* was affirmed by the ECtHR, see n.161 below.

[*Add to n.77*]   13–035

A majority of the House of Lords in *Re P (AP)* [2008] UKHL 38; [2009] 1 A.C. 173 accepted that there would be circumstances where it was legitimate for a domestic court to provide greater protection for fundamental rights than required by the Strasbourg jurisprudence. See further, J. Wright, "Interpreting Section 2 of the Human Rights Act 1998: Towards an Indigenous Jurisprudence of Human Rights" [2009] P.L. 595.

[*Add to n.79*]   13–036

The Court of Appeal may depart from one of its own decisions where it concludes that it is inconsistent with a subsequent decision of the ECtHR (*R. (RJM) v Secretary of State for Work and Pensions* [2008] UKHL 63; [2009] 1 A.C. 311 at [59]–[67] (Lord Neuberger)). In the same case, the House of Lords declined to depart from the ECtHR's decision in *Stec* on the basis that it was inconsistent with earlier Strasbourg case law, stating that it would be only in the most exceptional circumstances that such a course would be appropriate at [31] (Lord Neuberger). The House of Lords departed from its own decision in *Pretty* (n.148 below) on whether the right to respect for private life is engaged in cases concerning decisions to terminate one's own life in light of the ECtHR's decision in that case (*R. (Purdy) v Director of Public Prosecutions* [2009] UKHL 45; [2009] 1 Cr. App. R. 32 at [35]–[39] (Lord Hope)). The House declined to overturn its decision in *Kay* in light of the ECtHR's judgment in *McCann v UK* (2008) 47 E.H.R.R. 40 in *Doherty v Birmingham City Council* [2008] UKHL 57; [2009] 1 A.C. 367 at [56] (Lord Hope) and at [82]–[88] (Lord Scott).

The duty to interpret legislation compatibly with convention rights

[*Add to n.94*]   13–041

In *Connolly v DPP* [2007] EWHC 237 (Admin); [2008] 1 W.L.R. 276, the Divisional Court held that the prohibition on sending a communication of an indecent or grossly offensive nature with the purpose of causing distress or anxiety in the Malicious Communications Act 1988 should be read so as not to criminalise communications which fell within art.10 (as in the present case where the material was part of an anti-abortion claim) at [18] (Dyson L.J.).

Declaration of incompatibility

13–045 *[Add to n.104]*

The Annex to the Government's *Responding to Human Rights Judgments* (Cm 7524) up-dates the position to January 2009.

[Note 105 Amend reference to Lester and Pannick to Lester, Pannick and Herberg (2009) and add]

In *Doherty*, n.79 above, at [49]–[51] (Lord Hope), the majority of the House of Lords held that although the exclusion of gipsies from the protection of the Mobile Homes Act 1983 was incompatible with their rights under art.8 and the inconsistency could not be removed by interpretation, it would not make a declaration of incompatibility as legislation was already in place which would remove the exclusion (although without retrospective effect). See further, *Wright*, n.107 below.

13–046 *[Add to n.107]*

The court may express a view in making a declaration as to how the incompatibility can be removed. However, the court will be reluctant to do so where the incompatibility arises from the interaction of different elements of a statutory scheme or where there is likely to be comprehensive legislative reform of the whole area (*R. (Wright) v Secretary of State for Health* [2009] UKHL 3; [2009] 1 A.C. 739 at [39] (Baroness Hale)).

13–047 *[Add to n.112]*

See further n.104 above.

Ministerial statement of compatibility

13–049 *[Add to n.117]*

The decision to proceed with legislation and to make a statement under s.19(1)(b) of the HRA that the Government intended to introduce the legislation while acknowledging the doubt about whether the ban on the broadcasting of political advertising was consistent with art.10 of the ECHR was held to be an additional reason to attach weight to Parliament's view in *R. (Animal Defenders International) v Secretary of State for Culture, Media and Sport* [2008] UKHL 15; [2008] 1 A.C. 1312 at [33] (Lord Bingham). See n.231 below.

Time limits

[Add to n.125]   13–051

While not wishing to limit the factors which could be taken into account when exercising the court's discretion to extend time, the Court of Appeal has indicated that the length of, and reasons for, the delay, the impact of such delay on the cogency of evidence, whether the defendant might have contributed to such delay and the duration of any disability under which the claimant may have been labouring when the cause of action accrued will be relevant in certain cases (*Dunn v Parole Board* [2008] EWCA Civ 374; [2009] 1 W.L.R. 728 at [30]–[33] and [39] (Thomas L.J.). A claimant cannot circumvent the one-year time limit by combining a claim under the HRA with another claim with a longer limitation period (*Somerville v Scottish Ministers* [2007] UKHL 44; [2008] SC(HL) 45 at [71] (Lord Scott) and at [172]–[175] (Lord Mance)).

THE CONTENT OF CONVENTION RIGHTS UNDER THE HRA

Absolute Rights

The right to life

[Add to n.148]   13–060

The House of Lords has departed from its decision in *Pretty* and required the Director of Public Prosecutions to clarify prosecution policy on assisted suicide on the grounds that the uncertainty in the current policy does not satisfy the requirements of art.8(2) (*Purdy*, n.79 above, at [54]–[56] (Lord Hope)).

[Note 149 Delete the second sentence and add]   13–061

The ECtHR held in *Osman* that it is sufficient for an applicant to show that the authorities did not do all that could reasonably be expected of them to avoid a real and immediate risk to life of which they were, or ought to have been, aware. In *Van Colle v Chief Constable of Hertfordshire*

Police [2008] UKHL 50; [2009] 1 A.C. 225 at [36] (Lord Bingham), the House of Lords overturned an award of damages to the family of a victim who was a witness against the murderer on the basis that the latter's previous offences were relatively minor and did not give rise to a sufficiently real risk at the relevant time.

[Add to n.150]

In *Budayeva v Russia* [2008] ECHR 15339/02 at [147]–[165], the ECtHR found substantive and procedural violations of art.2 since the state had been warned of the risk of mud slides (which killed some of the applicants' relatives or destroyed their homes), but had taken no steps to prevent the harm and had dispensed with the criminal investigation too early and prevented the inquest from apportioning responsibility.

[Add to n.151]

The House of Lords provided guidance on the extent of a health authorities' duties to protect the lives of patients in hospital (particularly the most vulnerable) in *Savage v South Essex Partnership NHS Foundation Trust* [2008] UKHL 74; [2009] 1 A.C. 681 at [67]–[72] (Lord Rodger), and at [97]–[100] (Baroness Hale). It has been held that an NHS trust had no operational obligation under art.2 in respect of a patient who committed suicide after being allowed to leave hospital, as the patient was a voluntary mental patient who had not been detained under the Mental Health Act 1983: *Rabone v Pennine Care NHS Trust* [2009] EWHC 1827 (QB) (Simon J. holding at [55] that the operational duty in art.2 only arose in respect of "the exercise of coercive powers over an individual who (by reason) of the exercise of such powers is particularly vulnerable"). This question had been left open in *Savage*: at [101]–[102].

[Add to n.152]

There is no obligation under art.2 to hold an inquiry into the legality of a war in which the lives of British citizens were lost (*R. (Gentle) v Prime Minister* [2008] UKHL 20; [2008] 1 A.C. 1356 at [8]–[10] (Lord Bingham)). The procedural aspect of art.2 is dependent on being able to demonstrate at least an arguable substantive breach at [6]. See further, *Ramsahai v Netherlands* (2008) 46 E.H.R.R. 43 (in which the ECtHR found a number of failures in relation to the procedural obligation under art.2, including the fact that the initial 15 hours of the investigation were carried out by the police and officers involved were not separated at [326]–[335]).

[Add to n.153]

Lord Phillips identified six essential ingredients for an investigation. To comply with art.2, it must: be initiated by the state itself; be prompt and carried out with reasonable expedition; be effective; be carried out by a person who is independent of those implicated in the events being investigated; there must be a sufficient element of public scrutiny of the investigation or its results; and the next of kin of the victim must be involved in the procedure to the extent necessary to safeguard his or her legitimate interests (*R. (L (A Patient)) v Secretary of State for Justice* [2008] UKHL 68; [2009] 1 A.C. 588 at [35]). The case concerned an individual who attempted suicide while in custody and was left with a serious injury as a result (which carries a reduced art.2 obligation).

The right to be free from torture, inhuman and degrading treatment or punishment

[Add to n.157]   13–063

It was accepted in *E v Chief Constable of the RUC* [2008] UKHL 66; [2009] 1 A.C. 536 at [43] (Lord Carswell) that sectarian abuse and the throwing of missiles could constitute inhuman or degrading treatment of school children. However, there was no breach of art.3 on the facts as the police had discharged their obligations to take all reasonable steps to avoid it.

[Add to n.161]   13–064

In *R. (Wellington) v Secretary of State for the Home Department* [2008] UKHL 72; [2009] 1 A.C. 335, the House of Lords decided that there was no breach of art.3 in ordering Wellington's extradition to the United States where he would face a mandatory life sentence without the prospect of early release (save in the most exceptional circumstances). The majority also held that the desirability of extradition (as opposed to permitting a suspect to evade justice) could be taken into account when considering whether his treatment overseas would violate art.3, that is, that a relativist approach to art.3 was permissible (at [20]–[28] (Lord Hoffmann)). This latter finding appears to be in conflict with the clear terms of art.3 itself and the decision of the ECtHR in *Saadi v Italy* (2008) 24 B.H.R.C. 123 (see Lord Brown's dissent in *Wellington* at [85]–[87]).

In *N v United Kingdom* (2008) 47 E.H.R.R. 39 at [42]–[51], the ECtHR affirmed that it was only in the most exceptional circumstances (such as in *D v United Kingdom* (1997) 24 E.H.R.R. 423) that expulsion of a person with a serious illness to a country where the healthcare system was less effective would constitute a breach of art.3.

[Add to n.164]

As to the state's obligations to disclose information about allegations of torture, see *R. (Binyan Mohamed) v Secretary of State for Foreign and Commonwealth Affairs* [2008] EWHC 2048 and 2100 (Admin) and *R. (Al-Sweady) v Secretary of State for Defence* [2009] EWHC 2387 (Admin).

The prohibition on slavery and forced labour

13–065 *[Add to n.166]*

However, the imposition of a civic obligation only on members of one gender may violate art.4 read with art.14 (*Adami v Malta* (2007) 44 E.H.R.R. 49 at [47]).

The ban on punishment without lawful authority

13–067 *[Add to n.171]*

The ECtHR was not satisfied that the applicants homicide conviction arising from his actions in quelling a riot during the 1956 revolution was in accordance with such general principles as it was not clear that the victim had laid down his arms and could therefore properly have been regarded at the time as a non-combatant (*Korbely v Hungary* (2008) 25 B.H.R.C. 382 at [89]–[94]).

13–068 *[Add to n.172]*

Domestic courts have held that civil recovery orders and financial reporting orders are not penalties for the purposes of art.7 (on the latter, see *R. v Adams* [2008] EWCA Crim 914; [2009] 1 W.L.R. 301 at [25] (Latham L.J.)).

[Add to n.175]

The ECtHR held that it was reasonably foreseeable that the emerging Lithuanian government would be likely to take steps against the applicants for their attempts to overthrow it notwithstanding the fact that Lithuania was not yet an independent state (*Kuolelis v Lithuania* [2008] ECHR 74357/01 at [116]–[121]).

Limited rights

The right to liberty and security of the person

13–070 *[Delete second sentence of sub-paragraph (f) and add]*

Until a state has authorised entry to the country, detention is in order to prevent unauthorised entry, even where the individual has surrendered himself to the authorities and is openly pursuing the legal process to obtain lawful entry.[179]

[Delete n.179 and substitute]

[179] *Saadi v UK* (2008) 47 E.H.R.R. 17 at [65]–[66]. The ECtHR found that the UK had acted in good faith and to ensure a speedy resolution of asylum claims. The conditions of detention were also found to be adequate at [75]–[79]. In order to avoid arbitrariness, art.5 requires that the state must not act in bad faith, and for the purposes of art.5(1)(b), (d) and (e), the detention must be necessary at [69]–[71]. However, the specific reasons for detaining the applicant were not provided until 76 hours after his detention and then only orally. As such, there was a violation of art.5(2) at [84]–[85].

In *R. (James) v Secretary of State for Justice* [2009] UKHL 22; [2009] 2 W.L.R. 1149 at [14]–[15] (Lord Hope) and at [51] (Lord Brown), the House of Lords held that detention after conviction which is lawful under art.5(1)(a) may become arbitrary and unlawful if a prisoner sentenced to an indeterminate sentence for public protection is detained for a long period after the expiry of the tariff without a meaningful opportunity to demonstrate that his continued detention is no longer justified.

[Add to n.181]   13–071

JJ was distinguished in *Secretary of State for the Home Department v E* [2007] UKHL 47; [2008] 1 A.C. 499 at [11] (Lord Bingham) and [25] (Baroness Hale) where, analysing the core element of art.5 as confinement, the House of Lords held that the control order in that case (involving a 12-hour curfew and other restrictions) did not involve a deprivation of liberty. Similarly, a 16-hour curfew and a requirement to live 150 miles from London (where his family was located) was held (by a majority) not to breach art.5 in *AP v Secretary of State for the Home Department* [2009] EWCA Civ 731 at [31]–[33] (Maurice Kay L.J.).

In *Austin v Metropolitan Police Commissioner* [2009] UKHL 5; [2009] 1 A.C. 564 at [22]–[23] and at [34] (Lord Hope), the House of Lords held that although art.5 is expressed in absolute terms, there remains scope to consider the purpose of any restriction and the need to balance individual and collective interests. As such, confining a group of protestors to a small area for a period of hours in order to preserve public order did not infringe art.5. This outcome is questionable: the Article guarantees liberty (subject to limited exceptions) and does not only provide protection against arbitrary interferences with it.

[Add to n.182]

The ECtHR held that detaining illegal immigrants in the transit zone of an international airport for over 10 days was a deprivation of liberty under art.5 (*Riad and Idiab v Belgium* [2008] ECHR 29787/03 at [78] (French text)). The court went on to hold that being forced to live in a public place without proper facilities also violated art.3: at [104]–[108].

13–073 *[Note 185 delete citation for Brooke and add]*

[2008] EWCA Civ 29; [2008] 1 W.L.R. 1950 at [77]–[80] (Lord Phillips C.J.).

[Add to n.186]

In *James* (n.179 above) at [21] (Lord Hope) and at [60] (Lord Brown), the House of Lords held that art.5(4) is concerned exclusively with procedure. A majority of the House of Lords upheld the power of the Secretary of State to depart from the Parole Board's recommendation for release at the half-way stage of a determinate sentence against a challenge based on art.5(4) (*R. (Black) v Secretary of State for Justice* [2009] UKHL 1; [2009] 2 W.L.R. 282 at [78]–[85] (Lord Brown)).

On the admission of "closed" material and art.5(4), see *A v UK* (2009) 26 B.H.R.C. 1 and *Secretary of State for the Home Department v AF (No.3)* [2009] UKHL 28; [2009] 3 All E.R. 643.

The right to marry and found a family

13–076 *[Note 192]*

Delete *Secretary of State for the Home Department v Baiai* [2007] EWCA Civ 478 at [48]–[57] (Buxton L.J.).

[Add]

R. (Baiai) v Secretary of State for the Home Department [2008] UKHL 53; [2009] 1 A.C. 287 at [28]–[32] (Lord Bingham).

[Delete n.193 and substitute]

See *Dickson v UK* (2008) 46 E.H.R.R. 41 at [80]–[85], in which the ECtHR found the policy of denying artificial insemination facilities to prisoners to be in violation of art.8 and did not consider art.12 separately.

The right to education

13–077 *[Add to n.195]*

See further n.259 below on indirect discrimination in assigning Roma children to special schools. As a matter of domestic law, a rule which prevented the child of a convert to Judaism from entering a Jewish faith school was held to be directly and indirectly discriminatory in breach of the Race Relations Act 1976 (*R. (E) v The Governing Body of JFS* [2009] EWCA Civ 626 at [32]–[33] and at [45]–[46] (Sedley L.J.)).

[Add to n.198] **13–078**

The state was held to have crossed the line where there was very limited teaching of the Alevi faith although its followers represented a substantial minority (*Zengin v Turkey* (2008) 46 E.H.R.R. 44 at [60]–[70]). The ECtHR has held that the rules which permitted parents to request a partial exemption for their children from predominantly Christian religious and philosophical teaching was in breach of art.2 as it required parents to expose their own philosophical views to scrutiny and was based on an unrealistic distinction between observation of, and participation in, the classes (*Folgero v Norway* (2008) 46 E.H.R.R. 47 at [85]–[102]).

[Add to n.199]

The House of Lords' decision in *R. (SB) v Governors of Denbigh High School* [2006] UKHL 15; [2007] 1 A.C. 100 (n.226 below) has been applied to wearing a purity ring (*R. (Playfoot (A Child)) v Millais School Governing Body* [2007] EWHC 1698; [2007] H.R.L.R. 34 at [23] where the wearing of the ring was found not to be intimately linked to a belief in chastity before marriage) and the niqab (*R. (X) v Head Teachers and Governors of Y School* [2007] EWHC 298 (Admin); [2008] 1 All ER 249 at [30]–[36] (Silber J.) where an alternative school was available where the niqab was permitted).

Qualified rights

Prescribed by law

[Add to n.200] **13–080**

In *Liberty v UK* [2009] 48 E.H.R.R. 1 at [64]–[70], the ECtHR held that the provisions (which were neither legislative nor made public) used to justify the interception of communications from a number of groups between 1990 and 1997 were not in accordance with the law and in breach of art.8. See further, *Purdy*, n.79 above.

The right to respect for private and family life

[Note 214 delete second sentence and add] **13–085**

The House of Lords rejected a challenge to the hunting ban on the basis that it was fundamentally a public activity (*R. (Countryside Alliance) v Attorney General* [2008] UKHL 52; [2008] 1 A.C. 719 at [15] (Lord Bingham) at [54]–[55] (Lord Hope) at [90]–[100] (Lord Rodger) at [115]–[116] (Baroness Hale) and at [137]–[141] (Lord Brown)). The House of Lords held that art.8 may be engaged by being placed on a provisional list of carers considered unsuitable to work with vulnerable adults given its effect on livelihood (*Wright*, n.107 above). See *R. (on the application of G) v Nottinghamshire Healthcare NHS Trust* [2009] EWCA Civ 795 at [46]–[51] (art.8 was not engaged by a smoking ban inside and outside a high security psychiatric institution given the expectations of privacy in such accommodation and given that smoking was not sufficiently integral to a person's identity to engage art.8).

[Add to n.215]

Murray v Express Newspapers Plc [2008] EWCA Civ 446; [2008] 3 W.L.R. 1360 at [45]–[61] (Sir Anthony Clarke M.R.) involved a domestic application of the *Von Hannover* principle in a claim for damages arising from photographs of Mrs Murray's (the author J.K. Rowling's) two-year old son in the street. A reasonable expectation of privacy may extend to telephone calls, emails and internet usage at work if the employer has given no indication that such usage may be monitored (*Copland v UK* (2007) 45 E.H.R.R. 37 at [41]–[42]).

[Add to n.218]

The ECtHR held that the state had failed to provide sufficient protection for the applicant's reputation where national proceedings against the editor of a newspaper which had accused the applicant of hounding a pro-Nazi professor to death failed on the basis of fair comment (*Pfeifer v Austria* (2009) 48 E.H.R.R. 175 at [37]–[48]). This decision may require domestic courts to extend the scope of protection for reputation provided by the current law of defamation.

13–086 *[Delete n.220 and substitute]*

It has been invoked in relation to decisions to dismiss employees for sexual activity outside the workplace (*X v Y (Unfair Dismissal)* [2004] EWCA Civ 662; [2004] I.C.R. 1634 at [51] (Mummery L.J., no interference since the activity was found to take place in public)). In *Pay v UK* (2009) 48 E.H.R.R. 15, the ECtHR rejected as inadmissible the applicant's claim that his dismissal for taking part in bondage-domination-sado-masochistic floor shows in private clubs was a breach of art.8. The ECtHR did not express a concluded view on whether the activities fell within art.8. In *Mosley v News Group Newspapers Ltd* [2008] EWHC 1777; [2008] E.M.L.R. 20 at [98]–[109] (Eady J.), mild BDSM activities were held to fall within art.8 even when paid for and when they involved a number of participants.

Immigration authorities are required to take account of the impact of a proposed removal on the individual concerned and their family (usually a spouse or minor child) (*Beoku-Betts v Secretary of State for the Home Department* [2008] UKHL 39; [2009] 1 A.C. 115 at [41]–[44] (Lord

Brown)). In *EM (Lebanon) v Secretary of State for the Home Department* [2008] UKHL 64; [2008] 3 W.L.R. 931 at [7]–[18] (Lord Hope), the House of Lords found that there would be flagrant breach of art.8 in the exceptional circumstances of the case if the claimant were returned to Lebanon where under Sharia law, her son would be handed over to his abusive father who he had never met (cf. *RB (Algeria) v Secretary of State for the Home Department* [2009] UKHL 10; [2009] 2 W.L.R. 512 where the alleged risk of a breach of the essence of art.6 overseas was not sufficiently flagrant). The provisions of the Regulation of Investigatory Powers Act 2000 which permitted covert surveillance of those arrested in breach of their rights to legal professional privilege violated art.8 and a declaration of incompatibility was made (*McE v Prison Service of Northern Ireland* [2009] UKHL 15; [2009] 2 W.L.R. 782 at [96]–[105] (Lord Carswell)).

In an important decision, the ECtHR differed strongly from the House of Lords in holding that the indeterminate retention of fingerprints, DNA profiles and cellular samples from those arrested (even if subsequently acquitted) which bore no relation to the gravity of the offence or the individual's age at the time of the arrest was disproportionate (*S & Marper v UK* (2009) E.H.R.R. 50 at [105]–[125]).

The right to freedom of thought, conscience and religion

[Note 223 delete citation for *Countryside Alliance* and substitute n.214 **13–087** above.

[Add]

The belief should also be consistent with Convention values and worthy of respect in a democratic society. The Employment Appeal Tribunal relied on the ECtHR's jurisprudence under art.9 and art.2 of the First Protocol in holding that the opinion that children were better brought up by a heterosexual couples was not a philosophical belief as it was expressly stated to be based on evidence and logic (*McClintock v Department of Constitutional Affairs* [2008] I.R.L.R. 29 at [45] (Elias J.)).

A belief in the anthropogenic causes of climate change and human responsibility to address it can constitute a philosophical belief: *Grainger Plc v Nicholson* (EAT/0219/09) at [27]–[31] (Burton J.).

[Add to n.224]

The wearing of a purity ring was held not to be sufficiently intimately connected with Christian belief in *Playfoot* (n.199 above).

13–088 *[Add to n.225]*

The House of Lords upheld a decision not to exempt certain buildings owned by the Mormon church from business rates on the ground that they were not open to the public (*Gallagher (Valuation Officer) v Church of Jesus Christ of the Latter-Day Saints* [2008] UKHL 56; [2008] 1 W.L.R. 1852 at [12] (Lord Hoffmann)). The requirement that the building be open to the public was of general application and did not prevent the members of the church from manifesting their religion.

[Add to n.226]

The Court of Appeal upheld the decision not to grant an exemption from the policy on slaughtering cattle with bovine tuberculosis in relation to a Hindu community's temple bullock (*R. (Swaami Suryananda) v Welsh Ministers* [2007] EWCA Civ 893 at [51]–[60] (Pill L.J.)).

Freedom of expression

13–089 *[Add to n.228]*

The ECtHR may be moving towards greater protection for artistic expression. In *Vereinigung Blidender Kunstler v Austria* (2008) 47 E.H.R.R. 5 at [26]–[39], the court found an injunction which was unlimited in time and space preventing the display of a painting depicting a number of public figures engaged in sexual activities to be disproportionate.

[Add to n.229]

Some recent decisions of the ECtHR suggest that the protection of reputation and encouraging responsible standards of journalism are being given greater weight than the right to criticise public figures (see, for example, *Lindon, Otczakovsky-Laurnes & July v France* (2008) 46 E.H.R.R. 35 at [57]).

In contrast, in *Karako v Hungary*, App.No.39311/05, April 28, 2009 at [22]–[28], the ECtHR clearly distinguished between the right to personal integrity (which is protected by art.8) and the right to reputation.

13–090 *[Add to n.231]*

The House of Lords upheld the total ban on political advertising on the broadcast media (*Animal Defenders*, n.117 above). It remains unclear whether an absolute prohibition on political advertising is compatible with art.10 (*TV Vest v Norway* (2009) 48 E.H.R.R. 51 at [64]–[78]), particularly in relation to small parties. See T. Lewis and P. Cumper, "Balancing Freedom of Political Expression against Equality of Political Opportunity:

the Courts and the UK Broadcasting Ban on Political Advertising" [2009] P.L. 89.

[Add to n.233]

See further, I. Hare, "Extreme Speech Under International and Regional Human Rights Standards" in I. Hare and J. Weinstein (eds.), *Extreme Speech and Democracy* (2009) and *Soulas v France* [2008] ECHR 15948/04 at [36]–[48] (French version).

Freedom of assembly and association

[Add to n.236]   13–091

The ECtHR's decision in *Sorensen v Denmark* (2008) 46 E.H.R.R. 29 at [54]–[71] contains a useful discussion of the positive and negative aspects of freedom of association in the context of union membership.

[Add to n.238]   13–092

The earlier case law now needs to be reviewed in light of the ECtHR's judgment in *Demir and Baykara v Turkey* [2009] 48 E.H.R.R 54 at [153]–[154], in which the court held that as a result of international legal developments, the right to bargain collectively had become one of the essential elements of the right to join trade unions under art.11.

[Add to n.239]   13–093

The Court of Appeal rejected the justifications for prohibiting the women's peace camp which had been established for 23 years outside Aldermaston (*Tabernacle v Secretary of State for Defence* [2009] EWCA Civ 23 at [40]–[44] (Laws L.J.)).

[Add to n.241]

In *Bukta v Hungary* [2007] ECHR 25691/04 at [33]–[39], the ECtHR affirmed that notice requirements for a public demonstration were not necessarily inconsistent with art.11, but that a decision to close down a protest which was a justifiably spontaneous response to a recent event where there was no threat to public order was a disproportionate response. The House of Lords held that the Critical Mass cycle ride was a commonly or customarily held procession as it took place at the same time each month notwithstanding that it had no pre-determined route and was therefore not subject to the notice requirements of the Public Order Act 1986 (*Kay (FC) v Commissioner of Police for the Metropolis* [2008] UKHL 69; [2008] 1 W.L.R. 2723 at [16]–[25] (Lord Phillips)). The ECtHR's decision in *Tum Haber Sen* is reported at (2008) 46 E.H.R.R. 374.

The right to the enjoyment of possessions

13–094   *[Add to n.244]*

See further, the House of Lords decision in *RJM* (n.79 above).

13–095   *[Note 247 delete reference and substitute]*

(2008) 46 E.H.R.R. 45 at [64]–[66].

13–096   *[Note 250 delete reference for Countryside Alliance and substitute]*

(n.214 above).

[Add to n.251]

The Court of Appeal dismissed a challenge by shareholders of Northern Rock to the basis for the assessment of compensation following its "nationalisation" in *R. (SRM Global Master Finance Ltd) v Commissioners of Her Majesty's Treasury* [2009] EWCA Civ 788 at [73]–[77] (Laws L.J.). The court summarised the correct approach to the principles of balance, proportionality and the margin of appreciation by asking whether the state measure was manifestly without reasonable foundations.

The right to free elections

13–097   *[Add to n.253]*

The ECtHR upheld a requirement that candidates for election to the national parliament should provide information about their property and sources of income (*Russian Conservative Party of Entrepreneurs v Russia* (2008) 46 E.H.R.R. 39 at [62]). In the same case, the court rejected a challenge that a voter had not been able to vote for his party of choice as it had been denied registration at [78].

[Add to n.254]

Rules requiring the forfeiture of (modest) electoral deposits (*Sukhovetskyy v Ukraine* (2007) 44 E.H.R.R. 57 at [61]–[74]) and an electoral threshold of 10 per cent of the national vote to be represented in Parliament have been upheld (*Yumak and Sadak v Turkey* (2009) 48 E.H.R.R. 4 at [66]–[78]). The traditional (unelected) position of the Seigneur and Seneschal in Sark's unicameral legislature was held (by a majority) not to offend art.3 (*R. (Barclay) v Secretary of State for Justice* [2008] EWCA Civ 1319 at [121] (Jacob L.J.).

The prohibition on discrimination

[Add to n.257]   13–098

Compare *Runkee and White v UK* [2007] 2 F.C.R. 178 at [45] (violation of
art.14 read with art.1 of the First Protocol in relation to widowers; non-
entitlement to a widow's payment) to *Burden and Burden v UK*, n.73 above
at [53]–[61] (no violation of the same Convention rights where sisters
living together were not entitled to the same inheritance reliefs as married
couples or those with civil partnerships).

[Note 258 delete the second sentence and substitute]   13–099

In *RJM* (n.79 above), the House of Lords held that homelessness counted as
a personal characteristic. Lord Walker at [5] referred to certain innate and
immutable characteristics which are closely connected with an individual's
personality (such as gender, sexual orientation, colour, congenital dis-
abilities, nationality, language, religion and politics) and which are at the
core of art.14 and others (such as military status, residence and domicile,
past employment in the KGB) which are further outside. Lord Neuberger
stated that a personal characteristic was not determined by whether it was
voluntary or not at [47]. Ordinary residence was found to fall within art.14
in *Carson v UK* (2009) 48 E.H.R.R 41 at [76]. However, the challenge to
the UK's rules on drawing state pensions overseas failed as the applicants
were not in an analogous situation to UK resident pensioners and the
difference in treatment was, in any event, justified at [78]–[81].

[Delete n.259 and substitute]

The ECtHR has now held that art.14 prohibits indirect discrimination (*DH
v Czech Republic* (2007) 44 E.H.R.R. 37, [175–8] and [184–9]). The Court
accepted that the applicants' statistical evidence gave rise to a presumption
that the psychological tests used to determine school allocation had a
disparate impact on Roma children and that state had failed to discharge
the burden of demonstrating that they were objectively justified. The Court
therefore found there to be a violation of art.14 read with art.2 of the First
Protocol. This decision has potentially wide-ranging consequences. See
Baroness Hale's discussion of justification in *AL (Serbia) v Secretary of State
for the Home Department* [2008] UKHL 42; [2008] 1 W.L.R. 1434, [29–
49].

The Impact of the HRA

[Add to n.266]   13–101

See further, S. Shah and T. Poole, "The Impact of the Human Rights Act
on the House of Lords" [2009] P.L. 347.

13–102 *[Add to n.267]*

See further, Justice, A British Bill of Rights: Informing the debate (2007) (available from *http://www.justice.org.uk*) and the Joint Committee on Human Rights, A Bill of Rights for the UK (HL Paper 165–1); (HC Paper 150–1) (2007–08). The JCHR recommended supplementing the rights protected by the HRA with additional rights to trial by jury (in England and Wales), to administrative justice, to equality and, to a limited extent, to economic, social and cultural rights. The JCHR was skeptical of the Government wish to link rights to responsibilities. The Government has responded in A Bill of Rights for the UK? Government's Response to the Committee's Twenty-ninth Report of Session 2007–08 (HL Paper 15), (HC Paper 145) (2008–09) and its Green Paper, Rights and Responsibilities: Developing Our Constitutional Framework (Cm 7577) (2009) in which it proposes a new Bill of Rights and Responsibilities which would bring together Convention rights and fundamental common law and statutory rights (including some welfare entitlements). The Equality and Human Rights Commission (established under the Equality Act 2006) published its (broadly supportive) Human Rights Inquiry Report in June 2009 (available at *http://www.equalityhumanrights.com*). The debate about the effectiveness of the Human Rights Act continues: compare, K. Ewing and J. Tham, "The Continuing Futility of the Human Rights Act" [2008] P.L. 668 and A. Kavanagh, "Judging the Judges under the Human Rights Act: Deference, Disillusionment and the 'War on Terror'" [2009] P.L. 287.

[Note 268 should now read]

The Northern Ireland Human Rights Commission gave its final advice to the Secretary of State for Northern Ireland on a possible Bill of Rights for Northern Ireland on December 10, 2008, although there was no unanimity on which rights, in addition to those in the Convention, should be included (available at *http://www.nihrc.org*). See V. Bogdanor and S. Vogenauer, "Enacting a British Constitution: Some Problems" [2008] P.L. 38.

CHAPTER 14

REVIEW UNDER EUROPEAN COMMUNITY LAW

OVERVIEW OF THE EU LEGAL SYSTEM

Three pillars of the EU

[Add to end of para.14–005]   **14–005**

Article 47 TEU[26a] states that nothing in the EU Treaty shall affect the EC Treaty, and the ECJ has interpreted this to mean that it must ensure that acts falling within the scope of the EU Treaty do not encroach upon the powers conferred by the EC Treaty on the Community.[26b]

[26a] See also art.29 TEU.
[26b] Case C-440/05 *Commission v Council* [2008] 1 C.M.L.R. 22 at para.52; Case C-301/06 *Ireland v European Parliament* [2009] 2 C.M.L.R. 37 at para.75. By contrast, in the Lisbon Treaty (see para.14–012), it is envisaged that the Treaty on the Functioning of the Union ("TFU") (in which the current first and third pillars will reside) and the new EU Treaty ("TEU") (dealing with common foreign and security policy) will have equal legal value: art.1 TFU and arts 1 and 40 TEU.

Primacy of Community law

[Add to end of n.37]   **14–009**

For the lively debate on the extent to which, if at all, the principle of primacy applies to EU measures adopted pursuant to the second and third pillars, see: K. Lenaerts and T. Corthaut, "Of Birds and Hedges: The Role of Primacy in Invoking Norms of EU Law" (2006) 31 E.L. Rev. 287 at 289 and D. Nicol, "Democracy, Supremacy and the 'Intergovernmental' Pillars of the European Union" [2009] P.L. 218.

Direct effect of Community law measures

[Add to end of n.45]   **14–010**

; Case C-268/06 *Impact v Minister for Agriculture and Food* [2008] 2 C.M.L.R. 47 at paras 74–75 (art.5(2) of Council Directive 1999/70/EC, which assigned to Member States the general objective of preventing the abusive use of successive fixed-term employment contracts or relationships, was not capable of direct effect as "content comprising minimum protection in favour of individuals" could not be identified).

[Add to para.14–010 after ". . . other citizens"]

, trade unions[47a]

[47a] Case C-438/05 *International Transport Workers' Federation and Finnish Seamen's Union v Viking Line ABP and OÜ Viking Line Eesti* [2007] E.C.R. I–10779 at para.61.

REFORM

The proposed Reform Treaty

14–012 *[Paragraph 14–012]*

This paragraph should be read in light of the rejection of the Reform Treaty, or Lisbon Treaty as it is now more commonly known, by Ireland in a referendum in June 2008. Following a decision taken by the Heads of State or Government of the Member States on June 19, 2009[62a] to grant assurances to Ireland on issues which were regarded to be of importance to the people of Ireland—namely, the right to life, family and education; taxation; military neutrality, and workers' rights—a second referendum on the Lisbon Treaty in Ireland was held on October 2, 2009. This second referendum was passed and at the time of writing, only the Czech Republic has not yet ratified.

[62a] Council of the European Union, Presidency Conclusions, June 18/19, 2009, at paras 1–5 and Annexes 1–3. For discussion of the Irish rejection see S. Kingston, "Ireland's Options after the Lisbon Referendum: Strategies, Implications and Competing Visions of Europe" (2009) 34 E.L. Rev. 455.

14–013 *[Add to end of n.69]*

For useful discussions of the impact of the Lisbon Treaty, see, e.g. House of Lords European Union Committee, The Treaty of Lisbon: An Impact Assessment, 10th Report of Session 2007–08, Stationery Office, 2008, HL Paper No.62; House of Lords Constitution Committee Report, European Union (Amendment) Bill and the Lisbon Treaty: Implications for the UK Constitution, HL Paper No.84, 6th Report of Session 2007–08; C.

Harding, "From Past Imperfect to Future Perfect? A Longitudinal Study of the Third Pillar" (2009) 34 E.L. Rev. 25; S. Peers, "EU Criminal Law and the Treaty of Lisbon" (2008) 33 E.L. Rev. 507; P. Craig, "The Treaty of Lisbon, Process, Architecture and Substance" (2008) 33 E.L. Rev. 137; R. Schutze, "Lisbon and the Federal Order of Competences: A Prospective Analysis" (2008) 33 E.L. Rev. 709; J. Snell, "'European Constitutional Settlement', An Ever Closer Union, and the Treaty of Lisbon: Democracy or Relevance?" (2008) 33 E.L. Rev. 619; M. Dougan, "The Treaty of Lisbon 2007: Winning Minds, not Hearts" (2008) 45 C.M.L. Rev. 617.

SECONDARY LEGISLATION

Directives

Direct effect of directives

[Add to end of n.90]   14–023

For detailed criticism of this position, see P. Craig, "The Legal Effect of Directives: Policy, Rules and Exceptions" (2009) 34 E.L. Rev. 349.

[Add to end of n.92]   14–024

See also Case C-356/05 *Farrell v Whitty (MIBI)* [2007] E.C.R. I-3067 at paras 40–41 (Foster criteria approved, although insufficient information provided to the ECJ to determine whether the criteria satisfied); Case C-6/05 *Medipac-Kazantzidis AE v Venizeleio-Pananio (PESY KRITIS)* [2007] E.C.R. I–4557 at para.43.

[Add to n.104 after ". . . para.57"]   14–026

; Case C-152-154/07 *Arcor AG & Co KG v Germany* [2008] 3 C.M.L.R. 37 at para.36.

[Add to n.109 after ". . . para.39;"]

Case C-152/07 *Arcor AG & Co KG v Germany* [2008] 3 C.M.L.R. 37 at para.38 ("removal of benefits cannot be regarded as an obligation falling on a third party pursuant to the directives").

[Add new para.14–026A]   14–026A

In addition to these three established mitigations of the purely vertical direct effect of directives, it appears that a fourth qualification may also have emerged recently. Where a regulation refers to a directive, this may result in horizontal direct effect for the relevant directive provision. In the case of *Viamex*,[109a] payment of export refunds for live animals was dealt with through Regulation 615/98,[109b] which conditioned payment on compliance with rules concerning the welfare of live animals during transit set down in Directive 91/628.[109c] The German authorities refused to pay the refunds where the exporter had not complied with the 24-hour rest period for animals prescribed by the Directive.[109d] The ECJ stated that a directive cannot of itself impose obligations on an individual,[109e] but added that, it could not be:

> "precluded, in principle, that the provisions of a directive may be applicable by means of an express reference in a regulation to its provisions, provided that general principles of law and, in particular, the principle of legal certainty, are observed".[109f]

The ECJ found that there was no infringement of legal certainty since the purpose of the general reference in Regulation 615/98 to Directive 91/628 was to ensure compliance with the relevant provisions of the Directive on the welfare of live animals during transport. However, the reference to the Directive should not be interpreted as covering all the provisions in Directive 91/628 and, in particular, those provisions which have no connection with the principal objective pursued by that Directive.[109g]

[109a] Cases C-37 and 58/06 *Viamex Agrar Handels GmbH and Zuchtvieh-Kontor GmbH (ZVK) v Hauptzollamt Hamburg-Jonas* [2008] E.C.R. I–69.
[109b] Commission Regulation (EC) 615/98 of March 18, 1998 laying down specific detailed rules of application for the export refund arrangements as regards the welfare of live bovine animals during transport [1998] OJ L82/19.
[109c] Council Directive 91/628 EEC of November 19, 1998 on the protection of animals during transport and amending Directives 90/425 and 91/496 [1991] OJ L340/17, as amended by Council Directive 95/29/EC of June 29, 1995 concerning the protection of animals during transport [1995] OJ L148/52.
[109d] This rule is found in point 48(5) of Ch.VII of the Annex to Directive 91/628.
[109e] Cases C-37 and 58/06 *Viamex Agrar Handels GmbH and Zuchtvieh-Kontor GmbH (ZVK) v Hauptzollamt Hamburg-Jonas* [2008] E.C.R. I–69 at para.27.
[109f] Cases C-37 and 58/06 *Viamex Agrar Handels GmbH and Zuchtvieh-Kontor GmbH (ZVK) v Hauptzollamt Hamburg-Jonas* [2008] E.C.R. I–69 at para.28.
[109g] Cases C-37 and 58/06 *Viamex Agrar Handels GmbH and Zuchtvieh-Kontor GmbH (ZVK) v Hauptzollamt Hamburg-Jonas* [2008] E.C.R. I–69 at paras 29–30. See also Case C-207/06 *Schwaninger Martin Viehhandel—Viehexport v Zollamt Salzburg, Erstattungen*, July 17, 2008, ECJ.

The Charter of Fundamental Rights of the EU

[Add to end of n.123]   14–028

See C. Hilson, "Rights and Principles in EU Law: A Distinction without Foundation?" (2008) 15 Maastricht J. of European and Comparative L. 193.

Limited legal effect of the Charter

[Add to n.129 after ". . . para.38. See also"]   14–030

Case C-275/06 *Productores de Música de España (Promusicae) v Telefónica de España SAU* [2008] E.C.R. I–271 at para.64;

[Add to end of n.129]

; Case C-450/06 *Varec v Belgium* [2008] 2 C.M.L.R. 24 at para.48 (referring to the right to respect for private life which is "restated" in art.7 of the Charter); Case C-415/05 *Kadi and Al Barakaat International Foundation v Council* [2008] 3 C.M.L.R. 41 at para.335. Perhaps the ECJ's boldest invocation of the Charter to date is found in Case C-244/06 *Dynamic Medien Vertriebs GmbH v Avides Media AG* [2008] E.C.R. I–505 at para.41 (noting that the rights of the child are "enshrined" in the Charter—without mentioning that they were derived from Member State traditions).

[Add to end of para.14–030]

The Charter has subsequently been invoked by the ECJ in a range of cases, not involving a link to a directive.[129a]

[129a] See, e.g. Case C-438/05 *International Transport Workers' Federation and Finnish Seamen's Union v Viking Line ABP and OÜ Viking Line Eesti* [2007] E.C.R. I–10779 at para.43; Case C-341/05 *Laval v Svenska Byggnadsarbetareförbundet* [2007] E.C.R. I–11767 at para.90.

[Add to end of n.139]   14–031

; *Sumukan Ltd v Commonwealth Secretariat* [2007] EWCA Civ 1148; [2008] 1 Lloyd's Rep. 40 at para.51.

General Principles of Law

[Add new n.143a to para.14–033 after ". . . law applied by the ECJ."]   14–033

143a See U. Bernitz, J. Nergelius and C. Cardner, *General Principles of EC Law in a Process of Development* (Kluwer, 2008).

[Add to para.14–033 after ". . . against the EU under Art.288(2)[215(2)] EC."]

The ECJ has also held that an action in restitution can lie against Community institutions even though such an action is not expressly provided for in the EC Treaty, because unjust enrichment, is a source of non-contractual obligation common to the legal systems of the Member States, and the Community could not be dispensed from the application to itself of the same principles.144a

144a Case C-47/07P *Masdar (UK) Ltd v Commission* [2009] 2 C.M.L.R. 1 (Grand Chamber) at paras 44–48.

[Add to the end of para.14–033]

In addition, in the *Mangold* case,145a the general principle of equal treatment was found to be capable of creating obligations for private parties—although this holding has subsequently been distinguished by the ECJ145b and criticised by Advocates-General.145c

145a Case C-144/04 *Mangold v Helm* [2005] E.C.R. I–9981 at paras 75–77.
145b See, e.g. Case C-427/06 *Bartsch v Bosch und Siemens Hausgeräte (BSH) Altersfürsorge GmbH*, September 23, 2008.
145c Case C-411/05 *Palacios de la Villa v Cortefiel Servicios SA* [2007] E.C.R. I-8531 at paras 79–100, per A.G. Mazák (see L. Waddington, "Case C-411/05 *Félix Palacios de la Villa v Cortefi el Servicios SA*, Judgment of the Court (Grand Chamber) of 16 October 2007" (2008) 45 C.M.L. Rev. 895); Case C-55-56/07 *Michaeler v Amt für sozialen Arbeitsschutz and Autonome Provinz Bozen*, not yet reported, January 24, 2008, at paras 14–29 (A.G. Ruiz-Jarabo Colomer).

European Communities Act 1972

14–035 *[Add to end of para.14–035]*

After ratification of the Lisbon Treaty, this paragraph should be read in light of the amendment due to be introduced to s.2(1) of the European Communities Act 1972 by s.3(3) and Sch. Pt 1 of the European Union (Amendment) Act 2008, which has not yet entered into force, and which replaces the phrase "'enforceable Community right'" with the phrase "enforceable EU right".

[Add to end of para.14–036] **14–036**

After ratification of the Lisbon Treaty, this paragraph should be read in light of the amendments due to be introduced to s.2(2) of the European Communities Act 1972 by s.3(3) and Sch., Pt 1 of the European Union (Amendment) Act 2008, which has not yet entered into force, and which replaces references to "Community obligation" with references to "EU obligation."

[Add to end of para.14–038] **14–038**

After ratification of the Lisbon Treaty, this paragraph should be read in light of amendments due to be introduced to s.3(1) of the European Communities Act 1972 by s.3(3) and Sch. Pt 1 of the European Union (Amendment) Act 2008, which has not yet entered into force, and which replaces references to "Community instrument" with a reference to "EU instrument".

CHALLENGING A NATIONAL MEASURE IN A NATIONAL COURT

[Add to end of n.155] **14–039**

; *Fleming (t/a Bodycraft) v Customs and Excise Commissioners* [2008] UKHL 2; [2008] 1 W.L.R. 195 at [24] (as noted by Lord Walker, "[t]he provision is not made void but it must be treated as being (as Lord Bridge of Harwich put it in *R. v Secretary of State for Transport Ex p. Factortame* Ltd (No.1) [1990] 2 A.C. 85, 140) 'without prejudice to the directly enforceable Community rights of nationals of any member state of the EEC'"). Lord Walker also commented that disapplication is different from the obligation of conforming interpretation and "[t]he process of disapplication does not involve reading words into the national legislation (that would be, . . ., to confuse it with conforming interpretation": *Fleming* at [49]. See also *L v Human Fertilisation and Embryology Authority* [2008] EWHC 2149 (Fam) at [47]–[48]; *Test Claimants in the FII Group Litigation v Revenue and Customs Commissioners* [2008] EWHC 2893 at [142]–[146]; *Murphy v Media Protection Services Ltd* [2008] EWHC 1666 (Ch) at [64].

CHALLENGING A COMMUNITY MEASURE IN A NATIONAL COURT

[Add to end of n.167] **14–042**

; *R. (on the application of SPCM SA) v Secretary of State for the Environment, Food and Rural Affairs* [2007] EWHC 2610 (Admin) at [38] and [39] (the claimant's challenge to arts 5 and 6.1 of Regulation

1907/2006 was "unfounded" and not "arguable" and so a reference would not be made).

14–043 *[Add to n.168 after ". . . 4199, para.20"]*

See, e.g. *R. (on the application of SPCM SA) v Secretary of State for the Environment, Food and Rural Affairs* [2007] EWHC 2610 (Admin) at [23] (referring where there was a "serious issue" concerning the validity of art.6(3) of Regulation 1907/2006).

[Add to end of n.168]

; Case C-119/05 *Ministero dell'Industria, del Commercio e dell'Artigianato v Lucchini SpA* [2009] 1 C.M.L.R. 18 at para.53.

14–043 *[Add new para.14–043A]*

14–043A In the specific context of state aid, it has been held that the jurisdiction of national courts is limited. Proceedings concerning state aid might be commenced before national courts requiring those courts to interpret and apply the concept of aid contained in art.87(1) EC.[172a] Similarly, in order to be able to determine whether a state measure established without taking account of the preliminary examination procedure laid down by art.6 of Decision 3484/85 should or should not be made subject to that procedure, a national court might have occasion to interpret the concept of aid referred to in art.4(c) ECSC and art.1 of Decision 3484/85.[172b] However, national courts do not have jurisdiction to give a decision on whether state aid is compatible with the EC Treaty, as this is an assessment which falls exclusively within the competence of the Commission, subject to review by the Community courts.[172c]

[172a] Case C-119/05 *Ministero dell'Industria, del Commercio e dell'Artigianato v Lucchini SpA* [2009] 1 C.M.L.R. 18 at para.50.
[172b] Case C-119/05 *Ministero dell'Industria, del Commercio e dell'Artigianato v Lucchini SpA* [2009] 1 C.M.L.R. 18 at para.50.
[172c] Case C-119/05 *Ministero dell'Industria, del Commercio e dell'Artigianato v Lucchini SpA* [2009] 1 C.M.L.R. 18 at paras 51–52.

INTERPRETATION BY NATIONAL COURTS

14–044 *[Add to end of n.175]*

The CFI has observed that the art.10EC duty is "especially binding in the area of police and judicial cooperation in criminal matters": Case T-284/08 *People's Mojahedin Organization of Iran v Council* [2009] 1 C.M.L.R. 44 at para.52.

[Add to end of n.176]   14–045

; Case C-268/06 *Impact v Ministry of Agriculture and Food* [2008] 2 C.M.L.R. 47 at para.99.

[Add to n.180 after ". . . paras 41–43"]

; Case C-404/07 *Katz v Sós*, ECJ, October 9, 2008, at paras 48–49. *Pupino* has been followed by the House of Lords: *Pilecki v Circuit Court of Legnica, Poland* [2008] UKHL 7; [2008] 1 W.L.R. 325 at [32]–[33] (interpreting the Extradition Act 2003 in light of Council Framework Decision 2002/584/JHA of June 13, 2002 on the European arrest warrant and surrender procedures between Member States); *Caldarelli v Judge for Preliminary Investigations of the Court of Naples, Italy* [2008] UKHL 51; [2008] 1 W.L.R. 1724 at [22].

[Add to n.181]

; Case T-284/08 *People's Mojahedin Organization of Iran v Council* [2009] 1 C.M.L.R. 44 at para.52.

[Add to n.190 after ". . . Litster [1990] 1 A.C. 546;"]   14–048

Murphy v Media Protection Services Ltd [2007] EWHC 3091 (Admin) at [26] (the obligation is to "construe the provisions so nearly as possible as to achieve the result required by the relevant Directive, once the time for the implementation of the latter has passed");

[Add to end of n.191]

; *R. (on the application of Equal Opportunities Commission) v Secretary of State for Communities and Local Government* [2007] EWHC 483 (Admin) at [61] (it was not appropriate in this case to read the national legislation compatibly with the Directive because of the degree of reading down or transposition that would be required to render the provisions compliant with the Directive; in the alternative, it was not "possible" to do so because such extreme application of the requirement to interpret national legislation in accordance with directives would not be effective or sensible because of the need for clarity, certainty and comprehensibility).

[Add to para.14–048 after ". . . what is reasonable".[191]"]

The obligation has been described as not dissimilar to that found in s.3 of the Human Rights Act 1998[191a] and it has been suggested that interpretation should not create "a new and different scheme", offend the legislation's "cardinal principles", or remove the "core and essence" of the legislation.[191b]

[191a] See 13–040.
[191b] *Vodafone 2 v Revenue and Customs Commissioners* [2009] EWCA Civ 446 at [71].

[Add to end of n.192]

; Case C-268/06 *Impact v Minister for Agriculture and Food* [2008] 2 C.M.L.R. 47 at paras 100–103 (a national court was not required to interpret national legislation with retrospective effect where, as a matter of national law, legislation was not to be given retrospective effect unless there was a clear and unambiguous indication to the contrary).

14–049 *[Add to end of n.193]*

; Case C-268/06 *Impact v Ministry of Agriculture and Food* [2008] 2 C.M.L.R. 47 at para.101.

[Add to n.195 after ". . . [2000] E.C.R. I–4491"]

; Case C-404/06 *Quelle AG v Bundesverband der Verbraucherzentralen und Verbraucherverbande* [2008] 2 C.M.L.R. 49;

[Add to end of para.14–049]

The ECJ has indicated subsequently to *Pfeiffer* that the interpretive obligation is limited by the general principles of legal certainty and non-retroactivity and the obligation not to adopt an interpretation *contra legem*[195a]; however, it is clear that the interpretive obligation is "forceful".[195b]

[195a] See, e.g. Case C-268/06 *Impact v Ministry of Agriculture and Food* [2008] 2 C.M.L.R. 47 at paras 99–100.
[195b] P. Craig, "The Legal Effect of Directives: Policy, Rules and Exceptions" (2009) 34 E.L. Rev. 349, 359.

EFFECTIVE PROCEDURES AND REMEDIES

Principle of national procedural autonomy

14–052 *[Add to end of n.202]*

The Lisbon Treaty will introduce a new art.19(1) TEU, providing that "Member States shall provide remedies sufficient to ensure effective legal protection in the field covered by Union law".

[Add to end of n.203]

Cases C-95/07 and C-96/07 *Ecotrade SpA v Agenzia delle Entrate—Ufficio di Genova 3* [2008] E.C.R. I–03457 at para.46; Case C-2/06 *Willy Kempter KG v Hauptzollamt Hamburg-Jonas* [2008] 2 C.M.L.R. 21 at para.57; Case C-445/06 *Danske Slagterier v Bundesrepublik Deutschland* [2009] 3 C.M.L.R. 10 at para.48.

Principle of effective protection

[Add to end of n.210]   14–053

For comment, see G. Anagnostaras, "The Incomplete State of Community Harmonisation in the Provision of Interim Protection by the National Courts" (2008) 33 E.L. Rev. 586; A. Arnull, "Case C-432/05, *Unibet (London) Ltd and Unibet (International) Ltd v Justitiekanslern*, judgment of the Grand Chamber of 13 March 2007" (2007) 44 C.M.L. Rev. 1763; K. Lenaerts, "The Rule of Law and the Coherence of the Judicial System of the European Union" (2007) 44 C.M.L. Rev. 1625.

Balancing procedural autonomy and effective protection

[Add to end of n.217]   14–055

See also Case C-455/06 *Heemskerk BV, Firma Schaap v Productschap Vee en Vlees*, ECJ, November 25, 2008, at paras 44–48 (a Dutch court was not obliged to raise points of EC law of its own motion where examining EC law would result in denial of the principle of Dutch law that an individual bringing an action must not be placed in a less favourable position than if he had not brought that action (the principle of the prohibition of *reformatio in pejus*): such would undermine the rights of the defence, legal certainty and protection of legitimate expectations).

[Add to end of para.14–055]

A Dutch rule enabling a court to raise of its own motion public policy rules did not breach the principle of effectiveness on the basis that it did not have power to raise of its own motion EC rules, where those EC rules did not involve public policy: the rule safeguarded the rights of the defence and ensured the proper conduct of proceedings by, in particular, avoiding delays.[218a]

[218a] Case C-222/05 *Van der Weerd v Minister van Landbouw, Natuur en Voedselkwaliteit* [2007] E.C.R. I–4233 at paras 28–38.

Requirement of equivalence

14–056　*[Add to para.14–056 after ". . . action are similar.*[219]*"]*

In assessing equivalence, the national court must ask itself two "sub-questions": " (i) Is there a 'similar domestic action'? (ii) Are the rules applicable to the Community right 'not less favourable'?"[219a]

[219a] *Byrne v Motor Insurers' Bureau* [2008] EWCA Civ 574; [2009] Q.B. 66 at [22].

[Add to end of n.220]

; Case C-445/06 *Danske Slagterier v Bundesrepublik Deutschland* [2009] 3 C.M.L.R. 10 at paras 40–41.

Limitation Periods

14–057　*[Add to end of n.225]*

; Cases C-95/07 and C-96/07 *Ecotrade SpA v Agenzia delle Entrate—Ufficio di Genova 3* [2008] E.C.R. I–03457 at para.44 (the possibility of exercising a right to deduct tax without any temporal limit would be "contrary to the principle of legal certainty, which requires the tax position of the taxable person, having regard to his rights and obligations vis-à-vis the tax authority, not to be open to challenge indefinitely"); Case C-2/06 *Willy Kempter KG v Hauptzollamt Hamburg-Jonas* [2008] 2 C.M.L.R. 21 at para.58; Case C-445/06 *Danske Slagterier v Bundesrepublik Deutschland* [2009] 3 C.M.L.R. 10 at para.32 (time limits for *Francovich* damages actions); Case C-241/06 *Lämmerzahl* [2007] E.C.R. I–8415 at para.52; Cases C-95/07 and C-96/07 *Ecotrade SpA v Agenzia delle Entrate—Ufficio di Genova 3* [2008] E.C.R. I–03457 at para.46.

[Add to para.14–057 after ". . . guidance of the ECJ.[226]*"]*

In order to ensure legal certainty, however, limitation periods have to be fixed in advance. A situation marked by significant legal uncertainty might involve a breach of the principle of effectiveness, because reparation of the loss or damage caused to individuals by breaches of Community law for which a Member State could be held responsible might be rendered excessively difficult in practice if the individuals were unable to determine the applicable limitation period with a reasonable degree of certainty.[226a]

[226a] Case C-445/06 *Danske Slagterier v Bundesrepublik Deutschland* [2009] 3 C.M.L.R. 10 at paras 33–34.

[Add to end of n.227]

; Case C-445/06 *Danske Slagterier v Bundesrepublik Deutschland* [2009] 3 C.M.L.R. 10 at para.35.

[Add new para.14–057A]   14–057A

Where a Member State imposes a time limit within which a claim has to be made, either by introducing a new time limit or shortening an existing one, the House of Lords has indicated that the time limit has to be fixed in advance so as to provide legal certainty.[228a] In the situation where a retrospective time limit is introduced, the legislation has to include an adequate transitional period, so that those with accrued rights have a reasonable time limit within which to make their claims before the new retrospective time limit applies.[228b] The adequacy of the time limit is to be determined by reference to the principles of effectiveness and legitimate expectation, to ensure that the period is not so short as to render it practically impossible or excessively difficult for a person with an accrued right to make his claim.[228c] In the context of limitation periods for *Francovich* damages actions, the fact that institution of infringement proceedings by the Commission does not have the effect of interrupting or suspending the limitation period does not make it impossible or excessively difficult for individuals to exercise their Community rights or breach the principle of equivalence, since an individual may bring a *Francovich* action without having to wait until a judgment finding that the Member State has infringed Community law has been delivered.[228d] Where the complaint is that a directive has not been transposed or incorrectly transposed, EC law does not preclude the limitation from beginning to run on the date on which the first injurious effects of the incorrect transposition have been produced and further effects are foreseeable, even if that date is prior to the correct transposition of the directive.[228e]

[228a] *Fleming (t/a Bodycraft) v Customs and Excise Commissioners* [2008] UKHL 2; [2008] 1 W.L.R. 195 at [79(c)].
[228b] *Fleming (t/a Bodycraft) v Customs and Excise Commissioners* [2008] UKHL 2; [2008] 1 W.L.R. 195 at [79(d)].
[228c] *Fleming (t/a Bodycraft) v Customs and Excise Commissioners* [2008] UKHL 2; [2008] 1 W.L.R. 195 at [79(f)].
[228d] Case C-445/06 *Danske Slagterier v Bundesrepublik Deutschland* [2009] 3 C.M.L.R. 10 at paras 39, 45.
[228e] Case C-445/06 *Danske Slagterier v Bundesrepublik Deutschland* [2009] 3 C.M.L.R. 10 at para.56.

[Add to end of n.229]   14–058

In a number of cases, the ruling in *Emmott* has been described by the ECJ as "justified by the particular circumstances of that case": see, e.g. Case

C-445/06 *Danske Slagterier v Bundesrepublik Deutschland* [2009] 3 C.M.L.R. 10 at para.54.

[Add to end of n.230]

Case C-445/06 *Danske Slagterier v Bundesrepublik Deutschland* [2009] 3 C.M.L.R. 10 at para.54.

[Add to the end of n.232]

Contrast Cases C-95/07 and C-96/07 *Ecotrade SpA v Agenzia delle Entrate—Ufficio di Genova 3* [2008] E.C.R. I–03457 at para.48 (two year time limit did not render the exercise of a right to deduct tax virtually impossible or excessively difficult).

14–059   *[Paragraph 14–059]*

This paragraph should be read in light of *Cooper v Attorney General* [2008] EWHC 2178; [2008] 3 C.M.L.R. 45 in which the proposition that application of the judicial review time limit for bringing a challenge pursuant to the Environmental Impact Assessment Directive breached the principle of effectiveness, in circumstances where the claimant waited 42 months before bringing a challenge, was considered to be "unarguable": at [64]–[66].

No general obligation to reopen final judicial and administrative decisions

14–063   *[Add to end of para.14–063]*

The duty of res judicata in respect of a decision which is contrary to Community law does not extend to preventing recovery of state aid granted in breach of Community law which has been found to be incompatible with the Common Market in a decision of the Commission which has become final.[252a]

[252a] Case C-119/05 *Ministero dell'Industria, del Commercio e dell'Artigianato v Lucchini SpA* [2009] 1 C.M.L.R. 18 at para.63.

14–064   *[Add to end of para.14–064]*

The ECJ has subsequently clarified that the fourth requirement to seek review immediately cannot be interpreted as an obligation to make the application for review within a certain specified period and Member States remain free to set reasonable time limits for seeking remedies, in a manner consistent with the Community principles of effectiveness and equivalence.[254a]

254a Case C-2/06 *Willy Kempter KG v Hauptzollamt Hamburg-Jonas* [2008] 2 C.M.L.R. 21 at paras 56, 60.

[Add new para.14–064A]   14–064A

It has also been held that the duty to re-open administrative decisions is not dependent upon the litigant involved having relied upon Community law in the initial decision-making process. In the *Kempter* case, the ECJ observed that:

". . . while Community law does not require national courts to raise of their own motion a plea alleging infringement of Community law provisions where examination of that plea would oblige them to go beyond the ambit of the dispute as defined by the parties, they are obliged to raise of their own motion points of law based on binding Community rules where, under national law, they must or may do so in relation to a binding rule of national law."254a

The ECJ has located the Member State's duty in the duty of fidelity found in art.10 EC.254b

254a Case C-2/06 *Willy Kempter KG v Hauptzollamt Hamburg-Jonas* [2008] 2 C.M.L.R. 21 at para.45. See A. Ward, "Do unto Others as You Would have them do unto you: *Willy Kempter* and the Duty to Raise EC Law in National Litigation" (2008) 33 E.L. Rev. 739.
254b Case C-2/06 *Willy Kempter KG v Hauptzollamt* [2008] 2 C.M.L.R. 21 at para.38. See 14–044.

State liability in damages for breach of Community law

[Add to end of n.260]   14–066

See also Case C-445/06 *Danske Slagterier v Bundesrepublik Deutschland* [2009] 3 C.M.L.R. 10 (adopting a test for determining whether pig meat was unfit for human consumption which violated art.28 EC).

[Add to end of n.264]

For a discussion of the absorption of *Francovich* into national law, see M. Künnecke, "Divergence and the *Francovich* Remedy in German and English Courts" in S. Prechal and B. van Roermund (eds.), *The Coherence of EU Law: The Search for Unity in Divergent Concepts*, 2008 (OUP) p.233.

Sufficiently serious breach

14–069 *[Add to para.14–069 after ". . . their evaluation".[271]"]*

The "sufficiently serious" test is "not a hard-edged test" and "it requires a value judgment by the national court".[271a]

[271a] *Byrne v Motor Insurers' Bureau* [2008] EWCA Civ 574; [2009] Q.B. 66 at [45].

[Add to end of n.273]

Case C-452/06 *Synthon BV v Licensing Authority of the Department of Health*, ECJ, October 16, 2008, at paras 42–43 (a sufficiently serious breach arose where the Licensing Authority refused an application for mutual recognition of a product pursuant to Directive 2001/83, the relevant provision of which had been "clearly and precisely" worded: see also n.274 below).

[Add to end of n.274]

See also Case C-452/06 *Synthon BV v Licensing Authority of the Department of Health*, ECJ, October 16, 2008, at paras 41–43 (a sufficiently serious breach arose where the Licensing Authority refused an application for mutual recognition of a product pursuant to Directive 2001/83 which granted "only a very limited discretion" in relation to refusal).

[Add to end of n.280]

; *Byrne v Motor Insurers' Bureau* [2008] EWCA Civ 574; [2009] Q.B. 66 at [44] (the fact that the ECJ had given an "unambiguous statement" regarding the meaning of the Directive contributed to a finding of sufficiently serious breach).

[Add to end of para.14–069]

If the breach has "serious consequences", the national courts will also include this as a relevant factor to consider in determining whether there has been a "sufficiently serious breach".[284a] While a finding of breach by the ECJ is an important factor, it is not indispensable for establishing that the breach of Community law was sufficiently serious; an individual can bring an action for damages, without having to wait for a prior judgment by the ECJ that the Member State has breached Community law.[284b] Similarly, an individual's ability to take an action for damages cannot be dependent on the Commission's assessment of the expediency of taking action against a Member State pursuant to art.226 EC.[284c]

284a *Byrne v Motor Insurers' Bureau* [2008] EWCA Civ 574; [2009] Q.B. 66
at [45].
284b Case C-445/06 *Danske Slagterier v Bundesrepublik Deutschland* [2009]
3 C.M.L.R. 10 at paras 37 and 39.
284c Case C-445/06 *Danske Slagterier v Bundesrepublik Deutschland* [2009]
3 C.M.L.R. 10 at para.38.

Identifying the defendant

[Add to n.297 after ". . . question: paras 120–126"].   14–073

That a remedy of damages in respect of judicial decisions is reserved for
"exceptional cases" was emphasised recently in *Cooper v Attorney General*
[2008] EWHC 2178; [2008] 3 C.M.L.R. 45 at [55] (the claimant sought
damages in respect of a judgment of the Court of Appeal, acting as the
court of final instance, and it was held that it was "not appropriate to ask
simply whether the judicial error was inexcusable. Regard must be had to
the specific nature of the judicial function (which entails interpretation of
provisions of law) and to the legitimate requirements of legal certainty.)".

[Add new para.14–074A]   14–074

Mitigating Loss

Given that it is a general principle common to the legal systems of the   14–074A
Member States that an injured party must show reasonable diligence in
limiting the extent of loss or damage incurred, or risk having to bear the loss
or damage himself, in relation to the damages liability of a Member State for
breach of EC law, the ECJ has held that a national court may inquire
whether the injured person showed reasonable diligence in seeking to avoid
the loss or damage, or to limit its extent, and whether he availed himself in
time of all the legal remedies available to him.[301a] However, it is contrary to
the principle of effectiveness to oblige an injured party to have recourse
systematically to all the legal remedies available to it if that would give rise to
excessive difficulties or could not be reasonably required.[301b] The ECJ has
held that the fact that an alternative remedy may give rise to an art.234
preliminary reference is not a reason for concluding that the remedy is not
reasonable, given that the art.234 procedure is "an instrument of cooperation between the Court of Justice and the national courts".[301c]

301a Case C-445/06 *Danske Slagterier v Bundesrepublik Deutschland* [2009]
3 C.M.L.R. 10 at paras 60–61.
301b Case C-445/06 *Danske Slagterier v Bundesrepublik Deutschland* [2009]
3 C.M.L.R. 10 at para.62.
301c Case C-445/06 *Danske Slagterier v Bundesrepublik Deutschland* [2009]
3 C.M.L.R. 10 at paras 65–66.

Preliminary Rulings

14–076 *[Add to para.14–076 after ". . . given primary facts.[307]"]*

The ECJ will provide the national court with all the elements of interpretation of Community law which may be of use for deciding the case before it, whether or not that court has referred to them in the wording of its question.[307a]

[307a] Case C-275/06 *Productores de Música de España (Promusicae) v Telefónica de España SAU* [2008] 2 C.M.L.R. 17 at para.42.

[Add to end of n.309]

; Case C-250/06 *United Pan-Europe Communications Belgium SA v Belgium* [2007] E.C.R. I–11135 at paras 19–21 (a reference relating to competition law deemed inadmissible for want of precision in outlining the legal and factual context, and in particular for failing to indicate the relevant market in respect of which there was an alleged dominant position).

[Add to n.310 after ". . . [1992] E.C.R. I–4971;"]

Case C-333/07 *Société Régie Networks v Direction de Contrôle Fiscal Rhône-Alpes Bourgogne* [2009] 2 C.M.L.R. 20 (Grand Chamber) at paras 46–52. See also Case C-11/07 *Eckelkamp v Belgium* [2008] 3 C.M.L.R. 44 at para.28 (the court should only refuse to rule where it is "quite obvious" that the question is irrelevant to the main proceedings).

[Add to end of n.310]

; Case C-119/05 *Ministero dell'Industria, del Commercio e dell'Artigianato v Lucchini SpA* [2009] 1 C.M.L.R. 18 at para.44.

[Add to para.14–076 after ". . . relevant to the dispute.[310]"]

, although any question referred will enjoy a presumption of relevance.[310a] The fact that, following annulment of a decision, the EU institution may make a second decision with the same outcome for the applicant, does not, in itself, mean that a ruling will not be relevant for the main proceedings before the national court.[310b]

[310a] Case C-333/07 *Société Régie Networks v Direction de Contrôle Fiscal Rhône-Alpes Bourgogne* [2009] 2 C.M.L.R. 20 (Grand Chamber) at paras 46–52 (irrelevance should be "obviously" apparent).
[310b] Case C-333/07 *Societe Regie Networks v Direction de Controle Fiscal Rhone-Alpes Bourgogne* [2009] 2 C.M.L.R. 20 (Grand Chamber) at paras 53–61.

[Add to end of para.14–076]

Although it is unusual for a reference for a preliminary ruling to be made at the permission stage in judicial review proceedings, and before a fully reasoned judgment of an English court, such a reference may be made where it is both convenient and necessary to do so.[318a] A second reference in the same case on the same issue has also been sought where the meaning of the ECJ's first preliminary ruling was "not beyond reasonable argument".[318b]

[318a] *R. (on the application of Mellor) v Secretary of State for Communities and Local Government* [2008] EWCA Civ 213 (the unusual circumstances of the case justified making a reference at the permission stage: where Directive 85/337/EEC did not require that reasons be given for declining to have an environmental impact assessment, the question was whether a gap in the Directive should be filled by interpretation. That question of interpretation in turn involved a question of policy on which other Member States might have different views, and the ECJ would be better informed as to the policy considerations throughout the Community than the United Kingdom courts). The application for permission was refused, but the claimant sought a reference before pursuing his appeal.

[318b] *O'Byrne v Aventis Pasteur MSD Ltd* [2008] UKHL 34; [2008] 4 All ER 881 at [24].

[Add to end of n.322] **14–077**

; M. Broberg, "Acte Clair Revisited" (2008) 45 C.M.L. Rev. 1383.

[Add to end of n.323]

The House of Lords does not generally consider each of the *CILFIT* criteria but asks if the answer is "clear beyond the bounds of reasonable argument": *R. (on the application of Countryside Alliance) v Attorney General* [2007] UKHL 52; [2009] 1 A.C. 719 at [31]; *O'Byrne v Aventis Pasteur MSD Ltd* [2008] UKHL 34; [2008] 4 All ER 881 at [23]–[24].

DIRECT ACTIONS IN THE ECJ AND CFI

Review of legality

[Add to end of para.14–081] **14–081**

The ECJ and CFI do not however have jurisdiction, when exercising judicial review of legality under art.230 EC, to issue declaratory judgments or directions, even where they concern the manner in which their judgments are to be complied with.[334a]

[334a] Case T-145/06 *Omya AG v Commission* [2009] 4 C.M.L.R. 19 at para.23.

14–082 *[Add to para.14–082 after ". . .the person addressed".[338]]*

The requirement is generally interpreted restrictively. For example, where a provision of EC law requires a procedure to be followed for the adoption of an EC act, under which a person may claim rights such as a right to be heard, the procedural guarantee will enable the relevant person to satisfy the art.230 requirement in respect of a procedural infringement, but will not, in itself, suffice to satisfy the art.230 requirement in respect of infringement of a substantive rule of law.[338a]

[338a] Case C-260/05P *Sniace v Commission* [2007] E.C.R. I–10005 at para.53; Case C-355/08P *WWF-UK Ltd v Council*, at paras 43–47, ECJ, May 5, 2009, at paras 43–47.

[Add to end of n.339]

; Case C-260/05P *Sniace v Commission* [2007] E.C.R. I–10005 at para.53; Case C-355/08P *WWF-UK Ltd v Council* ECJ, May 5, 2009, at para.41; Case C-503/07P *Saint-Gobain Glass Deutschland GmbH v Commission*, April 8, 2008, at para.60; Joined Cases C-75/05P and C-80/05P *Germany v Kronofrance SA* [2009] 1 C.M.L.R. 3 at paras 35–36 . The CFI has also applied the test consistently after objecting in Case T-177/01 *Jégo-Quéré v Commission* [2002] E.C.R. II–2365: Case T-254/00 *Hotel Cipriani SpA v Commission* [2009] 1 C.M.L.R. 39 at paras 74–93 (holding that beneficiaries of an unlawful aid scheme were "individually concerned" as they constituted a "closed class"); Case T-95/06 *Federación de Cooperativas Agrarias de la Comunidad Valenciana v Community Plant Variety Office*, January 31, 2008, at paras 84–91.

[Add to n.343 after ". . . All E.R. (E.C.) 226"]

; Case C-119/05 *Ministero dell'Industria, del Commercio e dell'Artigianato v Lucchini SpA* [2009] 1 C.M.L.R. 18 at paras 54–56. For comment, see P. Nebbia "Do the Rules on State Aids have a life of their own? National Procedural Autonomy and Effectiveness in the Lucchini Case" (2008) 33 E.L. Rev. 427.

[Add new para.14–082A]

14–082A Community measures, even though irregular, are in principle presumed to be lawful and to produce legal effects until they are declared void.[343a] By way of exception to that principle, measures tainted by an irregularity the gravity of which is so obvious that it cannot be tolerated by the Community legal order must be treated as having no legal effect, even provisional, and must be regarded as legally non-existent.[343b] The ECJ has explained that the purpose of this exception is to maintain a balance between two fundamental, but sometimes conflicting, requirements with which a legal order must comply, namely, stability of legal relations and respect for legality. The gravity of the consequences attaching to a finding that a measure of a Community institution is non-existent means that, for reasons of legal certainty, such a finding may be reserved for quite extreme situations.[343c] Where a measure has been annulled for formal or procedural defects, the institution is entitled to adopt an identical measure afresh, having observed the formal and procedural requirements, and to give the new measure retroactive effect, if that is essential to the attainment of the public-interest objective pursued and if the legitimate expectations of the persons concerned are protected.[343d]

[343a] Case T-256/07 *People's Mojahedin Organization of Iran v Council,* October 23, 2008, at para.55.
[343b] Case T-256/07 *People's Mojahedin Organization of Iran v Council,* October 23, 2008, at para.56.
[343c] Case T-256/07 *People's Mojahedin Organization of Iran v Council,* October 23, 2008, at para.57.
[343d] Case T-256/07 *People's Mojahedin Organization of Iran v Council,* October 23, 2008, at para.65.

GROUNDS OF JUDICIAL REVIEW AGAINST COMMUNITY MEASURES: OVERVIEW

[Add to 14–083 after ". . . and protection of legitimate expectations."]   14–083

The ECJ has also held that even where a Community institution possesses broad discretion, the court is able to review the institution's interpretation of the relevant facts, and must not only establish whether the evidence relied on is factually accurate, reliable and consistent, but must also ascertain whether the evidence contains all the relevant information to be taken into account to assess the situation and whether it is capable of substantiating the conclusions drawn from it.[345a]

[345a] Case T-256/07 *People's Mojahedin Organization of Iran v Council,* October 23, 2008, at para.138; C-525/04P *Spain v Commission* [2007] E.C.R. I–9947 at para.57.

[Add new para.14–084A]   14–084

The ECJ has also made it clear that, for example, measures adopted by the Community for national security or anti-terrorism objectives will not be considered non-justiciable and they will not escape all review by the   14–084A

189

Community judicature.[348a] Likewise, Community measures adopted to give effect to UN measures will not be considered, for that reason, to be non-reviewable by the ECJ or CFI.[348b]

[348a] Joined Cases C-402/05P and C-415/05 *Kadi and Al Barakaat International Foundation v Council* [2008] 3 C.M.L.R. 41 (Grand Chamber) at para.343.

[348b] Joined Cases C-402/05P and C-415/05 *Kadi and Al Barakaat International Foundation v Council* [2008] 3 C.M.L.R. 41 (Grand Chamber) at paras 281–292 (see the Opinion of A.G. Maduro, noting, at para.28, that there was no basis in the EC Treaty from which it "could logically follow that measures taken for the implementation of Security Council resolutions have supraconstitutional status and are hence accorded immunity from judicial review").

GENERAL PRINCIPLES OF LAW

Non-discrimination

14–087 *[Add to end of n.355].*

[. . ., On age discrimination, see also Case C-388/07 *R. (on the application of The Incorporated Trustees of the National Council on Ageing (Age Concern England)) v Secretary of State for Business, Enterprise and Regulatory Reform* [2009] 3 C.M.L.R. 4; Case C-411/05 *Palacios de la Villa v Cortefiel Servicios SA* [2007] E.C.R. I–8531.

[Add to end of n.356]

; Case C-273/04 *Poland v Council* [2008] 1 C.M.L.R. 23 (Grand Chamber) at paras 87–89 (Poland's complaint about discrimination because of difference in treatment between old and new Member States in the context of the Common Agricultural Policy was rejected on the basis that the agricultural situation in the new Member States was "radically different" from that in the old Member States).

Proportionality

14–089 *[Add to end of n.363]*

; Case T-145/06 *Omya AG v Commission* [2009] 4 C.M.L.R. 19 at para.34 (a power of the Commission to request information from an undertaking should not constitute a burden on that undertaking which was disproportionate to the requirements of the inquiry).

[Add to para.14–091 after ". . . health,[373]"] 14–091

state aid[373a]

[373a] Case C-333/07 *Société Régie Networks v Direction de Contrôle Fiscal Rhône-Alpes Bourgogne* [2009] 2 C.M.L.R. 20 (Grand Chamber) at paras 77–78; Case T-254/00 *Hotel Cipriani SpA v Commission* [2009] 1 C.M.L.R. 39 at paras 280–290.

[Add to para.14–091 after ". . . discretion".[374]"]

The ECJ has explained that misuse of powers refers to cases where an authority has used its powers for a purpose other than that for which those powers had been conferred on it. Where more than one aim was pursued— even if the grounds of a decision include, in addition to proper grounds, an improper aim—that would not make the Decision invalid for misuse of powers, since it does not nullify the main aim.[374a]

[374a] Case T-145/06 *Omya AG v Commission* [2009] 4 C.M.L.R. 19 at para.99.

[Add new para.14–091A]

Even where the Community institutions are granted wide discretion by the 14–091A
court—such as in the context of anti-terrorism measures or economic assessments—the role of the Community judicature is not only to establish whether the evidence relied on is factually accurate, reliable and consistent, but to ascertain whether that evidence contains all the relevant information to be taken into account in order to assess the situation and whether it is capable of substantiating the conclusions drawn from it. When conducting such a review, the Community court must not substitute its own assessment of what is appropriate.[374a]

[374a] Case T-284/08 *People's Mojahedin Organization of Iran v Council* [2009] 1 C.M.L.R. 44 at para.55; Case C-525/04P *Spain v Commission* [2007] E.C.R. I-9947 at para.57.

[Add to n.374 after ". . . I–5755, at para.58"]

; Case T-145/06 *Omya AG v Commission* [2009] 4 C.M.L.R. 19 at para.32.

Legal certainty and legitimate expectations

[Add to end of para.14–093] 14–093

The principle also requires that penalties must have a proper legal basis, which requirement is not breached if the precise level of fine that might be imposed in respect of certain conduct is not known in advance.[380a]

[380a] Case T-69/04 *Schunk GmbH v Commission* [2009] 4 C.M.L.R. 2 at paras 27–29, 45–46.

[Add to n.376 after ". . . I-11261, at para.72"]

; Case T-24/07 *ThyssenKrupp Stainless AG v Commission*, July 1, 2009, at para.86 (the principles of legal certainty and legitimate expectations required application of the ECSC Treaty, rather than the EC Treaty, even though the ECSC Treaty had expired).

[Add to end of n.377]

See also Case T-99/04 *AC-Treuhand AG v Commission*, [2008] 5 C.M.L.R. 13 at para.113 (the general principles of Community law, including the principle of *nullum crimen, nulla poena sine lege*, as applicable to Community competition law, need not necessarily have the same scope as when they apply to a situation covered by criminal law in the strict sense).

14–094 *[Add to para.14–094 after ". . . principle of legal certainty".[381]"]*

The ECJ has emphasised that three conditions are required to be satisfied in order to claim entitlement to the protection of legitimate expectations: first, precise, unconditional and consistent assurances originating from authorised and reliable sources were required to have been given to the person concerned by the Community authorities; secondly, those assurances were required to be such as to give rise to a legitimate expectation on the part of the person to whom they were addressed; and thirdly, the assurances given were required to comply with the applicable rules.[381a]

[381a] Case T-145/06 *Omya AG v Commission* [2009] 4 C.M.L.R. 19 at para.117; Case C-47/07P *Masdar (UK) Ltd v Commission* [2009] 2 C.M.L.R. 1 (Grand Chamber) at paras 84, 86 (no legitimate expectation arose as to receipt of financial assistance where a contractor had not implemented a project in accordance with the conditions to which the grant of assistance was made subject and the contractor could not rely on "vague indications").

14–095 *[Add to end of n.390]*

; Case T-254/00 *Hotel Cipriani SpA v Commission* [2009] 1 C.M.L.R. 39 at paras 392–393 (the beneficiary of unlawful aid might not entertain a legitimate expectation that the aid was lawful where the aid scheme had not been notified and recovery of the aid was therefore a foreseeable risk); Case C-408/04 *Commission v Salzgitter* (Germany, intervening) [2008] 2 C.M.L.R. 52 (Grand Chamber) at paras 98–105; Case C-199/06 *Centre d'Exportation du Livre Français (CELF) v Société Internationale de Diffusion et d'Édition (SIDE)* [2008] 2 C.M.L.R. 20 at paras 65–68 (no legitimate expectation arose even if the Commission had initially decided not to raise any objections to the aid, so long as the Commission had not taken a decision approving aid, and so long as the period for bringing an action against such a decision had not expired).

Human rights

[Add to end of n.402]   14–098

; Case T-99/04 *AC-Treuhand AG v Commission* [2008] 5 C.M.L.R. 13 at para.45; Joined Cases C-402/05P and C-415/05 *Kadi and Al Barakaat International Foundation v Council* [2008] 3 C.M.L.R. 41 (Grand Chamber) at para.283.

[Add to end of n.405]

; Case C-438/05 *International Transport Workers' Federation and Finnish Seamen's Union v Viking Line ABP and OÜ Viking Line Eesti* [2007] E.C.R. I–10779 at para.43; Case C-341/05 *Laval v Svenska Byggnadsarbetareförbundet* [2007] E.C.R. I–11767 at para.90.

[Add to para.14–099 after ". . . trade union activity,[408]"]   14–099

which includes the right to strike,[408a]

[408a] Case C-438/05 *International Transport Workers' Federation and Finnish Seamen's Union v Viking Line ABP and OÜ Viking Line Eesti* [2007] E.C.R. I–10779 at paras 43–44; Case C-341/05 *Laval v Svenska Byggnadsarbetareförbundet* [2007] E.C.R. I–11767 at paras 90–91.

[Add to para.14–099 after ". . . expression,[412]"]

freedom to receive information,[412a]

[412a] Case C-336/07 *Kabel Deutschland Vertrieb und Service GmbH & Co KG v Niedersächsische Landesmedienanstalt für privaten Rundfunk* [2009] 2 C.M.L.R. 6 at para.33.

[Add to end of n.410]

; Case C-303/06 *Coleman v Attridge Law* [2008] 3 C.M.L.R. 27; Case C-267/06 *Tadao Maruko v Versorgungsanstalt der Deutschen Bühnen* [2008] E.C.R. I-1757 at paras 66–73.

[Add to end of n.412]

; Case C-336/07 *Kabel Deutschland Vertrieb und Service GmbH & Co KG v Niedersächsische Landesmedienanstalt für privaten Rundfunk* [2009] 2 C.M.L.R. 6 at para.37 (noting that the maintenance of pluralism which national legislation sought to guarantee was "connected with freedom of expression", which is protected by art.10 ECHR, and one of the "fundamental rights guaranteed by the Community legal order"); Case C-250/06 *United Pan-Europe Communications Belgium* [2007] E.C.R. I–11135 at para.41; Case C-73/07 *Tietosuojavaltuutettu v Satakunnan Markkinapörssi Oy and Satamedia Oy*, ECJ (Grand Chamber), December 16, 2008, at paras 52–57.

[Add to end of n.413]

; Case C-73/07 *Tietosuojavaltuutettu v Satakunnan Markkinapörssi Oy and Satamedia Oy*, ECJ (Grand Chamber), December 16, 2008, at paras 52–57 (right to privacy with respect to the processing of personal data); Case C-275/06 *Productores de Música de España (Promusicae) v Telefónica de España SAU* [2008] E.C.R. I–271 at para.64 (for discussion see: I. Davies and S. Helmer, "Case Comment: *Productores de Música de España ("Promusicae") v Telefónica de España SAU ("Telefonica")*" (2008) 30 European Intellectual Property Rev. 307; L. Hetherington, "Peer-to-Peer File Sharing—ISPS and Disclosure of User Identities" (2008) 19 Entertainment L. Rev. 81).

[Add to end of n.414]

; Case C-450/06 *Varec v Belgium* [2008] 2 C.M.L.R. 24 at para.48.

[Add to end of n.419]

; Joined Cases C-402/05P, *Yassin Abdullah Kadi and Al Barakaat International Foundation v Council and Commission*, ECJ (Grand Chamber), September 3, 2008, at paras 359–371; Case C-275/06 *Productores de Música de España (Promusicae) v Telefónica de España SAU* [2008] E.C.R. I–271 at para.62.

[Add to end of n.423]

; Joined cases C-402/05P and C-415/05 *Kadi and Al Barakaat International Foundation v Council* [2008] 3 C.M.L.R. 41 (Grand Chamber) at paras 333–353.

[Add to para.14–099 after ". . . the right to fair legal process within a reasonable period,[415]"]

the right to effective judicial protection,[415a]

[415a] Case C-432/05 *Unibet* [2007] E.C.R. I-2271 at para.37; Joined cases C-402/05P and C-415/05 *Kadi and Al Barakaat International Foundation v Council* [2008] 3 C.M.L.R. 41 (Grand Chamber) at para.335. The principle of effective judicial protection has also formed the basis of a decision of the ECJ to the effect that, even though there is provision in the EC Treaty, a right of action for unjust enrichment, must lie against the Community institutions: Case C-47/07P *Masdar (UK) Ltd v Commission* [2009] 2 C.M.L.R. 1 (Grand Chamber) at paras 50–51.

The right to be heard

Right to be heard in competition proceedings

[Add new para.14–103A] 14–103

Competition proceedings conducted pursuant to Regulation 17/2004[442a] 14–103A consist of two stages: a preliminary investigation and an inter partes stage, with the latter running from the Commission's notification of its Statement of Objections to the Final Decision.[442b] An undertaking is only able to rely in full on its rights of defence after the Commission's notification of its statement of objections, because otherwise the effectiveness of the preliminary investigation would be compromised.[442c] However, because the measures of inquiry undertaken by the Commission during its preliminary investigation suggest that an infringement has been committed and may have a significant impact on the undertaking, it is necessary to prevent the rights of the defence from being irremediably compromised during that stage of the administrative procedure, and once a measure has been taken in respect of an undertaking, such as a request for information, the Commission is required to inform the undertaking concerned of the subject matter and purpose of the investigation underway.[442d] Putative infringements must be specified and the fact that the undertaking may be faced with allegations related to that possible infringement, so that it can take the measures which it deems useful for its exoneration and prepare its defence at the inter partes stage of the administrative procedure.[442e]

[442a] Commission Regulation (EC) 17/2004 of January 7, 2004 laying down the reduction coefficient to be applied under the Community tariff quota for barley provided for by Regulation (EC) 2305/2003 [2004] OJ L4/7.
[442b] Case T-99/04 *AC-Treuhand AG v Commission* [2008] 5 C.M.L.R. 13 at paras 47–49.

442c Case T-99/04 *AC-Treuhand AG v Commission* [2008] 5 C.M.L.R. 13 at para.48.
442d Case T-99/04 *AC-Treuhand AG v Commission* [2008] 5 C.M.L.R. 13 paras 51–52.
442e Case T-99/04 *AC-Treuhand AG v Commission* [2008] 5 C.M.L.R. 13 at para.56

[Add new para.14–103B]

14–103B The ECJ has also held that although compliance with a reasonable time limit in the conduct of competition proceedings constitutes a general principle of Community law, its infringement justifies the annulment of a decision only insofar as it also constitutes an infringement of the rights of defence of the undertaking concerned.442f

442f Case T-145/06 *Omya AG v Commission* [2009] 4 C.M.L.R. 19 at paras 84–86; Case T-276/04 *Compagnie Maritime Belge SA v Commission* [2009] 4 C.M.L.R. 21 at para.45.

14–106 *[Add new para.14–106A]*

The right to be heard in anti-terrorism proceedings

14–106A One of the most notable situations in which the right to be heard has arisen recently has been in context of anti-terrorism measures. In the important *Kadi* case,452a at issue was the legality of a regulation,452b which implemented United Nations Security Council ("UNSC") Resolution 1390 (2002). The Resolution set up a system at the UNSC level listing suspected members of Al Qaeda and the Taliban: once a name is listed, various restrictions are imposed upon that person or organisation, including the freezing of their assets. Kadi and Al Barakaat were included on the UNSC list and in Annex 1 to the EC Regulation, and they sought annulment of the Regulation on a number of grounds,452c one of which was violation of their right to be heard. The ECJ found that the applicants' right to be heard had been violated, since at no stage had the Council informed the applicants of any of the evidence against them, nor had they been heard on that evidence.453d The ECJ reasoned that Community authorities could not be required to communicate the grounds justifying inclusion in the list before a person or entry is entered into the list for the first time as this would be liable to jeopardise the effectiveness of the freezing of funds and resources and undermine the "surprise effect".453e Similarly, the Community authorities were not bound to hear the appellants before including their names in the list.453f However, the ECJ described its judicial review task as being to accommodate legitimate security concerns about the nature and sources of information taken into account in the adoption of the act concerned and the need to accord the individual a sufficient measure of procedural justice.453g The problem with the Regulation was that it did not provide any procedure for communicating evidence justifying the inclusion of names in Annex 1 to that Regulation and for hearing those persons, either at the same time as that inclusion or within a reasonable time afterwards.[453h]

[452a] Case C-415/05 *Kadi and Al Barakaat International Foundation v Council* [2008] 3 C.M.L.R. 41 at para.335.

[452b] Council Regulation (EC) 881/2002 of May 27, 2002 imposing certain specific restrictive measures directed against certain persons and entities associated with Usama bin Laden, the Al-Qaida network and the Taliban, and repealing Council Regulation (EC) 467/2001 prohibiting the export of certain goods and services to Afghanistan, strengthening the flight ban and extending the freeze of funds and other financial resources in respect of the Taliban of Afghanistan ([2002] OJ L139/9).

[452c] The applicants' challenge on lack of Community competence to adopt the Regulation was unsuccessful: at para.226.

[453d] Case C-415/05 *Kadi and Al Barakaat International Foundation v Council* [2008] 3 C.M.L.R. 41 at paras 333–353.

[453e] Case C-415/05 *Kadi and Al Barakaat International Foundation v Council* [2008] 3 C.M.L.R. 41 at paras 338–340.

[453f] Case C-415/05 *Kadi and Al Barakaat International Foundation v Council* [2008] 3 C.M.L.R. 41 at para.341.

[453g] Case C-415/05 *Kadi and Al Barakaat International Foundation v Council* [2008] 3 C.M.L.R. 41 at para.344; see also Case T-284/08 *People's Mojahedin Organization of Iran v Council* [2009] 1 C.M.L.R. 44 at para.75.

[453h] Case C-415/05 *Kadi and Al Barakaat International Foundation v Council* [2008] 3 C.M.L.R. 41 at paras 345–348.

The requirement to state reasons

[Add to end of n.455]   **14–108**

; Case C-333/07 *Société Régie Networks v Direction de Contrôle Fiscal Rhône-Alpes Bourgogne* [2009] 2 C.M.L.R. 20 (Grand Chamber) at paras 62–63; Case T-254/00 *Hotel Cipriani SpA v Commission* [2009] 1 C.M.L.R. 39 at paras 296–298.

[Add to end of n.461]   **14–109**

; Case T-304/06 *Paul Reber GmbH & Co KG v Office for Harmonisation in the Internal Market (Trade Marks and Designs)* [2008] E.T.M.R. 68 at para.55 (the Boards of Appeal of the OHIM could not be required to provide an account that followed exhaustively and individually each element of the reasoning articulated by the parties before them).

14–111 *[Add to end of para.14–111]*

In the competition context, a decision adopted pursuant to art.82 EC, must mention facts forming the basis of the legal grounds of the measure and the considerations which have led to the adoption of the decision.[468a]

[468a] Case T-276/04 *Compagnie Maritime Belge SA v Commission* [2009] 4 C.M.L.R. 21 at para.82.

[Add new para.14–111A]

14–111A The question whether the grounds of a judgment of the CFI are contradictory or inadequate is a question of law which is amenable to review on appeal by the ECJ.[468b] However, the CFI is not obliged to respond in detail to every single argument advanced, particularly if the argument was not sufficiently clear and precise. The CFI is also not obliged to provide an account which follows exhaustively and one by one all the arguments put forward by the parties to the case; the CFI's reasoning may be implicit provided that it enables the persons concerned to know why the CFI has not upheld their arguments and provides the ECJ with sufficient material for it to exercise its power of review.[468b]

[468b] Case C-120/06P *Fabbrica Italiana Accumulatori Motocarri Montecchio SpA (FIAMM) v Council*, ECJ, September 9, 2008, at para.90.
[468c] Case C-120/06P *Fabbrica Italiana Accumulatori Motocarri Montecchio SpA (FIAMM) v Council*, ECJ, September 9, 2008, at paras 91, 96; Case C-440/07P *Commission v Schneider Electric SA*, ECJ (Grand Chamber), July 16, 2009, at para.135.

[Add new para.14–111B]

14–111B Where the Council takes a decision to freeze an individual's funds because of suspected engagement in terrorist activity, there is a requirement to refer not only to the legal conditions of application of the relevant regulation,[468c] but also to the actual and specific reasons why the Council considers that the person concerned must be made the subject of a measure freezing funds.[468d]

[468c] Council Regulation (EC) 2580/2001 December 24, 2001 on specific restrictive measures directed against certain persons and entities with a view to combating terrorism [2001] OJ L344/70.
[468d] Case T-256/07 *People's Mojahedin Organization of Iran v Council*, October 23, 2008, at para.81.

GROUNDS FOR JUDICIAL REVIEW OF NATIONAL MEASURES

[Add to end of n.475]   **14–113**

; *R. (on the application of Equal Opportunities Commission) v Secretary of State for Communities and Local Government* [2007] EWHC 483 (Admin) (the Employment Equality (Sex Discrimination) Regulations 2005 were found not to have properly implemented Directive 2002/73/EC of the European Parliament and of the Council of September 23, 2002 amending Council Directive 76/207/EEC on the implementation of the principle of equal treatment for men and women as regards access to employment, vocational training and promotion, and working conditions [2002] OJ L269/15).

Failure to state reasons

[Add to para.14–117 after ". . . have been commenced."]   **14–117**

The ECJ has explained that the duty to state reasons is linked to the principle of effective judicial review,

> "which must be able to cover the legality of the reasons for the contested decision, presupposes in general, that the court to which the matter is referred may require the competent authority to notify its reasons. However where it is more particularly a question of securing the effective protection of a right conferred by Community law, interested parties must also be able to defend that right under the best possible conditions and have the possibility of deciding, with a full knowledge of the relevant facts, whether there is any point in applying to the courts. Consequently, in such circumstances, the competent national authority is under a duty to inform them of the reasons on which its refusal is based, either in the decision itself or in a subsequent communication made at their request."[486a]

The subsequent communication may take the form, not only of an express statement of the reasons, but also of information and relevant documents being made available in response to the request made.[486b]

[486a] Case C-75/08 *R. (on the application of Mellor) v Secretary of State for Communities and Local Government*, April 30, 2009, ECJ, at para.59.
[486b] Case C-75/08 *R. (on the application of Mellor) v Secretary of State for Communities and Local Government*, April 30, 2009, ECJ, at para.60.

Implementation of Community law

14–120 *[Add new para.14–120A]*

14–120A The ECJ has stressed also that when transposing directives which leave discretion to them, Member States must interpret the directives in a manner which allows a fair balance to be struck between the various fundamental rights protected by the Community legal order. Further, when implementing the measures transposing those directives, the authorities and courts of the Member States must not only interpret their national law in a manner consistent with those directives but also make sure that they do not rely on an interpretation of them which would be in conflict with those fundamental rights or with the other general principles of Community law, such as the principle of proportionality.[491a]

[491a] Case C-305/05 *Ordre des barreaux francophones et germanophone* [2007] E.C.R. I–5305 at para.28); Case C-275/06 *Productores de Música de España (Promusicae) v Telefónica de España SAU* [2008] E.C.R. I–271 at para.68

The principle of proportionality

14–124 *[Add new n.501a after "ends and means".]*

[501a] To comply with the principle of proportionality, Member States must employ means which, whilst enabling them effectively to attain the objectives pursued by their domestic laws, cause the least possible detriment to the objectives and principles laid down by the relevant Community legislation: Case C-271/06 *Netto Supermarkt GmbH & Co OHG v Finanzamt Malchin* [2008] E.C.R. I–771 at para.19; Case C-409/04 *R. (on the application of Teleos Plc) v Customs and Excise Commissioners* [2008] 1 C.M.L.R. 6 at para.52.

14–126 *[Add to end of n.506]*

See also Cases C-11/06 and C-12/06 *Rhiannon Morgan v Bezirksregierung Köln* [2007] E.C.R. I–9161 at para.46.

14–128 *[Add to end of para.14–128]*

Similarly, while the objective of preventing tax evasion justifies stringent requirements as regards the obligations of persons liable to payment of value added tax, the principle of proportionality requires that the taxable person not be held liable for the entire shortfall in tax caused by fraudulent acts of third parties over which he has no influence.[509a]

509a Case C-271/06 *Netto Supermarkt GmbH & Co OHG v Finanzamt Malchin* [2008] E.C.R. I–771 at para.23.

[Add new para.14–132A] **14–132**

In areas where the Community's competence is weaker, the test of **14–132A** proportionality will be applied flexibly. For example, states have a "wide discretion" to determine what constitutes a service of general economic interest, for the purposes of arts 16 and 86 EC.518a

518a Case T-289/03 *British United Provident Association Ltd (BUPA) v Commission* [2008] E.C.R. II–81 at para.166.

Equality

[Add to end of n.520] **14–134**

See also *R. (on the application of Partridge Farms Limited) v Secretary of State for Environment, Food and Rural Affairs* [2009] EWCA Civ 284 at paras 58 and 79 (accepting that the principle of equality was one of the "fundamental principles of Community law", but that the claimant had not succeeded in persuading the court that the Compensation (England) Order 2006 (SI 2006/168) breached the principle of equality by not making provision for high pedigree cattle in setting compensation for cattle slaughtered on account of tuberculosis: "As the European Court has emphasised, the principle of equality does not preclude legislation of general application from affecting different persons in different ways provided it is determined on the basis of objective criteria formulated to meet the relevant objective" (Collins L.J.)).

[Add new n.524a after "the ECJ's finding."] **14–136**

524a For interesting examples of this approach being adopted at national level, see: *Deane Public Works Ltd v Northern Ireland Water Ltd* [2009] NICh 8 (general principles of non-discrimination and equal treatment implied into a tender contract to create obligations for a contracting authority in the public procurement context even though no requirement in the relevant procurement directive and implementing regulations); *Federal Security Services Ltd v Chief Constable of the Police Service of Northern Ireland* [2009] NICh 3 (relying on the general principles of transparency, equal treatment and non-discrimination to impose a stand-still requirement between the contract award decision and the conclusion of the contract in circumstances where such was not required by either national regulations or even the relevant EC directive).

Protection of legitimate expectations

14–138 *[Add to end of para.14–138]*

In the tax context, the ECJ has held that it would be contrary to the principle of legal certainty if a Member State, which had laid down the conditions for the application of the exemption from value added tax by prescribing a list of the documents to be presented to the competent authorities and which had accepted the documents presented by a supplier as establishing entitlement to the exemption, could subsequently require that supplier to account for the VAT, where it emerged that because of a third party's fraud, of which the supplier had and could have had no knowledge, the conditions for the exemption were in fact not met.[531a]

[531a] Case C-271/06 *Netto Supermarkt GmbH & Co OHG v Finanzamt Malchin* [2008] E.C.R. I–771 at para.26.

Part III

PROCEDURES AND REMEDIES

CHAPTER 15

THE HISTORICAL DEVELPMENT OF JUDICIAL REVIEW REMEDIES AND PROCEDURES

There is no update to this historical account.

CHAPTER 16

CPR PT 54 CLAIMS FOR JUDICIAL REVIEW

SCOPE

[Note 8 should now read]   16–002

For practical guidance, see also: B. Lang (ed.), *Administrative Court: Practice and Procedure* (2006); C. Lewis, *Judicial Remedies in Public Law*, 2008 4th edn Ch. 9; M. Supperstone and L. Knapman (eds), *Administrative Court Practice*, 2008; J. Halford, "Strategy in Judicial Review: Using the Procedure to the Claimant's Advantage" [2006] J.R. 153; A. Lidbetter, "Strategy in Judicial Review for Defendants" [2007] J.R. 99.

THE ADMINISTRATIVE COURT

[Note 18 delete "Practice Direction 54, para.3" and substitute]   16–003

Practice Direction 54D—Administrative Court (Venue)

[Add at end of n.18]

Regionalisation of the Administrative Court began on April 21, 2009 when offices of the court were established in the District Registries of the High Court in Birmingham, Cardiff, Leeds and Manchester (Regionalisation was foreshadowed in *Justice Outside London: Report of the Judicial Working Group* (led by May L.J.) in January 2007). The regional offices do not just deal with the administrative side of the court's business (issuing proceedings and so on), but also hear cases in the region with which the claimant has the closest connection. The following considerations are also relevant to determining the appropriate venue for proceedings: the reason expressed by any party for a particular venue; where the defendant is based; where the claimant's legal representative is based; the ease and cost of travelling to a venue; the availability of suitable alternative means of attending a hearing (such as by video-link); media interest in a particular area; the volume of cases at a particular venue; whether there are similar claims already outstanding at a particular venue; and whether there are devolution issues which would render Cardiff the appropriate venue (see Practice Direction 54D—Administrative Court (Venue) para.5.2). The standard forms for issuing and defending judicial review proceedings (Forms N461 and N462) now have a section in which the parties may indicate their preference and new forms N464 (application for directions as to venue) and N465 (response to applications for directions as to venue) have been produced. Paragraph 4 makes provision for urgent cases. S. Nason, "Regionalisation of the Administrative Court" [2009] J.R. 1. The decision as to venue is a judicial one. Certain matters will remain in London. These include proceedings relating to: control orders (under CPR Pt 76); financial restrictions (CPR Pt 79) and the Proceeds of Crime Act 2002; confiscation and forfeiture (RSC Order 115); terrorism; extradition; and the discipline of solicitors. Proceedings before the Divisional Court and where a special advocate is appointed will also continue to be heard in London (PD 54D para.3.1). For an example of the impact of hearing a case out of London, see *R. (on the application of McDougal) v Liverpool City Council* [2009] EWHC 1821 (Admin) at [4] (Silber J.: "I heard this case in Liverpool and a large number of people connected with the School came to listen to the case. Their presence in such large numbers and the dignified way in which they all listened to the legal submissions was very impressive. I was left in no doubt that many people in the Croxteth area were very troubled by the plans of the Council to close the School.")

EXHAUSTION OF OTHER REMEDIES AND ADR

16–014 *[Add to end of n.45]*

A remedy will not be considered to be ineffective just because it is not legally binding if in practice the body against whom it is ordered undertakes to comply with it: *R. (on the application of Carnell) v Regent's Park College* [2008] EWHC 739; [2008] E.L.R. 268 at [24]. It was also held in *Carnell* that where a claimant seeks judicial review without exhausting an alternative remedy, and the time limit for pursuing the alternative remedy expires while seeking judicial review, that will not justify allowing the judicial review proceedings to proceed: at [31]–[33].

Alternative (or substitute) remedies

Avenues of appeal or review by statute

16–020 *[Add to end of n.61]*

On proposals to bring AIT within the unified tribunal structure, see 1–094 above.

Other avenues of legal challenge

[Add to end of n.71]   16–021

Judicial review should not be sought where it is "not likely" to be quicker than the alternative remedy: *R. (on the application of Carnell) v Regent's Park College* [2008] EWHC 739; [2008] E.L.R. 268 at [25].

Alternative Dispute Resolution (ADR)

[Note 81 delete "para.34" and substitute]   16–022

para.3.4

Exchange of letters before claim

[Note 86 delete "PD58, para.8" and substitute]   16–025

Pre-action Protocol, para.8.

GATHERING EVIDENCE AND INFORMATION

Freedom of Information Act 2000

[Add to end of n.96]   16–027

; J. Macdonald and C. Jones (eds), *The Law of Freedom of Information*, 2009 (2nd edn.); and P. Coppel (ed), *Information Rights*, 2007 (2nd edn.).

[Add to end of n.98]

See further, *B.B.C. v Sugar* [2009] UKHL 9; [2009] 1 W.L.R. 430 [24]– [27] (Lord Phillips).

[Add to end of para.16–028]   16–028

An appeal from the Information Tribunal lies to the High Court: see, e.g. *HM Treasury v Information Commissioner* [2009] EWHC 1811 (Admin) (a successful appeal relating to a request for the legal advice which led HM Treasury to declare that the Financial Services and Markets Act 2000 was compatible with the HRA).

Environmental Information Regulations 2004

16–030 *[Add to n.101]*

See *R. (Office of Communications) v Information Commissioner* [2009] EWCA Civ 90 at [34]–[66] (Richards L.J.).

Access requests under the Data Protection Act 1998

16–034 *[Add to n.108]*

See *Quinton v Peirce* [2009] EWHC 912 (QB); [2009] F.S.R. 17 at [87]–[94] (Eady J.) for an unsuccessful attempt to enforce the data protection principles in the context of a local election dispute.

PREPARING THE CLAIM FORM

16–040 *[Note 128 delete "54" and substitute]*

54A

PERMISSION

16–043 *[Note 134 delete "see PD54, para.2.4"]*

See PD54, para.2.4

The timing of the application for permission

16–050 *[Note 158 delete "54" and substitute]*

54A

[Note 161 delete "54" and substitute]

54A

16–057 *[Add to n.181]*

R. (Lower Mill Estate Limited) v Commissioners of Her Majesty's Revenue and Customs [2008] EWHC 2409 (Admin).

Challenging the refusal of permission

[Note 196 delete "PD52, para.15.3"] 16–061

INTERLOCUTORY STAGE

Application by interveners

[Note 203 delete "54" and substitute] 16–064

54A

Disclosure

[Add to n.209] 16–067

See further, *R. (on the application of Mohamed) v Secretary of State for Foreign and Commonwealth Affairs* [2008] EWHC 2048 (Admin) where disclosure was ordered under *Norwich Pharmacal* principles in relation to allegations that the claimant had been tortured while in custody of the Pakistani authorities. See also *R. (Al-Sweady) v Secretary of State for Defence* [2009] EWHC 2387 (Admin).

[Note 218] 16–069

Preparation of skeleton arguments

[Delete:] [Note 219 delete "54" and substitute] 16–070

54A

Discontinuing and orders by request

[Add n.220A] 16–071

PD 54A, para.17 and Practice Direction (Administrative Court: Uncontested Proceedings) [2008] 1 W.L.R. 1377.

FUNDING JUDICIAL REVIEW

16–082 *[Add to n.244]*

The current guidance on the Funding Code (July 2009) is available on the LSC website.

[Note 245 delete "17–00" and substitute]

16–041–16–044

COSTS

Protective costs orders in public interest cases

16–089 *[Add to n.266]*

G. Opperman, M. Gullick and C. Stone, "*Corner House Revisited*: The Law Governing Protective Costs Orders" [2009] J.R. 43

16–090 *[Add to n.272]*

Important guidance on the application of the *Corner House* principles has been provided by the Court of Appeal in *R. (Compton) v Wiltshire Primary Care Trust* [2008] EWCA Civ 749; [2009] 1 W.L.R. 1436 at [10]–[24] (Waller L.J.) and *R. (Buglife-The Invertebrate Conservation Trust) v Thurrock Thames Gateway Development Corporation* [2008] EWCA Civ 1209 at [18]–[28] (Sir Anthony Clarke M.R.).

16–091 *[Add to n.276]*

and *Buglife*, n.272 above at [29]–[36].

Costs before and at permission stage

16–093 *[Add to n.282]*

As to the amount of such costs, see the guidance in *R. (Roudham & Larling Parish Council) v Breckland Council* [2008] EWCA Civ 714 at [25]–[31] (Buxton L.J.). See also *R. (on the application of Davey) v Aylesbury Vale District Council* [2007] EWCA Civ 1166; [2008] 1 W.L.R. 878 which adds further guidance on the amount of costs at the permission stage. If awarding costs against the claimant, the judge should consider whether they are to include preparation costs in addition to acknowledgment costs. Acknowledgement costs are those costs incurred in preparing and serving an acknowledgement of service with grounds of opposition. Preparation costs refer to other pre-permission costs, such as pre-issue costs. It will be for the defendant to justify the latter costs by showing that it was reasonable and proportionate to incur such cost. There may be no sufficient reason why such costs, if incurred, should be recoverable: at [21]. If the claimant wishes to submit that any or all the costs which would be otherwise recoverable should not be recovered, however reasonable and proportionate they were, it is for him to persuade the court to that effect: at [30]. It is highly desirable that these questions should be dealt with by the trial judge and left to the costs judge only in relation to the reasonableness of individual items: at [21]. If, at the conclusion of such proceedings, the judge makes an undifferentiated order for costs in a defendant's favour (a) the order has to be regarded as including any reasonably incurred preparation costs; but (b) Practice Statement (Judicial Review: Costs) [2004] 1 W.L.R. 1760 should be read so as to exclude any costs of opposing the grant of permission in open court, which should be dealt with on the *Mount Cook* principles: at [21].

[Note 283 delete "54" and substitute]

54A

CHAPTER 17

OTHER JUDICIAL REVIEW PROCEEDINGS

SPECIAL PROCEDURE FOR REVIEW OF ASYLUM AND IMMIGRATION DECISIONS

[Add new para.17–009A after para.17–009]   17–009

Transfer of immigration and asylum adjudication to the unified tribunal system

In early 2010, the jurisdiction of the Asylum and Immigration Tribunal 17–009A
(AIT) will be transferred to new immigration and asylum chambers in the
First-tier Tribunal and the Upper Tier Tribunal (see 1-094). The single-
tier AIT will cease to exist and the current process of reconsideration by
the AIT will end. In the new system, initial appeals will be dealt with by
the First-tier Tribunal; there will be an appeal on points of law to the
Upper Tier Tribunal (requiring the permission of the First-tier Tribunal
or the Upper Tribunal). From the Upper Tribunal an appeal will lie on
points of law, with permission, to the Court of Appeal (or Court of
Session in Scotland). The role of the Administrative Court in determining
challenges to the AIT's refusal to reconsider and in relation to "opt ins"
will end. The Upper Tribunal is a superior court of record and so will not
routinely be amenable to judicial review.

The Borders, Citizenship and Immigration Act 2009 s.53 provides for
the transfer of judicial review applications from the High Court of
England and Wales to the Upper Tribunal which deal with "fresh claims"
cases (i.e. they call into question a decision by the Home Secretary not to
treat submissions as an asylum or human rights claim within the meaning
of Pt 5 of the Nationality, Immigration and Asylum Act 2002 wholly or
partly on the basis that they are not significantly different from material
that has been previously considered). Similar provision is made for
transfers from the High Court of Northern Ireland and the Court of
Session in Scotland. The Administrative Court has discretion to transfer
other immigration and asylum judicial review claims to the Upper
Tribunal for determination.

HABEAS CORPUS

17–010 *[Add to end of n.35]*

In 2007, the Administrative Court received 27 applications for habeas corpus and one was determined: Ministry of Justice, *Judicial and Court Statistics 2007*, Table 1.14.

17–012 *[Add to end of n.42]*

And see *Wells v Parole Board; Walker v Secretary of State for the Home Department; Secretary of State for Justice v Walker* [2009] UKHL 22; [2009] 2 W.L.R. 1149 at [5] (Lord Hope of Craighead: "As Simon Brown L.J. said in *R. v Oldham Justices Ex p. Cawley* [1997] Q.B. 1, 13, where there has been a criminal conviction the courts have firmly excluded collateral attack by habeas corpus, holding that the only proper remedy lies by way of appeal. Sentences of imprisonment for public protection are sentences for an indefinite period, subject to the provisions of Ch II of Pt II of the Crime (Sentences) Act 1997 as to the release of prisoners and duration of licences: Criminal Justice Act 2003, s.225(4). There is no entitlement to release until release has been directed by the Parole Board, and a direction to that effect cannot be given until the Board is satisfied that detention is no longer necessary for the protection of the public. Mandatory orders may be obtained to ensure that the system works properly. But it is not open to the courts to set that system aside by directing release contrary to the provisions of the statute").

CORONERS

17–044 *[Add new para.17–044A after para.17–044]*

17–044A The Coroners and Justice Bill, introduced to Parliament in the 2008-09 session, will create a new legal framework for coroners.

HOMELESS APPEALS

17–045 *[Add to n.143]*

In May 2008, the Law Commission report *Housing Disputes: Proportionate Dispute Resolution* (Law Com No.309/Cm 7377) made several recommendations for reform, including that the county court should have powers to grant interim relief pending the outcome of a local authority's internal review of homelessness cases. The Government rejected this proposal on the ground that there was "a significant risk that any changes in this area would be exploited to circumvent these procedures to the detriment of those who are genuinely homeless and in priority need" (Ministry of Justice statement, July 16, 2009).

CHAPTER 18

JUDICIAL REVIEW REMEDIES

REMEDIES AGAINST THE CROWN AND MINISTERS

Ministers are officers of the Crown

[Add to n.14]   18–006

The Secretary of State would have no immunity from a prohibiting order (or any other judicial review remedy) to prevent him from laying draft Orders in Council before Her Majesty if such draft Orders constituted an abuse of power (*R. (Bancoult) v Secretary of State for Foreign and Commonwealth Affairs (No.2)* [2007] EWCA Civ 498; [2008] Q.B. 365 at [34]–[36] (Sedley L.J.) (overturned on other grounds in *Bancoult* [2008] UKHL 61; [2009] 1 A.C. 453).

INTERIM REMEDIES

Interim injunctions

Approach in judicial review claims

[Add to n.40]   18–015

R. (Debt Free Direct Ltd) v Advertising Standards Authority Ltd [2007] EWHC 1337 (Admin).

Bail

[Add to n.59]   18–022

R. (Mongan) v Isleworth Crown Court [2007] EWHC 1087 (Admin) (application allowed in a case where a material change of circumstance made reconsideration appropriate).

FINAL REMEDIAL ORDERS

Mandatory orders

18–024 *[Add to n.68]*

Striking recent examples of mandatory orders include that the Director of Public Prosecutions should promulgate a specific policy in relation to assisted suicide (*R. (Purdy) v Director of Public Prosecutions* [2009] UKHL 45; [2009] 3 W.L.R. 403 at [56] (Lord Hope)) and that the claimant's son should be admitted to the faith school which had excluded him on racial grounds (*R. (E) v The Governing Body of JFS* [2009] EWCA Civ 626).

Quashing and prohibiting orders

Substituting a decision

18–032 *[Delete "Secondly, CPR r.54.19(3) . . . take the decisions itself)." and substitute]*

Secondly, CPR r.54.19 provides:

"(1) This rule applies where the court makes a quashing order in respect of the decision to which the claim relates.
(2) The court may—
(a) (i) remit the matter to the decision-maker; and
(ii) direct it to reconsider the matter and reach a decision in accordance with the judgment of the court; or
(b) in so far as any enactment permits, substitute its own decision for the decision to which the claim relates."

18–033 *[Delete "On the face of it . . . substitutes words in an inquisition" and substitute]*

The power to substitute is confined to cases where three conditions are made out: that the decision in question was made by a court or tribunal; that the decision is quashed on the ground of error of law; and that, without the error, there would only have been one decision which the court or tribunal could have reached.[82] Unless the court directs otherwise, a substituted decision under CPR r.19(2)(b) has effect as if it were a decision of the relevant court or tribunal.[83]

[82] Senior Courts Act 1981 s.31(5A).
[83] Senior Courts Act 1981 s.31(5B).

DISCRETION IN GRANTING AND WITHHOLDING REMEDIES

Remedy would serve no practical purpose

[Note 137 delete reference and substitute] 18–055

[2008] UKHL 22; [2008] 1 W.L.R. 1587 at [62]–[65] (Lord Hoffmann). K. Yates, "Appealing the Discretionary Grant or Refusal of Relief in Judicial Review Proceedings" [2009] J.R. 129.

CHAPTER 19

MONETARY REMEDIES IN JUDICIAL REVIEW

SCOPE

[Add to n.1]   19–001

T. Cornford, *Towards a Public Law of Tort*, 2008 (Aldershot: Ashgate Publishing).

Other sources of compensation

[Add to end of n.9]   19–003

On the withdrawal of the common law ex gratia scheme for compensating victims of miscarriages of justice, see *R. (on the application of Niazi) v Secretary of State for the Home Department* [2007] EWHC 1495 (Admin); [2007] A.C.D. 75 (held: no procedural or substantive legitimate expectation). The statutory scheme under the Criminal Justice Act 1998 s.133 continues (for a challenge to a decision under which, see *R. (on the application of Miller) v Independent Assessor* [2009] EWCA Civ 609).

NEGLIGENCE

[Add new n.162a after "Thus where the purpose of the duty is to protect 19–045 *health and safety this is seen as impliedly excluding any greater common law duty (e.g. to prevent economic loss arising from a defective building)."]*

[162a] See, in a different context, *Trent SHA v Jain* [2009] UKHL 4; [2009] 2 W.L.R. 248 (for comment, see L. Blom-Cooper, "When the private lawyer should go public" [2009] P.L. 195): owners of a care home, erroneously shutdown by a regulatory body after a without notice hearing, were owed no duty of care in respect of the catastrophic financial loss they suffered.

REFORM FOR TORT LIABILITY

19–071 *[Add new para.19–071A after para.19–071]*

19–071A In July 2008, the Law Commission published a consultation paper entitled *Administrative Redress: Public Bodies and the Citizen* (Consultation Paper No.187) containing proposals for wide ranging reform. The paper suggested that the torts of breach of statutory duty and misfeasance in public office might be abolished. A new regime, in place of the common law of negligence, was outlined for "truly public" activities, based on what is called "the principles of modified corrective justice". Claimants would have to show "serious fault" by the public authority. For academic commentary see: T. Cornford, "Administrative Redress: the Law Commission's Consultation Paper" [2009] P.L.70; M. Fordham, "Monetary Awards in Judicial Review" [2009] P.L. 1; C. Brasted and J. Potter, "Damages in Judicial Review: The Commercial Context" (2009) 14 J.R. 53; and J. Morgan, "Policy reasoning in tort law: the courts, the Law Commission and the critics" (2009) 125 L.Q.R. 215.

COMPENSATION UNDER THE HUMAN RIGHTS ACT

19–081 *[Add at end of n.302]*

And see J. Steele, "Damages in tort and under the Human Rights Act: remedial or functional separation?" (2008) 67 C.L.J. 606.

Index

225